DATA ANALYTICS 2020

The Ninth International Conference on Data Analytics

October 25 - 29, 2020

DATA ANALYTICS 2020 Editors

Manuela Popescu, IARIA, EU/USA

Arianna Agosto, Post-doctoral Researcher, Department of Economics and Management, University of Pavia, Italy

Paolo Giudici, Professor of Statistics, FinTech laboratory, University of Pavia, Italy

Les Sztandera, Thomas Jefferson University, USA

Printed from e-media with permission by:

Curran Associates, Inc.
57 Morehouse Lane
Red Hook, NY 12571

Some format issues inherent in the e-media version may also appear in this print version.

International Academy, Research, and Industry Association (IARIA)
412 Derby Way
Wilmington, DE 19810

Phone: (408) 893-6407
Fax: (408) 527-6351

petre@iaria.org

Additional copies of this publication are available from:

Curran Associates, Inc.
57 Morehouse Lane
Red Hook, NY 12571 USA
Phone: 845-758-0400
Fax: 845-758-2633
Email: curran@proceedings.com
Web: www.proceedings.com

Table of Contents

DATA ANALYTICS 2020

Forward

The Ninth International Conference on Data Analytics (DATA ANALYTICS 2020), held on October 22-29, 2020, continued the series on fundamentals in supporting data analytics, special mechanisms and features of applying principles of data analytics, application-oriented analytics, and target-area analytics.

Processing of terabytes to petabytes of data, or incorporating non-structural data and multi-structured data sources and types require advanced analytics and data science mechanisms for both raw and partially-processed information. Despite considerable advancements on high performance, large storage, and high computation power, there are challenges in identifying, clustering, classifying, and interpreting of a large spectrum of information.

The conference had the following tracks:

- Application-oriented analytics
- Big Data
- Sentiment/opinion analysis
- Data Analytics in Profiling and Service Design
- Fundamentals
- Mechanisms and features
- Predictive Data Analytics
- Transport and Traffic Analytics in Smart Cities

We take here the opportunity to warmly thank all the members of the DATA ANALYTICS 2020 technical program committee, as well as all the reviewers. The creation of such a high quality conference program would not have been possible without their involvement. We also kindly thank all the authors that dedicated much of their time and effort to contribute to DATA ANALYTICS 2020. We truly believe that, thanks to all these efforts, the final conference program consisted of top quality contributions.

We also gratefully thank the members of the DATA ANALYTICS 2020 organizing committee for their help in handling the logistics and for their work that made this professional meeting a success.

We hope that DATA ANALYTICS 2020 was a successful international forum for the exchange of ideas and results between academia and industry and to promote further progress in the field of data analytics.

DATA ANALYTICS 2020 Steering Committee

Sandjai Bhulai, Vrije Universiteit Amsterdam, the Netherlands
Ivana Semanjski, Ghent University, Belgium
Les Sztandera, Thomas Jefferson University, USA
Kerstin Lemke-Rust, Hochschule Bonn-Rhein-Sieg, Germany
Wolfram Wöß, Institute for Application Oriented Knowledge Processing | Johannes Kepler University, Linz, Austria
George Tambouratzis, Institute for Language and Speech Processing, Athena R.C., Greece

DATA ANALYTICS 2020 Publicity Chair

Daniel Andoni Basterrechea, Universitat Politecnica de Valencia, Spain

DATA ANALYTICS 2020

COMMITTEE

DATA ANALYTICS Steering Committee

Wolfram Wöß, Institute for Application Oriented Knowledge Processing | Johannes Kepler University, Linz, Austria
George Tambouratzis, Institute for Language and Speech Processing, Athena R.C., Greece
Ivana Semanjski, Ghent University, Belgium
Kerstin Lemke-Rust, Hochschule Bonn-Rhein-Sieg, Germany
Les Sztandera, Thomas Jefferson University, USA
Sandjai Bhulai, Vrije Universiteit Amsterdam, The Netherlands

DATA ANALYTICS 2020 Publicity Chair

Daniel Andoni Basterrechea, Universitat Politecnica de Valencia, Spain

DATA ANALYTICS 2020 Technical Program Committee

Abderazek Ben Abdallah, The University of Aizu, Japan
Arianna Agosto, University of Pavia, Italy
Madyan Alsenwi, Kyung Hee University, Global Campus, South Korea
Jam Jahanzeb Khan Behan, Université Libre de Bruxelles (ULB), Belgium / Universidad Politécnica de Cataluña (UPC), Spain
Rudolf Berrendorf, Bonn-Rhein-Sieg University, Germany
Flavio Bertini, University of Bologna, Italy
Nik Bessis, Edge Hill University, UK
Sandjai Bhulai, Vrije Universiteit Amsterdam, Netherlands
Jean-Yves Blaise, UMR CNRS/MC 3495 MAP, Marseille, France
Savong Bou, Toyota Technological Institute, Japan
Ozgu Can, Ege University, Turkey
Juan Vicente Capella Hernández, Universitat Politècnica de València, Spain
Julio Cesar Duarte, Instituto Militar de Engenharia, Rio de Janeiro, Brazil
Daniel B.-W. Chen, Monash University, Australia
Monica De Martino, National Research Council - Institute for Applied Mathematics and Information Technologies (CNR-IMATI), Italy
Corné de Ruijt, Vrije Universiteit Amsterdam, Netherlands
Konstantinos Demertzis, Democritus University of Thrace, Greece
Marianna Di Gregorio, University of Salerno, Italy
Ivanna Dronyuk, Lviv Polytechnic National University, Ukraine
Magdalini Eirinaki, San Jose State University, USA
Nadia Essoussi, University of Tunis - LARODEC Laboratory, Tunisia
Panorea Gaitanou, Greek Ministry of Justice, Athens, Greece
Raji Ghawi, Technical University of Munich, Germany
Ana González-Marcos, Universidad de La Rioja, Spain
Gregor Grambow, Aalen University, Germany

Copyright Information

A New Proposal to Improve Credit Scoring Model Predictive Accuracy

Arianna Agosto and Paolo Giudici

Department of Economics and Management
University of Pavia, Italy

Email: arianna.agosto@unipv.it
paolo.giudici@unipv.it

Emanuela Raffinetti

Department of Economics,
Management and Quantitative Methods
University of Milan, Italy

Email: emanuela.raffinetti@unimi.it

***Abstract*—Machine Learning models and Artificial Intelligence algorithms are required to provide powerful predictions to support the decision process of operators in the FinTech sector, characterised by an extensive use of credit scoring models and digitalised financial services. In such a context, the model predictive accuracy assessment represents a basic requirement. On the one hand, literature provides several predictive accuracy measures but, on the other hand, these measures are typically computationally intensive or are based on subjective criteria. In this paper a solution is provided through a novel predictive accuracy measure, we called Rank Graduation Accuracy (RGA), which is based on the distance between the predicted and observed ranks of the response variable. The RGA presents properties which allow to fulfill the need of ensuring reliable predictions improving the model predictive accuracy assessment in highly complex situations.**

Keywords–Machine Learning models; Artificial Intelligence-based systems; Predictive accuracy; Credit Scoring models.

I. INTRODUCTION

A very key point in the application of Machine Learning (ML) and Artificial Intelligence (AI) methods is the evaluation of their predictive accuracy. The predictive accuracy requirement is basic especially in banking and FinTech sectors where data have to be exploited in order to draw conclusions from them and predict future trends. To do this, more accurate results have to be performed to allow organizations to detect new risks (in terms of default predictive accuracy). This objective is more evident when dealing with AI systems, which have a black-box nature resulting in automated decision making which in turn can classify a user into a class associated with the prediction of the individual behavior, without explaining the underlying rationale. In order to avoid that wrong actions are taken as a consequence of "automatic" choice, predictive accuracy measures have to be as much as possible reliable.

Several researchers have proposed, along the years, statistical measures aimed at evaluating predictive accuracy [4] [7]. Likewise, the increasing availability of computational power has allowed to translate these measures in statistical softwares giving rise to direct comparisons between different types of predictive models on the same data. But model comparison methods are not universal, since depending on the nature of response variable to be predicted. Our proposal is motivated by the several applications of machine learnings models in credit rating, where the response variable usually takes a binary nature. In this case, predictive accuracy can be assessed in terms of false positive and false negative predictions providing, for a given set of cut-off points, the Receiver Operating Characteristic (ROC) curve, whose main summary measure corresponds to the area under it (Area Under the Receiver Operating Characteristic curve - AUROC). If on the one hand, the AUROC is widely employed, on the other hand it suffers from some drawbacks due to subjective choice of the cut-off points. With the aim of overcoming this restriction, [10] proposes to resort to the Somers' D measure [11] in the context of credit rating accuracy measurement. Even if the Somers' D is independent on the subjective choice of cut-off points, Somers' D is highly computational intensive.

Our purpose is to introduce a new predictive accuracy measure which, due to its construction, is based on objective criteria and less computational intensive than its main competitors. The novel predictive accuracy measure appears as a derivation of a recent research contribution in the field of dependence analysis illustrated by [3] and is based jointly on the comparison between the observed and the predicted response variable ranks and on the employment of the actual values of the response variable corresponding to both ranks.

The rest of the paper is organized as follows. In Section II, an overview of the mainly used predictive accuracy measures is introduced. In Section III, our new proposed predictive accuracy measure is presented and discussed. In Section IV, an application to credit scoring data is illustrated. In Section V, concluding remarks, together with details on future works, are provided.

II. BACKGROUND

Credit scoring models typically involve a binary response variable denoting the borrower's default. Given the binary nature of the response variable, the most commonly employed predictive accuracy measure is the AUROC [2] [7].

Let n denote the total number of borrowers, such that $n = n_D + n_{ND}$, where D and ND are the defaulting and non-defaulting borrower sets. Let S_D and S_{ND} be the credit score random variable, for the defaulting and non-defaulting borrowers, respectively.

For a specific cut-off value c, $F_D(c)$ and $F_{ND}(c)$ are the sensitivity (true positive rate) and 1-specificity (false positive rate) of a credit scoring model based on the cut-off value c. Let $F_D(c)$ and $F_{ND}(c)$ be the sensitivity (true positive rate) and 1-specificity (false positive rate) of a credit scoring model based on the cut-off value c, such that $F_D(c) = P(S_D \leq c)$ and $F_{ND}(c) = P(S_{ND} \leq c)$ [1].

For a given set of cut cut-off values $c = \{1, \ldots, C\}$, the ROC curve is characterised by the set of points with coordinates $(F_D(c), F_{ND}(c))$ or, equivalently, by (G_{ND_i}, G_{D_i}), where $G_{ND_i} = \sum_{i=1}^{n} p_{ND_i}$, $G_{D_i} = \sum_{i=1}^{n} p_{D_i}$, $p_{ND_i} = P(S_{ND_i} = s_i)$, $p_{D_i} = P(S_{N_i} = s_i)$ and $i = 1, \ldots, n$. From this, it follows that the AUROC is computed as

$$AUROC = \frac{1}{2} \sum_{i=1}^{n} (G_{D_i} + G_{D_{i-1}})(G_{ND_i} - G_{ND_{i-1}}).$$

The AUROC maesure is equal to 0.5 for a random model without any predictive accuracy and is equal to 1 for a perfect model. In the intermediate situations, AUROC takes values in the range $(0.5, 1)$.

An alternative measure of predictive performance is the Somers' D measure [11]. Let Y be a response variable and X be a predictor variable, and let us denote with n the total number of borrowers. Let the variable Y values be arranged in a non-decreasing sense, i.e., $Y_i \leq Y_j$ for $i < j$. Thus, we can define the quantity c_{ij} as follows

$$c_{ij} = \begin{cases} +1, & \text{if } X_i < X_j, Y_i < Y_j \\ -1, & \text{if } X_i > X_j, Y_i < Y_j \\ 0, & \text{otherwise.} \end{cases} \tag{1}$$

The Somers' D measure, pointed out with D_{XY}, is formalized as follows:

$$D_{XY} = \frac{1}{n_u} \sum_{i=1}^{n} \sum_{j>i} c_{ij}, \text{ with } n_u = \sum_{i=1}^{n} \sum_{j>i} 1_{[Y_i \neq Y_j]}. \tag{2}$$

Some specifications are needed:

- D_{XY} takes values in the close range $[-1, +1]$ and does not depend on the chosen cut-off points;
- D_{XY} is computational intensive since, given N observations to be predicted, it computes $\binom{N}{2}$ combinations;
- in the case of a multivariate model, depending on more than one explanatory variable, the Somer's D can be extended by replacing the values of X with the predictions derived from the model, which can be function of all the explanatory variables. Let us denote this extension with $D_{\hat{Y},Y}$;
- since the focus is not on the direction of concordance, the absolute value of $D_{\hat{Y},Y}$ has to be considered.

III. METHODOLOGY

Let $\boldsymbol{y}$ be a vector of the observed values to be predicted and let $\hat{\boldsymbol{y}}$ be the vector of the corresponding predicted values, computed through a specific model $f(\boldsymbol{X})$, where $\boldsymbol{X}$ is the matrix containing the observations on the explanatory variables. Our goal is to compare different models: $\hat{y} = f^1(\boldsymbol{X})$, $\hat{y} = f^2(\boldsymbol{X})$, ..., using a general methodology based on the concordance curve.

A. The concordance curve

Let Y be a target variable and let $X_1, X_2, \ldots, X_p$ be a set of p explanatory variables. The Y values, re-ordered in non-decreasing sense, can be used to build the Y Lorenz curve, denoted with L_Y. More formally, the curve is characterised by the following pairs: $(i/n, \sum_{j=1}^{i} y_{r_j})$, for $i = 1, \ldots, n$, where r_i indicates the (non-decreasing) ranks of Y.

The same Y values can also be used to build the Y dual Lorenz curve, denoted with L_Y', obtained by re-ordering the Y variable values in a non-increasing sense. More formally, the curve is characterised by the following pairs: $(i/n, \sum_{j=1}^{i} y_{d_j})$, for $i = 1, \ldots, n$, where d_i indicates the (non-increasing) ranks of Y.

Likewise, the predicted $\hat{Y}$ values can also be re-ordered, in a non-decreasing sense. Let $\hat{r}_i$, for $i = 1, \ldots, n$, indicate the (non-decreasing) ranks of $\hat{Y}$. A third curve, named concordance curve and denoted with C_Y, can be provided by ordering the Y values with respect to the ranks of the predicted $\hat{Y}$ values, $\hat{r}_i$. Formally, the concordance curve is characterised by the pairs: $(i/n, \sum_{j=1}^{i} y_{\hat{r}_j})$, for $i = 1, \ldots, n$, where $\hat{r}_i$ indicates the (non-decreasing) ranks of $\hat{Y}$.

To illustrate the previous concept, Figure 1 reports, for a given set of test values Y, and the corresponding predictions $\hat{Y}$: the Lorenz curve, the dual Lorenze curve and the concordance curve, together with the bisector curve $(i/n, i/n)$, for $i = 1, \ldots, n$. To ease the illustration, all values have been normalised using the sum of all Y values: $(n\bar{y})$, where $\bar{y}$ indicates the mean of Y.

From Figure 1, we note that the Lorenz curve and its dual are symmetric around the bisector curve, and that the concordance curve lies between them. Note also that, when $\hat{r}_i = r_i$, for all $i = 1, \ldots, n$, the concordance curve is equal to the Lorenz curve, and a perfect concordance between the Y values and the corresponding predictions arises. On the other hand, when $\hat{r}_i = d_i$, the concordance curve is equal to the dual Lorenz curve and a perfect discordance between the Y values and the corresponding predictions emerges. In general, for any given point, a discrepancy between the Lorenz curve and the concordance curve arises only when the predicted rank is different from the observed one. We finally remark that, when the $\hat{Y}$ values are all equal each other, the concordance C_Y curve perfectly overlaps with the bisector curve. In this case, the model has no predictive capability, as it coincides with a random prediction of the Y values.

B. Our proposal: the RGA predictive accuracy measure

The concordance curve, and its relationship with the Lorenz and the dual Lorenz curve can be exploited to summarise the "distance" between the Y and the $\hat{Y}$ values, in terms of the "discrepancy" between their corresponding ranks. In this way, we fully address the ordinal requirement for credit scores. A novel predictive accuracy measure, we call Rank Graduation Accuracy (RGA), is introduced starting from a function C of C_Y and L_Y defined as:

$$C = \frac{\sum_{i=1}^{n} \{i/n - (1/(n\bar{y})) \sum_{j=1}^{i} y_{\hat{r}_j}\}}{\sum_{i=1}^{n} \{i/n - (1/(n\bar{y})) \sum_{j=1}^{i} y_{r_j}\}}, \tag{3}$$

where y_{r_j} are the Y variable values ordered according to the ranks r_j; $y_{\hat{r}_j}$ are the same values but ordered according to the ranks $\hat{r}_j$.

From (3), we note that the C index is a function of the y-axis values of the points lying on the concordance curve C_Y and of the y-axis values of the points lying on the Lorenz curve L_Y. Indeed the numerator of the index in (3) compares the distance between the set of points lying on the bisector curve and the set of points lying on the concordance curve

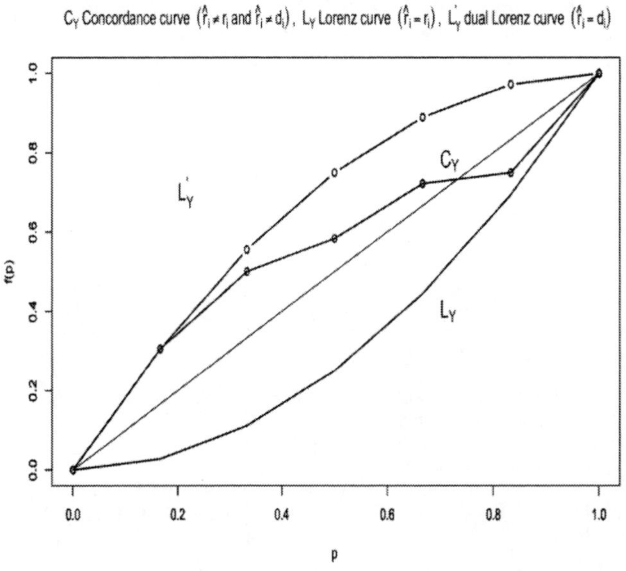

Figure 1. The L_Y and $L_Y^{'}$ Lorenz curves and the C_Y concordance curve.

C_Y, while the denominator compares the distance between the set of points lying on the bisector curve and the set of points lying on the Lorenz curve L_Y.

It can be shown that C fulfills the following properties, whose proofs can be found in [5]:

- $-1 \leq C \leq +1$: specifically, when $0 < C \leq +1$, Y and $\hat{Y}$ are concordant and when $-1 \leq C < 0$ they are discordant;
- $C = +1$ if and only if $C_Y = L_Y$ (full concordance): the concordance curve C_Y overlaps with the Lorenz curve L_Y;
- $C = -1$ if and only if $C_Y = L_Y^{'}$ (full discordance): the concordance curve C_Y overlaps with the dual Lorenz curve $L_Y^{'}$.

Remark Note that, when some of the $\hat{Y}$ values are equal to each other, the original Y values associated with the equal $\hat{Y}$ values can be substituted by their mean, as suggested by [3]. This adjustment is coherent with the definition of a model without predictive capability. To illustrate this point, suppose to consider a general model $f(X)$ with only one explanatory variable, such that $\hat{Y} = E(Y|X) = E(Y) = \bar{y}$ holds for any value of X. Since a re-ordering problem arises if the response variable values are associated with equal estimated values, the response variable values corresponding to the same estimated values are replaced by their mean. As a result, the resulting concordance curve C_Y overlaps with the bisector curve, whose co-ordinates are given by the set of pairs $(i/n, i/n)$. This can be easily shown considering the normalised set of pairs $(i/n, \sum_{j=1}^{i} y_{\hat{r}_j}/n\bar{y})$, characterising the concordance curve C_Y. In the case in which $\hat{y}_i = \bar{y}$, $\forall i = 1, \ldots, n$, we obtain $(i/n, \sum_{j=1}^{i} y_{\hat{r}_j}/n\bar{y}) = (i/n, \sum_{j=1}^{i} \bar{y}/n\bar{y}) = (i/n, i\bar{y}/n\bar{y}) = (i/n, i/n)$.

Looking more closely at (3) note that, when different models are compared, the denominator does not change, while the numerator does. It is therefore intuitive to compare models in terms of differences between the distances expressed by the numerator of formula (3), leading to the following:

$$C_{num} = \sum_{i=1}^{n} \left\{ i/n - (1/(n\bar{y})) \sum_{j=1}^{i} y_{\hat{r}_j} \right\}. \quad (4)$$

The above measure suffers from a drawback: positive values of the index may be compensated by negative values, leading C_{num} to take a value equal to zero. To overcome this problem, we resort to the squared distance between the set of points lying on the concordance curve C_Y and the set of points lying on the bisector curve. Indeed, as the bisector curve defines the situation of a random, non predictive model, for which the Y values are independent on the $\hat{Y}$, we can interpret the squared distance as the difference between the observed and the expected concordance values of Y, where by expected we mean the concordance values that we would have with a random model. If we divide the difference by the expected values themselves, we obtain the RGA (Rank Graduation Accuracy) measure as:

$$RGA = \sum_{i=1}^{n} \frac{\left\{ (1/(n\bar{y})) \sum_{j=1}^{i} y_{\hat{r}_j} - i/n \right\}^2}{i/n}. \quad (5)$$

Through some manipulations, an equivalent version of (5) can be further derived as

$$RGA = \sum_{i=1}^{n} \frac{\{C(y_{\hat{r}_i}) - i/n\}^2}{i/n}, \quad (6)$$

which emphasises the role of the quantity $C(y_{\hat{r}_j}) = \frac{\sum_{j=1}^{i} y_{\hat{r}_j}}{\sum_{i=1}^{n} y_{r_i}}$, that represents the cumulative values of the (normalised) response variable.

Note that the RGA index takes values between 0 and its maximum value RG_{max}, which is obtained when the predicted ranks order the response variable values in full concordance (full discordance) with the observed ranks. It can be used to normalise the values of the RGA index, obtaining a measure that is bounded between 0 and 1. It is worth remarking that all models with the same predicted ranks provide the same value of the RGA index. This issue has not to be intended as a limitation of our proposal being the goal of the measure to assess the model attitude in providing a re-ordering of the observed values, which is as much as possible similar to the original ordering.

C. The RGA for scoring models

When assessing the predictive accuracy of credit scoring models in terms of our diagnostic measure, the response variable Y values can be re-ordered according to the predicted values $P(y_i = 1)$, which indeed take real values. Thus, the computation of the RGA index involves only the values 0 or 1, according to the absence or the presence of the attribute of interest, which in this case is the non-default or default occurance.

The possible behaviors of the concordance curve in the binary case is illustrated in Figure 2. Figure 2 illustrates the three alternative scenarios that can arise, if Y and $\hat{Y}$ are: a) perfectly concordant, b) perfectly discordant and c) partially concordant (discordant). Looking more closely at Figure 2 note that the C_Y concordance curve has a behavior which is similar to the ROC curve. However, while the ROC curve is built ordering cut-off points in an arbitrary way, the C_Y concordance overcomes this subjectivity issue, as the ordering is based on the predicted values themselves. This is indeed a further advantage of our proposal presenting as an objective predictive accuracy diagnostics.

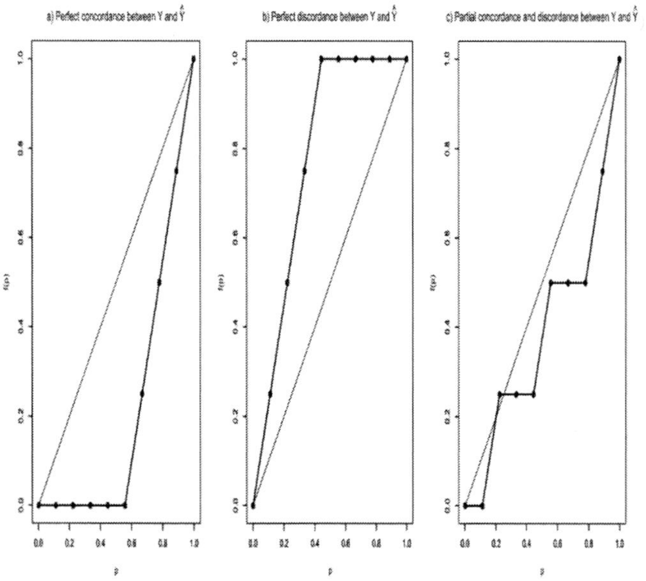

Figure 2. The L_Y and L'_Y Lorenz curves and the C_Y concordance curve.

We finally remark that, in the binary case, the number of points on which the concordance curve is constructed is equal to the number of observations. For each observation, the RGA index compares the values of the actual response, which in the binary case can be either 0 or 1, ordered in one case according to the ranks of the observed response, in the other according to the ranks of the predicted response. We have perfect concordance (Figure 2 a)) when the ranks coincide on all observations; perfect discordance (Figure 2 b)) when the ranks are in reverse correspondence.

IV. Application to Credit Scoring Models

The aim of this section is to show the RGA measure behavior when assessing the predictive accuracy of alternative logistic regression models employed in credit scoring applications. The models are applied to data supplied by a European External Credit Assessment Institution (ECAI), specialized in credit scoring for P2P platforms and focused on SME commercial lending. The dataset includes a set of information on the end-of-year 2015 financial ratios (calculated from balance-sheet variables) related to 15,045 South-European SMEs, for which the specification about the status (0 = active, 1 = defaulted) one year later (2016) is provided. For more details about the data, see [6].

In Table I, the financial ratios employed to predict company's status are reported. Table I shows that, to predict the company's status in 2016, 23 financial ratios from 2015 are available.

TABLE I. LIST OF FINANCIAL RATIOS EMPLOYED AS EXPLANATORY VARIABLES.

ID	Formula or Description
1	Total Assets/Equity
2	(Long term debt + Loans)/Shareholders Funds
3	Total Assets/Total Liabilities
4	Current Assets/Current Liabilities
5	(Current assets - Current assets: stocks)/Current liabilities
6	Shareholders Funds + Non current liabilities)/Fixed assets
7	EBIT/interest paid
8	(Profit or Loss before tax + Interest paid)/Total assets
9	Return on Equity (ROE)
10	Operating revenues/Total assets
11	Sales/Total assets (Activity Ratio)
12	Interest paid/(Profit before taxes + Interest paid)
13	EBITDA/interest paid (Solvency ratio)
14	EBITDA/Operating revenues
15	EBITDA/Sales
16	EBIT Dummy (=1 if EBIT<0, 0 otherwise)
17	Profit before tax Dummy (=1 if Profit before tax<0, 0 otherwise)
18	Financial Profit Dummy (=1 if Financial Profit<0, 0 otherwise)
19	Net Profit Dummy (=1 if Net Profit<0, 0 otherwise)
20	Trade Payables/Operating Revenues
21	Trade Receivables/Operating Revenues
22	Inventories/Operating Revenues
23	Turnover

Following the standard cross-validation approach, the dataset is split into a training and a test subsample, corresponding to 70% and 30% of the sample. A stepwise logistic regression is performed on the training dataset. From Figure 3, which provides the `R` output of the stepwise procedure, it results that that 17 variables over the original 23 variables are selected with $\alpha = 5\%$. For each variable, the corresponding estimated coefficients are also reported. In order to fulfill the model parsimony requirement, variables which are not significant at a level of 1%, are removed leading to select only 9 variables.

By using the estimated coefficient values reported in Figure 3 and derived from the implemented stepwise procedure, the predicted response values $\hat{Y}$ are computed for a set of models that are obtained considering all the subsets of the 9 selected predictors, whose number of predictors is let vary from 1 to 8. For each model, the RGA, Somers' D and AUROC are determined.

A comparison of the measures in terms of model selectivity is also provided by assessing the capability to order models by performance and choose the best among them. We first assess selectivity, for a given model dimension. To this aim, the boxplots in Figure 4 represent the distribution of the three measures for different model dimensions: from 1 predictor to 8 predictors. From the boxplots in Figure 4, it arises that the variability of the RGA measure across the models of the same dimension is always larger than that associated with the other measures, except in the case of only one predictor. This result shows the attitude of the RGA measure to order models and discriminate between them, by resorting to their predictive accuracy. On the contrary, Somers' D works better in the one dimensional case and this is motivated by the usual use of Somers' D as an exploratory tool for variable selection. From a methodological viewpoint, the better model selection power of the RGA measure, with respect to the AUROC, stems from the different construction. While the AUROC is calculated at a selected set of cut-off points, the RGA is calculated at all response values making it more sensible to model variations. Moreover, if on the one hand increasing the number of cut-off points would improve the AUROC performance making it similar to that associated with the RGA, this "modus operandi" may lead the AUROC-based approach more computationally intensive. Somers' D is also calculated at all response values but, differently from RGA, employs an additional data transformation, based on the binarisation of model errors, which makes it less sensible than the RGA.

As the last step, model selectivity is assessed by comparing different model dimensions. To do this, RGA, Somers' D and AUROC measures are computed on the best model - the one for which the analyzed measure is maximum - for model dimensions that go from 1 to 8. Figure 5 displays the relative change in the maximum value of the three measures, as the number of predictors increases. From Figure 5, it arises that the RGA measure dominates the others in terms of relative change, for all dimensions, allowing us to further show the RGA measure superiority in ordering models and discriminating between them.

```
Coefficients:
              Estimate Std. Error z value Pr(>|z|)
(Intercept) -1.768e+00  1.715e-01 -10.309  < 2e-16 ***
id_1         3.212e-03  1.521e-03   2.112  0.03465 *
id_3        -5.538e-01  1.144e-01  -4.839 1.30e-06 ***
id_4        -3.351e-01  6.943e-02  -4.826 1.39e-06 ***
id_6         4.775e-03  1.584e-03   3.015  0.00257 **
id_7         3.418e-03  1.645e-03   2.078  0.03773 *
id_8        -2.829e+00  3.588e-01  -7.884 3.18e-15 ***
id_9        -6.001e-02  4.175e-02  -1.438  0.15058
id_10       -2.745e-01  1.615e-01  -1.699  0.08923 .
id_11        3.717e-01  1.602e-01   2.320  0.02034 *
id_13       -3.029e-03  1.347e-03  -2.249  0.02451 *
id_15       -4.749e-01  1.973e-01  -2.407  0.01608 *
id_20        1.849e-03  2.954e-04   6.260 3.85e-10 ***
id_21        7.038e-04  2.681e-04   2.625  0.00867 **
id_23       -2.245e-05  7.658e-06  -2.932  0.00337 **
id_17        4.770e-01  1.631e-01   2.924  0.00345 **
id_19        6.236e-01  1.538e-01   4.055 5.01e-05 ***
---
Signif. codes:  0 '***' 0.001 '**' 0.01 '*' 0.05 '.' 0.1 ' ' 1
```

Figure 3. Logistic regression output for the model selected trough the R stepwise procedure.

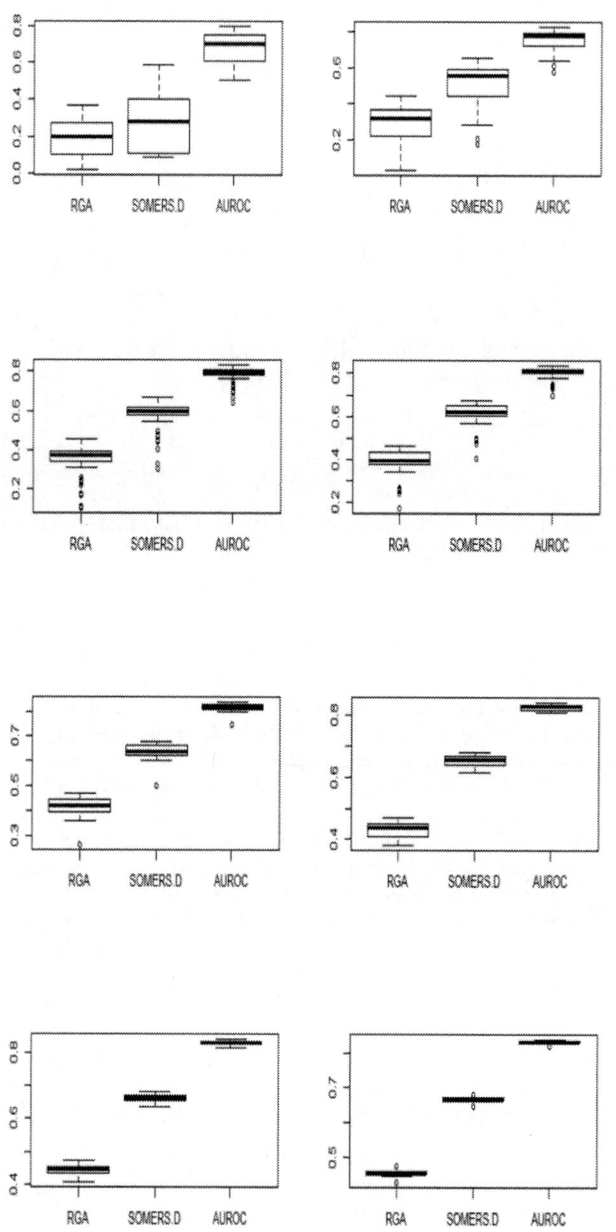

Figure 4. Distribution of RGA, Somers' D and AUROC over the models estimated on credit rating data. The eight plots correspond to different model dimensions; reading from left to right, and from top to bottom: models with 1, 2, 3, 4, 5, 6, 7 and 8 predictors.

V. Conclusions and Future Work

In this paper, a new measure to evaluate the predictive accuracy of a credit scoring model was presented.

The new measure, called RGA, is based on the computation of the cumulative values of the response variable, reordered according to the ranks of the values predicted by a given model.

Compared with the other most commonly used predictive accuracy measures, the RGA has the advantage of respecting the ordering requirement for borrowers, and of being independent on the choice of cut-off points, differently from the AUROC, and similarly to Somers' D. Nevertheless, on the contrary of the Somers' D, the RGA is less computational intensive.

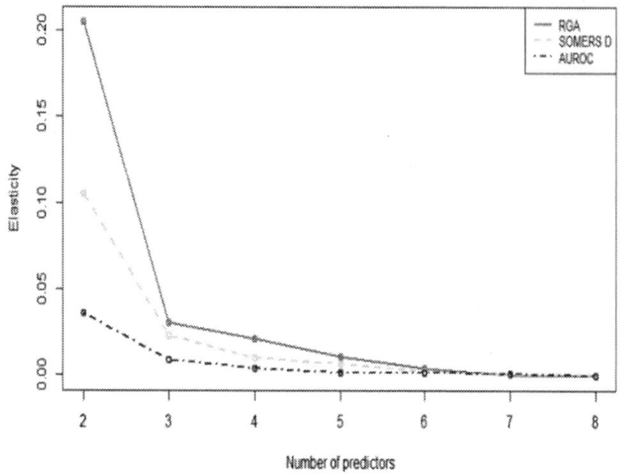

Figure 5. Relative change of RGA, Somers' D and AUROC, as a function of the number of predictors.

The proposed measure appears mathematically sound and easy to implement. Moreover, it has been found quite effective in both a real and a simulated credit scoring application. It overperforms Somers' D and AUROC in model ordering and in discriminating between "good" and "bad" models.

Due to its properties, we believe that the main beneficiaries of the proposed measure may be regulators and supervisors, interested in assessing and validating the credit risk models employed by banks and financial technology companies.

Future extensions of the research will be addressed both to the methodological and application contexts. In the former case, the development of a statistical testing procedure would provide to the predictive accuracy assessment a significance measure. In the latter case, the extensive application to several other application fields, involving the implementation of other machine learning models, would further shed light on the adequacy of our proposal as a suitable criterion for the evaluation of the predictive accuracy in multiple scenarios.

ACKNOWLEDGMENT

The work in the paper has received support from the European Union's Horizon 2020 training and innovation programme "FIN-TECH", under the grant agreement No. 825215 (Topic ICT-35-2018, Type of actions: CSA, https://www.fintech-ho2020.eu).

REFERENCES

[1] B. Engelmann, Measures of a Rating's Discriminative Power-Applications and Limitations. The Basel II Risk Parameters, Springer, 2006, ISBN: 978-3-540-33087-5.

[2] T. Fawcett, "An introduction to ROC analysis," Pattern Recognition Letters, vol. 27, 2006, pp. 861–874, ISSN: 0167-8655.

[3] P. A. Ferrari and E. Raffinetti, "A Different Approach to Dependence Analysis," Multivariate Behavioral Research, vol. 50, 2015, pp. 248–264, ISSN: 1532-7906.

[4] P. Giudici, Applied Data Mining: Statistical Methods for Business and Industry. Wiley, Hoboken, 2003, ISBN: 978-0470871409.

[5] P. Giudici and E. Raffinetti, *Multivariate Ranks-Based Concordance Indexes*, Advanced Statistical Methods for the Analysis 465 of Large Data-Sets, Studies in Theoretical and Applied Statistics, Springer-Verlag Berlin Heidelberg, 2012, ISBN: 978-3-642-21037-2.

[6] P. Giudici, B. Hadji-Misheva, A. Spelta, "Network based credit risk models," Quality Engineering, vol. 32, 2020, pp. 199–211, ISSN: 1532-4222.

[7] D. Hand, H. Mannila and P. Smyth, Principles of data mining. Adaptive Computation and Machine Learning Series. MIT Press, 2001, ISBN: 978-0262082907.

[8] M. O. Lorenz, "Methods of Measuring the Concentration of Wealth," Journal Publications of the American Statistical Association, vol. 9, 1905, pp. 209–219.

[9] D. McFadden, Conditional logit analysis of qualitative choice behavior. In Frontiers in Econometrics, ed. P. Zarembka, New York: Academic Press, 1974, ISBN: 0127761500.

[10] W. Orth, "The predictive accuracy of credit ratings: Measurement and statistical inference," International Journal of Forecasting, vol. 28, 2012, pp. 288–296, ISSN: 0169-2070.

[11] R. H. Somers, "A new asymmetric measure of association for ordinal variables," American Sociological Review, vol. 27, 1962, pp. 799–811, ISSN: 1939-8271.

Seasonality Modeling through LSTM Network in Inflation-Indexed Swaps

Looking for a bridge between the traditional standard pricing approach and the new FinTech techniques

Pier Giuseppe Giribone
Department of Economics (DIEC)
University of Genoa
Genoa, Italy
e-mail: pier.giuseppe.giribone@economia.unige.it

Abstract—**An Inflation-Indexed Swap (IIS) is a derivative in which, at every payment date, the counterparties swap an inflation rate with a fixed rate. For the calculation of the Inflation Leg cash flows, it is necessary to build a mathematical model suitable for the Consumer Price Index (CPI) projection. For this purpose, quants typically start by using market quotes for the Zero-Coupon swaps in order to derive the future trend of the inflation index, together with a seasonality model for capturing the typical periodical effects. In this study, I propose a forecasting model for inflation seasonality based on a Long Short-Term Memory (LSTM) network: a deep learning methodology particularly useful for forecasting purposes. Thanks to its architecture, able to capture highly nonlinear relationships, and to the design of a careful training, able to satisfy both statistical and econometric features, the proposed methodology can be considered more accurate rather than the traditional one. As a result, the study shows how the CPI predictions, conducted using a FinTech paradigm, can be integrated in the respect of the traditional quantitative finance theory developed in this research field.**

Keywords-Inflation-Indexed Swap (IIS); Year-on-Year Inflation-Indexed Swap (YYIIS); Zero-Coupon Inflation-Indexed Swap (ZCIIS); Seasonality model; CPI bootstrap; Machine Learning (ML); Deep Learning; Long Short-Term Memory (LSTM) Network.

I. INTRODUCTION

Machine learning methodologies are increasingly spreading in the financial sector. Among the numerous examples of applications proposed by the literature, the most popular ones are mainly aimed at solving the following problems: input data quality [15], innovative algo-trading techniques [5], optimal portfolio management [7], pattern recognition and classification [11], financial time-series forecasting as an alternative to traditional econometric approaches, such as: Autoregressive Integrated Moving Average (ARIMA), Bayesian Vector AutoRegression (BVAR), Generalized AutoRegressive Conditional Heteroskedasticity (GARCH) [13] [17].

It is more difficult to find evidence in literature of artificial intelligence methodologies applied to exotic financial instruments pricing or about the integration of traditional quantitative finance theory with the new FinTech methodologies. The traditional implementation regards the numerical solution of the so-called fundamental Black-Scholes-Merton PDE through Radial Basis Functions [4].

Only more recently, the application of Regressive Neural Networks together with the Monte Carlo method was suggested for evaluating early-exercise features in American and Bermuda option pricing in accordance with the Longstaff-Schwartz methodology [12]. This study aims to extend the existing literature concerning the integration of FinTech in Quantitative Finance through the design of a LSTM network for the seasonality modeling in inflation indexed swaps.

The paper is structured according to the following sections: the next part illustrates briefly the pricing framework; section 3 deals with the traditional standard method for the forecast of CPI values (trend + seasonality); section 4 describes the LSTM architecture; section 5 focuses on CPI projections (also called CPI bootstrap) and section 6 concludes with a real market case: the two methodologies are used for computing the fair-value for an Inflation-Indexed Swap and the model risk is quantified.

II. THE PRICING FRAMEWORK

An Inflation-Indexed Swap (IIS) is a swap deal in which, for each payment date, $T_1, \dots, T_M$, counterparty A pays to counterparty B the inflation rate in the considered period, while counterparty B pays to counterparty A the fixed rate.

The inflation rate is calculated as the percentage return of the Consumer Price Index (CPI) over the reference time interval. There are two main types of IIS traded on the market: the Zero-Coupon Inflation-Indexed Swap (ZCIIS) and the Year-on-Year Inflation-Indexed Swap (YYIIS) [2].

In a ZCIIS, at maturity date T_M, assuming $T_M = M$ years, counterparty B pays to counterparty A the fixed quantity:

$$N[(1+K)^M - 1] \quad (1)$$

where K and N are the fixed interest rate and the principal, respectively.

In return for this fixed payment, at the maturity date T_M, counterparty A pays to counterparty B the floating amount:

$$N\left[\frac{I(T_M)}{I_0} - 1\right] \quad (2)$$

In a YYIIS, for each payment date T_i, counterparty B pays to counterparty A the fixed amount:

$$N\varphi_i K \quad (3)$$

where φ_i is the year fraction of the fixed swap leg in the range $[T_{i-1}, T_i]$, $T_0 := 0$ and N is the principal of the deal.

Counterparty A pays to counterparty B the floating amount equals to:

$$N\varphi_i\left[\frac{I(T_i)}{I(T_{i-1})}-1\right] \quad (4)$$

ZCIIS and YYIIS are typically quoted in terms of the corresponding equivalent fixed rate K.

Based on these quotes and using stochastic calculus, pricing formulas can be derived for both classes of derivatives. Readers, interested in this quantitative financial part, can find the rigorous pricing formulas derivations in [2] [9] [10] and [14].

In particular Kazziha [10] derived the CPI forward values, $\Im_i$:

$$\Im_M(0) = \Im_{REF}(0)\cdot[1+K(T_M)]^M \quad (5)$$

where:

$\Im_{REF}(0)$ is the CPI reference value. It corresponds to the one set n months back in relation to the settlement date. Typically, the standard time lag is 3 months.

$K(T_M)$ is the Inflation Zero Swap Rate quoted on the market in correspondence to the maturity T_M.

III. CPI INDEX TRADITIONAL SIMULATION

Through (5), we are able to project the index values in the future according to the swap rates listed on the market following the pricing framework. Since the frequency with which the index is published is monthly, it is necessary to provide a simulation of the CPI with such periodicity [3].

The missing curve points are therefore estimated by adding the logarithm of the monthly increase between a calculated value $\Im_M(0)$ and its subsequent value $\Im_{M+1}(0)$:

$$\Delta\Im_M = \frac{\ln\left(\frac{\Im_{M+1}(0)}{\Im_M(0)}\right)}{12\cdot\tau} \quad (6)$$

where τ is the time interval expressed in year fraction between $\Im_M(0)$ and $\Im_{M+1}(0)$.

The points making up the simulated curve of the consumer price index are defined by the formula:

$$\Im_{i+1} = \Im_i \exp(\Delta\Im_M + \Re_M), \Im_M(0) \le \Im_i \le \Im_{M+1}(0) \quad (7)$$

The standard methodology, suggested by the main benchmark info provider pricing modules, takes into account the index seasonality algebraically adding the normalized residuals $\Re_M$ obtained from the historical values of the CPI, in accordance with the expression (8):

$$\Re_M = \frac{\sum_{i=1}^{seasyear}\ln\left[\frac{\Im_{i+1}^{Monthly}}{\Im_i^{Monthly}}\right]}{seasyear} - \frac{\sum_{i=1}^{12\cdot seasyear}\ln\left[\frac{\Im_{i+1}^{Monthly}}{\Im_i^{Monthly}}\right]}{12\cdot seasyear} \quad (8)$$

where $\Re_M$ are the standardized residuals obtained from the effect of seasonality over *seasyear* years. The first contribution is the logarithmic variation of the CPI values on the considered month; the second one represents the overall logarithmic variation recorded in the time period considered for seasonality. The objective of this study is to propose a deep learning methodology (LSTM network) able to simulate the seasonality of the inflation index. In this way, in addition to introducing a more robust and flexible econometric methodology than the standard one, the integration between the classic quantitative finance theory together with the Fintech paradigms can be considered an interesting feature [1]. In fact, the determination of the swap fair value is implemented by applying the formulas described above for the ZCIIS and YYIIS and therefore in total agreement with canonical principles; moreover, a Long Short-Term Memory network will be implemented for a more reliable simulation of the CPI seasonality. The next section deals with the explanation of the architecture and the training phase for the implemented LSTM network.

IV. LSTM NETWORK ARCHITECTURE AND TRAINING

LSTM networks are also able to learn long-term relationships between the time intervals of a time series, therefore without the need to pre-set the number of time lags, as occurs in other dynamic recurrent networks, such as Nonlinear AutoRegressive (NAR) and Nonlinear Auto-Regressive with exogenous variables (NARX) [6].

A common LSTM unit is composed of a cell, an input gate and a forget gate. The cell remembers values over arbitrary time intervals and the three gates regulate the flow of information into and out of the cell. Intuitively, the cell is responsible for keeping track of the dependencies between the elements in the input sequence. The input gate controls the extent to which a new value flows into the cell, the forget gate controls the extent to which a value remains in the cell and the output gate controls the extent to which the value in the cell is used to compute the output activation of the LSTM unit [8]. The activation function of the LSTM gates is often the logistic sigmoid. Figure 1 shows how the flux of a data sequence Y with C features (or channels) of length S has been processed into a LSTM layer. In the block diagram, h_t and $c(t)$ are, respectively, the output (also known as hidden state) and the cell state at time t.

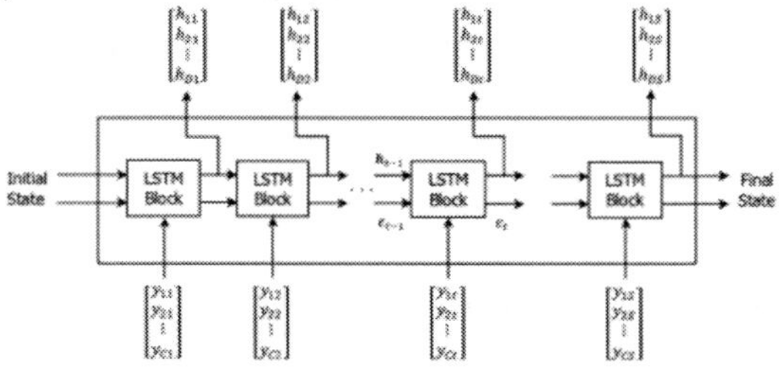

Figure 1. LSTM network architecture.

The first LSTM block uses the initial state of the network and the first time-step of the sequence in order to compute the first output and the first update of the cell state. At time t, the block uses the current state of the network (c_{t-1}, h_{t-1}) and the next step of the sequence for estimating the output and updating the current state of the cell c_t. The layer state is characterized by the hidden state (also known as the output state) and the cell state. The hidden state at time step t contains the output of the LSTM layer for the current time step. The cell state contains the information learnt in the previous steps. For each time step, the layer adds or removes information from the cell state. The layer controls these updates using gates. The following components control the cell state and the hidden state of the layer [8]:

- Input gate (i): Control level of cell state update.

- Forget gate (f): Control level of cell state reset (forget).
- Cell candidate (g): Add information to cell state.
- Output gate (o): Control level of cell state added to hidden state.

Figure 2 shows how the gates (i, f, g, o) process the signal at time t.

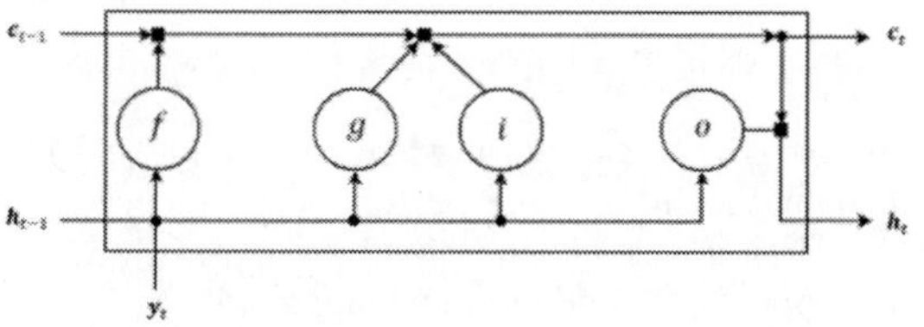

Figure 2. Signal processed by the gates (i, f, g, o).

In a LSTM, the parameters that are subjected to calibration are: the input weights (W), the recurrent weights (R) and the biases (b) [6]. W, R and b are the arrays built through the concatenations of such parameters for each component: $W = \left(W_i, W_f, W_g, W_o\right)^{\mathrm{T}}$, $R = \left(R_i, R_f, R_g, R_o\right)^{\mathrm{T}}$ and $b = \left(b_i, b_f, b_g, b_o\right)^{\mathrm{T}}$ where i, f, g and o denote the input gate, the forget gate, the cell candidate and the output gate, respectively.

At time step t, the cell state is given by:

$$c_t = f_t \odot c_{t-1} + i_t \odot g_t \quad (9)$$

where $\odot$ is the Hadamard product operator.

At time step t, the hidden state is given by:

$$h_t = o_t \odot \sigma_c(c_t) \quad (10)$$

where σ_c is the activation function of the state (typically a hyperbolic tangent).

The following equations define the components at time step t:

- Input gate (i):

$$i_t = \sigma_g(W_i y_t + R_i h_{t-1} + b_i) \quad (11)$$

- Forget gate (f):

$$f_t = \sigma_g\left(W_f y_t + R_f h_{t-1} + b_f\right) \quad (12)$$

- Cell candidate (g):

$$g_t = \sigma_c\left(W_g y_t + R_g h_{t-1} + b_g\right) \quad (13)$$

- Output gate (o):

$$o_t = \sigma_g(W_o y_t + R_o h_{t-1} + b_o) \quad (14)$$

σ_g is the activation function of the gate, typically a sigmoid.

LSTMs are supervised networks, as a result, after the design of the model, it is essential to implement a robust algorithm for the training phase. This is the part in which the designer decides how many neurons must be implemented in order to make reliable predictions. In order to obtain valid models for forecasting purposes it is necessary to conduct statistical and econometric tests. The objective of the first kind of test is to tune the LSTM in order to have a good fitting of the training dataset. The gap between the target and the model output is reduced through an ADAM optimizer as the network training process progresses, so it may happen that the estimated relationship returns a perfect fit of the sampled data (in-sample), making vain the attempt at generalization, fundamental for making the network capable of processing different data (out-of-sample). For this reason and especially in the field of deep learning where there is a huge number of parameters to tune in order to capture highly non-linear relationships, special measures for avoiding overfitting must be taken into consideration. As a result, the first intervention, shared also with traditional recurrent networks, such as NAR and NARX, is to work directly on the dataset through a random-splitting method.

The data set configuration used for the network is:

- 70% of the set will form the training set, thus the optimization will be carried out with respect to its loss function (J) only.
- 15% of the set will be assigned to the validation set, thus, despite the weights are updated with respect to the train set, the algorithm saves the weights that minimize J on the validation set, in order to avoid data overfitting and trying to reach a good generalization.
- 15% of the data set will form the test set, so that the network performance can be measured on data that it has never seen before, as the ultimate objective of a neural network user is to employ the network on completely new data.

The second kind of statistical measures, which are traditionally applied in the field of deep learning, work directly on the network. The implemented measures can be summarized as follows:

- Adding a term to the traditional loss function (RMSE) which put in a penalty (the λ coefficient) if a further weight (ω) associated to an arch has been activated: $J = RMSE + \frac{1}{2}\lambda\|\omega\|^2$
- Dropout, which is a technique consisting of training only a group of randomly selected neurons rather than the entire network: a percentage (a popular choice is 25%) determines how many neurons to choose and the remaining ones are deactivated. Since the neurons and the relative weights are continuously modified, it is thus possible to avoid overfitting.

These precautions are thus implemented in the forecaster in order to have a reliable fitting.

Given that the objective is to perform a prediction of the most reasonable CPI projections, the second test has an econometric nature. It is based on the verification of the autocorrelation error absence so that the model error is unstructured and the predicted values can be econometrically reliable.

V. Comparison between Standard and LSTM Techniques for the CPI Projection

In order to compare the standard inflation bootstrap methodology with the LSTM approach, we use the market data retrieved from Bloomberg on 30th June 2020. Swap rate values, $K(T_M)$, quoted by the market at the reference date are reported in Table I, together with the estimation of the CPI projections, $\Im_M(0)$ and the $\Delta\Im_M$, according to (5) and (6). The estimation of $\Delta\Im_M$ is useful in order to have the inflation values expressed on a monthly basis [3].

TABLE I. $K(T_M)$, $\Im_M(0)$ AND $\Delta\Im_M$ (30TH JUNE 2020)

T_M	***Mid Price*** $K(T_M)$	$\Im_M(0)$	$\Delta\Im_M$
1	-0.071	104.69561	0.0382
2	0.19375	105.17638	0.0543
3	0.347	105.86444	0.0787
4	0.497	106.86841	0.0721
5	0.57125	107.79688	0.0804

According to (7), this information allow us to project the CPI values for the next years using a market-oriented approach without taking into account the seasonality. In order to add this essential contribution for the forecast into the model, we have to consider the monthly normalized residuals, $\Re_M$, calculated starting from the past CPI realizations. The traditional way to implement this task is to apply (8).

Using the traditional market standard preference to consider the previous five years of the CPI time-series, we get the following $\Re_M$, from January to December: -0.011959, 0.001761, 0.008373, 0.00266, 0.000828, 0.00018,-0.005856, 0.000625, 0.002751, 0.00105, -0.002176, 0.001764.

Applying recursively (7), the projections for the CPI are obtained for the following years. These simulations are reported in Figure 3 together with the past values.

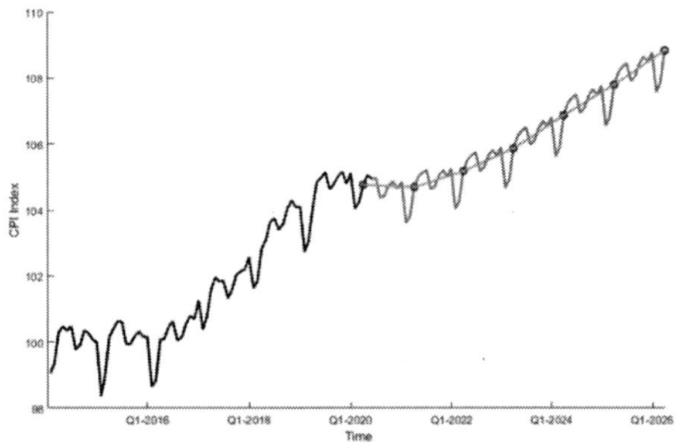

Figure 3. CPI time-series and its projection (traditional methodology). Black line: past CPI values. Green line: CPI projection without seasonality. Red Line: CPI projection with seasonality (traditional model). Blue points: market-implied CPI estimation

- the black line represents the past five years CPI values used for the estimation of the seasonality effect.
- the green line represents the CPI projections without seasonality: it connects the blue dots which are the $\Im_M(0)$ whose estimations are strictly connected to the $K(T_M)$ quotation.
- the red line represents the projections of the CPI index taking into account the seasonality through the monthly annualized residuals $\Re_M$.

The idea is to use a LSTM network with the aim of providing a better model for the seasonality. For the training set, we use the monthly return of the index computed in the last 5 years: $\ln\left[\frac{\Im_{i+1}^{Monthly}}{\Im_i^{Monthly}}\right]$, according to the market standard convention. The number of hidden units in the LSTM block is tuned in function of the performances recorded by the network. Using a layer made by 100 neurons, adopting an ADAM optimizer and implementing all the described techniques in order to avoid overfitting, we can achieve excellent results in the training phase [6]. From a statistical point of view, we obtain an R^2 close to 1, as a result the fitting over the historical time series is extremely good. From an econometric point of view, the auto-correlation error for the tuned model has been kept under an acceptable threshold for the non-zero lags [16], with a confidence interval equal to 95%.

Having checked the forecasting reliability of the LSTM network, we proceed to compute the following 6 years returns (72 values). Figure 4 and Figure 5 show the difference between the two approaches: the black line represents the realized past returns of the last five years and the red line represents the forecasted returns.

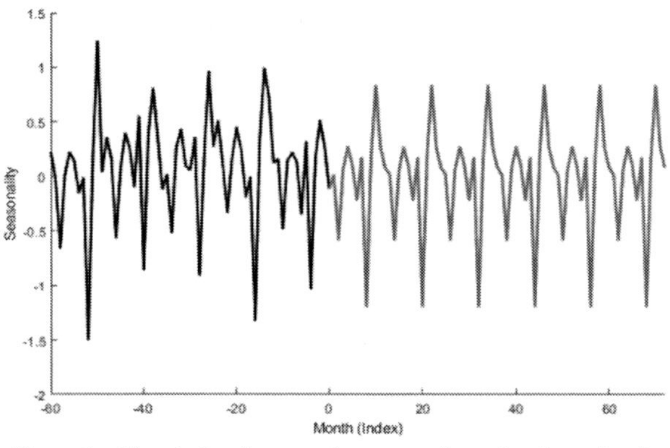

Figure 4. Historical and prospective seasonality estimation using the standard technique. Black line: realized past returns. Red line: forecasted returns

It is sufficient to look at the figures to realize that the red line (i.e. the projected time-series) obtained from the traditional method has a behavior which is too simplified. In fact, it is based on the estimation of the twelve normalized residuals of the previous months which are repeated equal for the future values. Implementing a properly trained LSTM allows to use a model able to capture highly nonlinear relationship among the time-series in accordance with the rigorous statistical and econometric tests [16] described in Section IV.

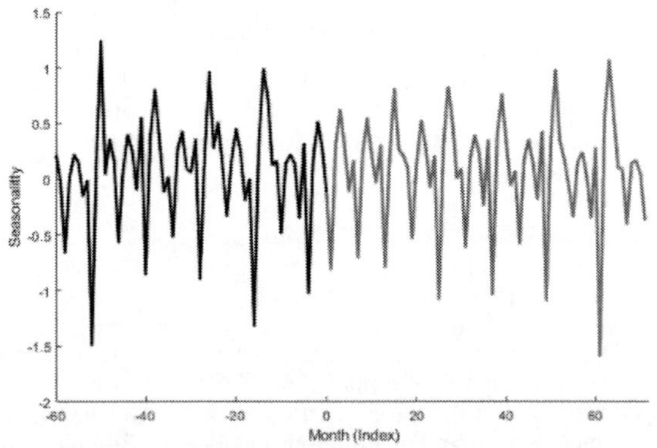

Figure 5. Historical and prospective estimation for seasonality using Deep Learning. Black line: realized past returns. Red line: forecasted returns

As a result, facing the forecasting problem with the FinTech approach, the red line has a more realistic forward-looking behavior thanks to both the advanced technology (deep learning) and the careful tuning. As we will see in the market case, which regards the pricing of a YYIIS, these differences in the simulation of the seasonality cause an impact on the derivative fair-value that is not always negligible.

VI. Market Case: YYIIS pricing

In this section, we proceed with the valorization of a YYIIS using the two approaches previously described. The main financial characteristics are reported in Table II. The valuation date of the "In Arrears" swap is 30th June 2020, as a result we use the historical and prospective inflation data already computed in the previous sections. Regarding the discount curve we use, according to the new benchmark standard for collateralized derivatives, the EUR OIS ESTR term structure. As a result, zero rates and discount factors used for pricing are those implied from the new market benchmark curve. Using the pricing framework described in section II, we proceed with the estimation of the future cash-flows for the swap and then we go through the discounting process for obtaining the NPVs for the two legs. The difference between the two NPVs gives the price of the swap.

TABLE II. YYIIS financial characteristics

	Receiving Leg	*Paying Leg*
Leg Type	Y-o-Y Inflation	Fixed
Notional	10 MM	10 MM
Currency	Euro	Euro
Index	CPTFEMU Index	Fixed Coupon: 0.5%
Effective Date	30th June 2020	30th June 2020
Maturity Date	30th June 2026	30th June 2026
Lag	3 Month	-
Interpolation	Monthly	-
Spread	0	-
Reset Frequency	Semi-Annual	-
Payment Freq.	Semi-Annual	Annual
Day Count	ACT/ACT	ACT/ACT
Discount Curve	EUR-OIS-ESTR	EUR-OIS-ESTR

The discounted Cash Flows for the fixed paying leg of the swap are equal to -306,314.62 Euro (Table III).

TABLE III. YYIIS Paying Leg

Payment Date	*Payment*	*Discount Rate*	*Present Value*
06/30/2021	-49,930.76	1.006019	-50,231.30
06/30/2022	-50,000.00	1.012638	-50,631.89
06/30/2023	-50,000.00	1.019137	-50,956.87
06/30/2024	-49,796.02	1.025040	-51,042.90
06/30/2025	-50,203.98	1.030223	-51,721.29
06/30/2026	-50,000.00	1.034607	-51,730.37

The discounted Cash Flows for the inflation-indexed receiving leg of the swap using the standard seasonality approach are equal to +391,740.5 Euro (Table IV).

TABLE IV. YYIIS Receiving Leg (standard approach)

Date	*Reset CPI*	*Payment*	*Discount*	*PV*
12/31/2020	104.74729	-2,185.66	1.002913	-2192.02
06/30/2021	104.69561	-4,894.44	1.006019	-4923.89
12/31/2021	105.06038	35,066.31	1.009331	35393.52
06/30/2022	105.17638	10,944.48	1.012638	11082.8
12/30/2022	105.6452	44,597.45	1.015884	45305.83
06/30/2023	105.86444	20,674.18	1.019137	21069.82
12/29/2023	106.49159	58,904.25	1.022122	60207.33
06/28/2024	106.86841	35,225.72	1.02504	36107.77
12/31/2024	107.45914	56,181.35	1.027729	57739.21
06/30/2025	107.79688	31,122.41	1.030223	32063.02
12/31/2025	108.44679	60,603.27	1.032507	62573.3
06/30/2026	108.84187	360,65.68	1.034607	37313.81

The discounted Cash Flows for the inflation-indexed receiving leg of the swap using the deep learning architecture are equal to +371,023.4 Euro (Table V).

It is interesting to highlight that, in correspondence with the dates where the CPI values can be directly implied by the market using (5), both methodologies are consistent with the values reported in Table I. This shows a good integration between traditional quantitative finance principles and new FinTech paradigms.

TABLE V. YYIIS RECEIVING LEG (LSTM APPROACH)

Date	*Reset CPI*	*Payment*	*Discount*	*PV*
12/31/2020	104.80403	3274,34	1.002913	3283.87
06/30/2021	104.69561	-10265.09	1.006019	-10326.88
12/31/2021	104.75465	5683.47	1.009331	5736.51
06/30/2022	105,17638	39847.66	1.012638	40351.25
12/30/2022	105.33777	15375.28	1.015884	15619.50
06/30/2023	105.86444	49737.38	1.019137	50689.20
12/29/2023	106.18170	29841.55	1.022122	30501.70
06/28/2024	106.86841	64287.66	1.02504	65897.43
12/31/2024	107.14643	26480.24	1.027729	27214.51
06/30/2025	107.79688	60025.26	1.030223	61839.40
12/31/2025	108.13120	31220.98	1.032507	32235.88
06/30/2026	108.63801	46376.07	1.034607	47981.01

According to the traditional pricing approach, the fair value for the analyzed YYIIS is +85,425.87. On the other hand, if we would have used the proposed and more advanced approach, its value would have been +64,708.77.

The gap between the values from the two pricing methodologies is equal to 20,717.1, an amount that can be considered significant enough for causing a percentage error higher than 20% compared to the Mark to Market of the analyzed derivative.

VII. CONCLUSION

This study shows how a Deep Learning methodology can be usefully implemented in a pricing framework aimed at determining the fair value of derivatives linked to the inflation index. The Long Short-Term Memory has allowed to identify the effect of seasonality more reliably than the traditional standard methodology. In fact, the proposed technique is able to simulate the future values of the time series by applying the described rigorous statistical and econometric tests, reasonably guaranteeing the reliability of the forecast. On the contrary, the traditional approach, based on the estimation of the historical normalized residuals, does not consider these important tests and it is not able to capture highly nonlinear relationships as a LSTM network does. It is particularly interesting considering how artificial intelligence paradigms can be integrated with traditional pricing methodologies in the quantitative finance field. For the continuation of the study, it is interesting to apply the suggested technology to derivatives written on an underlying which differs from inflation, where the seasonality modeling is of fundamental importance, such as commodity and energy derivatives.

ACKNOWLEDGMENT

I would like to thank Banca CARIGE for providing me market data through the Bloomberg® platform and the computational power needed for my researches over these past twelve years.

REFERENCES

[1] S. Bonini, G. Caivano, P. Cerchiello and P. G. Giribone, "Artificial Intelligence: Applications of Machine Learning and Predictive Analytics in Risk Management" AIFIRM (Italian Association of Financial Industry Risk Managers) position paper, N. 14, pp. 1–164, 2019.

[2] D. Brigo and F. Mercurio, "Interest Rate Models: Theory and Practice with smile, inflation and credit" Springer Finance, 2006.

[3] O. Caligaris and P. G. Giribone, "Modeling seasonality in inflation indexed swap through machine learning techniques: analysis and comparison between traditional methods and neural networks" Risk Management Magazine, vol. 13, N. 3, pp. 37–53, December 2018.

[4] R. Company, V. N. Egorova, L. Jodar and F. Soleymani, "A local radial basis function method for high-dimensional American option pricing problems" Mathematical Modelling and Analysis, vol. 23, N. 1, pp. 117–138, 2018.

[5] M. L. De Prado, "Advances in Financial Machine Learning", Wiley, 2018.

[6] M. de Simon-Martin et al., "Electricity Spot Prices Forecasting for MIBEL by using Deep Learning: a comparison between NAR, NARX and LSTM networks" 20th International Conference on Environment and Electrical Engineering (IEEE-EEEIC) 2020 Proceedings, 11th June 2020

[7] J. B. Heaton, N. Polson and J. H. Witte, "Deep Learning for Finance: Deep Portfolios" Applied Stochastic Models in Business and Industry, vol. 33, N. 1, pp. 3-12, 2017.

[8] S. Hochreiter and J. Schmidhuber, "Long Short-Term Memory" Neural Computing, vol. 9, N. 8, pp. 1735–1780, 1997.

[9] R. Jarrow and Y. Yildirim, "Pricing Treasury Inflation protected securities and related derivatives using an HJM model" Journal of Financial and Quantitative Analysis, vol. 38, N. 2, pp. 337–358, June 2003.

[10] S. Kazziha, "Interest rate models, inflation-based derivatives, trigger notes and cross-currency swaptions", PhD Thesis, Imperial Collage of Science, Technology and Medicine, London, 1999.

[11] P. Kim, "MATLAB Deep Learning with Machine Learning, Neural Networks and Artificial Intelligence" Apress, 2017.

[12] J. Lelong and B. Lapeyre, "Longstaff Schwartz algorithm and Neural Network regression" Advances in Financial Mathematics, Paris, 2020, unpublished.

[13] S. Mammadi, "Financial time series prediction using artificial neural network based on Levenberg-Marquardt algorithm" Procedia Computer Science, vol. 120, pp. 602–607, 2017.

[14] F. Mercurio, "Pricing inflation-indexed derivatives" Quantitative Finance, vol. 5, N. 3, pp. 289–302, June 2005.

[15] V. Pendyala, "Veracity of Big Data: Machine Learning and other approaches to verifying truthfulness" Apress, 2018.

[16] R. S. Tsay, "Analysis of Financial Time series" Third Edition, Wiley, 2010.

[17] C. Yanui, H. Kaijian and K. F. Geoffrey, "Forecasting crude oil prices: a deep learning based model" Procedia Computer Science, vol. 122, pp. 300–307, 2017.

Breast Cancer Dataset Analytics

Kevin Daimi
Department of Electrical, Computer Engineering and Computer Science
University of Detroit Mercy
Detroit, USA
daimikj@udmercy.edu

Noha Hazzazi
Electrical Engineering and Computer Science
Howard University
Washington DC, USA
noha.hazzazi@howard.edu

***Abstract*—Breast cancer is a disease that causes the cells of the breast to uncontrollably grow. It is the most occurring cancer in females worldwide. The type of breast cancer is governed by to breast cells that turn into cancer. Breast cancer can begin in different parts of the breast including lobules, ducts, and connective tissue. The clinical prognostic (the likelihood or expected development of a disease) stage depends on a number of factors including tumor size, lymph node status, whether the cancer has spread to other parts of the body, the cancer grade, Estrogen status, and Progesterone status. In this paper, the clinical prognostic stage (referred to as 6th Stage in this study) will be predicted using both a Python program and the Weka tool. The three algorithms, Neural Networks, Support Vector Machines, and Random Forest will be applied to the SEER Breast Cancer Dataset to classify the 6th Stage, which includes five classes.**

Keywords–Classification; Breast Cancer; Neural Networks; Support Vector Machines; Random Forest; Python; Weka.

I. INTRODUCTION

Breast cancer kicks off when cells in the breast start to grow out of control. These out of control cells usually develop a tumor that can be observed with an x-ray or sensed as a lump. The tumor is characterized as malignant (cancer) if the cells grow into surrounding tissues or spread to distant areas of the body. Breast cancer spreads when the cancer cells move to the blood or lymph system and are transferred to other parts of the body. Breast cancer occurs mainly in women, but men can also get it. Most breast cancers are introduced in the ducts that carry milk to the nipple (ductal cancers). Others develop in the glands that produce breast milk (lobular cancers) [1]. Breast cancer can span different ages. It is rare in very young women, but it has distinctive aspects that are not spotted in older patients. Young age breast cancer has aggressive biological characteristics and is liable to be diagnosed at an advanced stage providing poorer outcomes as compared to breast cancer in older premenopausal and postmenopausal women [2]. Cancer treatment is costly, especially in developing and under developing countries. Cost-effectiveness analyses can offer valuable information for planning and developing a breast cancer control policy. Such analyses can drive budget development, substantiate allocation of limited resources to national breast cancer control programs, improve breast cancer education, and pinpoint the most effective approaches of carrying out diagnostic and treatment services [3]. There are a number of breast cancer detection techniques. Among these are the mammographic images analysis. Kashyap, Bajpai, and Khanna [4] proposed a method to segment and classify abnormalities found in mammograms. They concluded that the removal of improved preprocessed and improved inverted preprocessed image enhances the detection of suspicious region in mammograms. Furthermore, edges of the skeptical region are sharpened by including thorough coefficients of the wavelet decomposition with the filtered image. Nugroho, Faisal, Soesanti, and Choridah [5] attempted to implement and analyze the contrast enhancement and feature selection technique to build a CAD(Computer Aided Design) system to differentiate normal, benign, and malignant. Preprocessing was required to improve the poor quality of images and remove the pieces added by the preprocessing step. The region of interest (suspicious area) was segmented and then extracted by texture feature method. The high dimensionality of features was identified by a feature selection technique. The digital mammogram images were taken from the Private Database of Oncology Clinic Kotabaru Yogyakarta. The dataset involved 40 mammogram images with 14 benign cases, 6 malignant cases, and 20 normal cases. Further mammograms analysis approaches can be found in [6]–[9]. Wang [10] provided an overview of recent advances in microwave sensors for biomedical imaging applications focusing on breast cancer detection. The electric characteristics of biological tissues at microwave spectrum, microwave imaging approaches, microwave biosensors, and current challenges in the field were also covered.

Breast cancer detection, diagnosis, and analysis paved the path for many machine learning applications. Gupta and Gupta [11] applied the machine learning techniques; Linear regression, Random Forest, Multi-layer Perceptron, and Decision Trees (DT) to the Wisconsin Breast Cancer Dataset. This dataset is made up of 569 samples (rows). Only the performance measures including accuracy, recall, and precision were summarized. No details for further conclusions were provided. Agarap [12] compared the performance of Linear regression, Multi-layer Perceptron, K-Nearest Neighbor (KNN), Softmax Regression, and Support Vector Machines (SVM) when applied to the Wisconsin Breast Cancer Dataset. The tool used was not specified and no details were provided. It is not that clear how the paper concluded that SVM performed the best. The two studies above involved a binary classification (benign or malignant tumor) of breast cancer tumor. Binary classification of the breast cancer using Naive Bayes and K-Nearest Neighbor was carried out in [13]. Their results showed that KNN achieved the highest accuracy of 97.51% with the lowest error rate (96.19%) than Naive Bayes. No details were provided apart from the well-known details of the algorithms. Bazazeh and Shubair [14] studied breast cancer binary classification using Support Vector Machines, Random

Forest, and Bayesian Networks. They also applied them to the Wisconsin Breast Cancer Dataset. They concluded Bayesian Networks had the best performance. A hybridized classifier for breast cancer diagnosis was proposed in [15]. They combined Self-Organizing Maps (unsupervised artificial neural network) method with the supervised classifier Stochastic Gradient Descent (SGD) to perform binary (cancer/no cancer) classification on the Wisconsin Breast Cancer Dataset. They compared the results of this combination with the outcomes of Decision Trees (DTs), Random Forests (RF) and Support Vector Machine (SVM). They concluded their combination resulted in excellent accuracy. Another approach was based on first using image processing techniques to prepare the mammography images for the feature and pattern extraction phase, and then feeding the extracted features to Back Propagation Neural Networks (BPNN) and Logistic Regression (LR) models [16]. They concluded BPNN performed the best. Similar approaches with different algorithms were proposed in [17]–[19]. A number of studies concentrate on using Convolutional Neural Networks for the analysis of breast tumors. Pawar and Patil [20] used Backpropagation Neural Network and compared the results with Radial Basis Function Network. Using the Wisconsin Breast Cancer Dataset and relying on MATLAB, it was concluded that a neural network with nine neurons in the hidden layer provided an accuracy of 99%. Convolutional Neural Networks was applied to the detection of breast cancer using Mammograms-MIAS dataset with 322 mammograms in which 189 images were normal and 133 abnormal breasts tumors [21]. The authors stressed that the experimental results depicting the efficacy of deep learning for breast cancer detection in mammogram images was promising and suggested using deep learning for various medical imaging. Further work on applying Artificial Neural Networks, Convolutional Neural Networks, and both Convolutional Neural Networks and Support Vector Machines to classifying breast cancer as either cancerous (malignant), non-cancerous (benign) could be found in [22]–[24].

All of the above studies concentrated on binary classification. In other words, they aimed at determining whether a tumor is benign or malignant. In general, they relied on the Wisconsin Breast Cancer Dataset with 569 samples. In this paper, a multi-class classification using the SEER Breast Cancer Dataset [25] with 4024 samples will be implemented. Members of IEEE can download this dataset. The attribute that will be the goal of this classification is the 6th Stage (S_Stage). It has five classes, as explained in Section II. Three classification methods were used: Neural Networks, Support Vector Machines, and Random Forest. Those were first included in a Python program and then run through the Weka tool [26]. Analysis of the outcomes are then provided. The remainder of the paper is organized as follows: Section II describes the SEER Breast Cancer Dataset and its preparation. Section III deals with the classification of the 6th Stage using a Python program. The classification of the 6th Stage using Weka is presented in Section IV. Section V deliberates on possible predictions on the SEER Dataset. The discussion of the outcomes is depicted in Section VI, and the paper is concluded in Section VII.

II. SEER BREAST CANCER DATASET

The Breast Cancer Dataset contains fifteen attributes (columns) and 4024 rows. Some attributes have been renamed for programming purpose. Those are enclosed in parentheses below.

A. Dataset Description

The attributes used in dataset are described below. The type of data and the values they can take are also stated. A sample of this dataset is presented in Table **??**. The rows appear as columns.

1) *Age: This represents the age of the patient. It is a continuous numerical attribute.*
2) *Race: A nominal attribute that has three values: White, Black, and Other (American Indian / AK Native, Asian / Pacific Islander) (See table 9).*
3) *Marital Status (M_Status): A nominal attribute with five different values: Married (including common law), Divorced, Single (never married), Widowed, and Separated (See table* **??***).*
4) *T-Stage: The letter "T" followed by a number (1-4) refers to the size and location of the tumor including how much the tumor has grown into nearby tissues. This Nominal variable takes the values; T1, T2, T3, and T4 (See table* **??***) [27].*
5) *N-Stage: The letter "N" followed by a number (1-3) stands for lymph nodes. Most often, the more lymph nodes with cancer, the larger the number assigned. N1, N2, and N3 are the possible values for this nominal attribute (See table* **??***).*
6) *6 th Stage (S_Stage): This nominal attribute takes the values IIA, IIB, IIIA, IIIB, and IIIC in this database. There are other values that are not included. The values (stages) of this attribute are based on a number of factors including type (invasive/inflammatory) of breast cancer, tumor found, tumor size, breast cancer cells found in the lymph nodes, number of auxiliary lymph nodes that the cancer spread to, number of lymph nodes near the breastbone that the cancer spread to, cancer spreading to the chest wall and/or skin of the breast, and redness/swelling/ulcer/warmness in large portion of the breast skin. Details of this categorization can be found in [27]. This attribute represents the class for this study (See table* **??***)*
7) *Grade: The grade refers to the amount of cancer cells that look like healthy cells when observed under a microscope. There are four grades (I-IV) for this nominal attribute: Well differentiated, Moderately differentiated, Poorly differentiated, and Undifferentiated; anaplastic (See table* **??***).*
8) *A Stage (A_Stage): The A Stage has two values: 'Reginal' indicating a neoplasm that has spread directly into surrounding organs or tissues, and 'Distant' indicating a neoplasm has spread to parts far from the primary tumor (See table* **??***).*
9) *Tumor Size (Tumor_Size): represents the size of the tumor in centimeters. It is a continuous numerical attribute.*
10) *Estrogen Status (E_Status): This nominal attribute has two values, positive if the breast cancer has*

estrogen receptors, and negative otherwise. These receptors are proteins that allow normal and some cancerous breast cells to grow (See table ??).

11) *Progesterone Status (P_Status): This nominal attribute has two values; positive if the breast cancer has progesterone receptors, and negative otherwise. Progesterone receptors enable normal and some cancerous breast cells to grow.*
12) *Regional Node Examined (RN_Exam): Represents the total number of regional lymph nodes that were removed and examined by the pathologist.*
13) *Regional Node Positive (RN_Pos): A continuous value that reflects the exact number of regional lymph nodes examined by the pathologist and found to contain metastases (development of secondary malignant growths at a distance from a primary site of cancer).*
14) *Survival Months (S_Months): A continuous attribute indicating the number of months a patient will survive.*
15) *Status: The status of the patient. The nominal attribute has two values; Dead and Alive.*

TABLE I. SAMPLE DATASET

Attribute	Row1	Row2	Row3
Age	43	67	58
Race	Other	White	Black
M_Status	Married	Divorced	Widowed
T_Stage	T2	T2	T1
N_Stage	N3	N1	N1
S_Stage	IIIC	IIB	IIA
Grade	II	III	II
A_Stage	Regional	Regional	Regional
Tumor_Size	40	25	11
E_Status	Positive	Positive	Positive
P_Status	Positive	Positive	Positive
RN_Exam	19	4	16
RN_Pos	11	1	1
S_Months	1	2	9
Status	Alive	Dead	Alive

B. Dataset Preparation

The preparation and cleaning of the dataset went through a number of steps. These steps are explained below. Some sample Python code will be shown.

1) *The Status column that has values "Dead" and "Alive" was completely removed. This has no impact on the classification.*

```
BC= pd.read\_csv(`BreastCancer2.csv',
    ↪ encoding=``latin-1")

BC1=BC.drop([`Status'], axis=1)
BC1.to\_csv(`BreastCancer3.csv')
```

2) *In this step, the nominal values were replaced by numbers as in the following Tables. The Python code for T_Type will be shown. The rest have similar code.*

Note that Estrogen Status and Progesterone Status values are similar. This should explain the absence of Progesterone Status values table.

```
initialization;
with (open('BreastCancer4.csv', 'w')) as predictfile:
  writer = csv.writer(predictfile, delimiter=',') x = 1
while x < 3409 do
    instructions;
    if lines[x][2] == 'White': then
        lines[x][2] = '1';
        if lines[x][2] == 'Black': then
            1
        else
            i
        end
        nes[x][2] = '2';
    else
        if lines[x][2] == 'Other (American Indian/AK
          Native, Asian/Pacific Islander)': then
            1
        else
            i
        end
        nes[x][2] = '3';
    end
    x = x +1
end
```

Algorithm 1: Python code for T_Type

TABLE 2. RACE VALUES

Race	Value
White	1
Black	2
Other	3

TABLE 3. MARTIAL STATUS VALUES

M_Status	Value
Married	1
Divorced	2
Single	3
Widowed	4
Separated	5

TABLE 4. T-STAGE VALUES

T-Stage	Value
T1	1
T2	2
T3	3
T4	4

TABLE 5. N-STAGE VALUES

N-Stage	Value
N1	1
N2	2
N3	3

TABLE 6. 6th-STAGE VALUES

Grade	Value
IIA	1
IIB	2
IIIA	3
IIIB	4
IIIC	5

TABLE 7. GRADE VALUES

Grade	Value
Grade I: well differentiated	1
Grade II: moderately differentiated	2
Grade III: poorly differentiated	3
Grade IV: undifferentiated	4

C. Understanding the Datasets

To better understand the dataset, the method "describe" was used as below. Table 10 provides insight into the dataset.

TABLE 8. A-STAGE VALUES

A-Stage	Value
Regional	1
Distant	2

TABLE 9. ESTROGEN STATUS VALUES

E_Status	Value
Positive	1
Negative	2

Percentile 25, 50, and 75 have been omitted in this table. Note that the actual maximum for Age, Tumor Size. Regional Node Examined, Regional Node Positive, and Survival months are 69, 140, 61, 41, and 107, respectively.

TABLE 10. DATASET STATISTICS

Attribute	Mean	STD	Min	Max
Age	53.968361	8.968991	30.000000	69.00000
Race	1.231440	0.580434	1.000000	3.000000
M_Status	1.646986	1.010138	1.000000	5.000000
T_Stage	1.783259	0.764173	1.000000	4.000000
N_Stage	0.693169	0.693169	1.000000	3.000000
S_Stage	2.320877	1.266084	1.000000	5.000000
Grade	2.150722	0.638458	1.000000	4.000000
A_Stage	1.022920	0.149666	1.000000	2.000000
Tumor Size	30.40059	20.95136	1.000000	140.0000
E_Status	1.067015	0.250080	1.000000	2.000000
P_Status	1.173642	0.378849	1.000000	2.000000
RN_Exam	14.358744	8.095945	1.000000	61.00000
RN_Pos	4.157200	5.110535	1.000000	46.00000
S_Months	71.286746	22.926034	1.000000	107.0000

```
BCS= pd.read\_csv(`FullNormalizedBC.csv')\\
df=BCS.describe(include = `all')\\
tp = dict(df)\\
print( tp, ``\n")
```

III. CLASSIFYING 6TH STAGE USING PYTHON

The 6th Stage (S_Stage) will be classified using Neural Network (MLPClassifier), Support Vector Machine (SVC), and Random Forest techniques. The dataset contains 1303 rows for class 1, 1126 for class 2, 1049 for class 3, 66 for class 4, and 470 for class 5. 70% of the dataset is used for training, and 30% for testing for both Sections III and IV. The resulting classification model will be saved and used to classify unseen data.

A. *S_Stage Classification Using Neural Networks*

After executing training and testing on the dataset, the resulting model is saved and then used to classify the 6th Stage for a dataset of 10 rows that does not contain values for S_Stage (no column existed for this attribute). The simple code used will be depicted below. It applies to all the methods with the expectation of fitting the method to the training data. Therefore, only this part of code will be shown for the other methods in B and C below.

```
# Fitting Linear Regression to the Training set
   from sklearn.neural_network import
       ↪ MLPClassifier
lm = MLPClassifier(solver='lbfgs', alpha=1e-5,
    ↪ hidden_layer_sizes=(150, 10), random_state
    ↪ =1)
lm.fit(X_train, y_train)
#Testing
classifications = lm.predict(X_test)
```

```
# Saving model to disk to predict unkown 6\
    ↪ textsuperscript{th} Stage
pickle.dump(lm, open(`NN_BC_model.pkl',`wb'))
# Loading the model
model = pickle.load(open(`NN_BC_model.pkl',`rb'))
```

Table 11 depicts classified S_Stage values for ten randomly selected rows of the test data together with the actual values of this attribute in the same rows of the test data. The abbreviations NN, SVM, and RF will be used to denote Neural Networks, Support Vector Machines, and Random Forest, respectively.

TABLE 11. ACTUAL AND PREDICTED VALUES OF S_STAGE

Row #	Actual	NN-Pred	SVM_Pred	RF_Pred
1213	1	1	1	1
3181	3	2	1	3
3228	3	3	2	3
560	1	1	1	1
1707	2	2	2	2
1624	2	1	2	2
3223	1	1	1	1
102	2	2	2	2
2719	5	5	3	5
906	5	5	3	5

height

The accuracy of the NN classifier on training set is 0.79, and the accuracy of the NN classifier on test set is 0.79. The Confusion Matrix is given below. It summarizes the results of classifications based on the test data. Each column represents the classifications for one of the classes. It is obvious there is a problem with class 4. The dataset has only 67 rows containing the value 4. Out of 135 class 5, only 126 were classified correctly (TP=126), and 9 incorrectly classified (FN=9). There were also 14 test data rows that were incorrectly classified as class 5 (FP=14). This will leave TN=1056.

$$\begin{array}{c c} & \begin{array}{ccccc} \mathbf{1} & \mathbf{2} & \mathbf{3} & \mathbf{4} & \mathbf{5} \end{array} \\ \begin{array}{c} \mathbf{1} \\ \mathbf{2} \\ \mathbf{3} \\ \mathbf{4} \\ \mathbf{5} \end{array} & \begin{pmatrix} 338 & 43 & 0 & 0 & 0 \\ 53 & 189 & 91 & 0 & 3 \\ 1 & 19 & 301 & 0 & 5 \\ 0 & 0 & 21 & 0 & 1 \\ 1 & 2 & 11 & 0 & 126 \end{pmatrix} \end{array}$$

The classification report is given in Table 12 below. Note that *Accuracy* is the number of correct predictions divided by the total number of predictions and multiplied by 100 to get a percentage. *Recall* is the ratio of the total number of correctly classified positive examples divide by the total number of positive examples. High recall is an indication that the class is correctly identified. Dividing the total number of correctly classified positive rows by the total number of predicted positive rows provides *Precision*. High precision indicates examples identified as positive are in fact positive (This indicates small FP). *F1 Score* (or *F Measure*) is a measurement that includes both recall and precision. In other words, it is the weighted average of both. The F-Measure will always be close to the minimum of Precision and Recall. Finally, Support depicts the number of examples of the true response that lie in that class. The Python code to print all these is as follows:

```
print(`Accuracy of NN classifier on training set:
    ↪ {:.1f}'
.format(lm.score(X_train, y_train)))
```

```
print(`Accuracy of NN classifier on test set:
    ↪ {:.1f}'
.format(lm.score(X_test, y_test)))
print(``\n")
print(``Confusion Matrix and classification
    ↪ Report for NN", ``\n")
print(confusion_matrix(y_test, classifications),
    ↪ ``\n")
print(classification_report(y_test,
    ↪ classifications), ``\n")
```

TABLE 12. NN CLASSIFICATION REPORT

Class	Precision	Recall	F1-Score	Support
1	0.86	0.89	0.87	381
2	0.75	0.56	0.64	336
3	0.71	0.92	0.8	326
4	0	0	0	22
5	0.93	0.9	0.92	140

Finally, the models were applied to ten rows that have not been used before with either training or testing step. These ten rows are shown in Table 13. The actual classes that were not provided to the models are: 5, 2, 1, 2, 3, 1, 5, 2, 2, 4.

TABLE 13. UNSEEN DATA FOR CLASSIFYING S_STAGE

Dataset Rows												
[53	1	1	4	3	2	1	043	1	1	13	10	034]
[49	1	1	2	1	2	1	035	1	1	14	2	070]
[46	1	3	1	1	2	1	013	1	1	9	2	093]
[65	1	1	2	1	2	1	035	1	1	7	1	093]
[62	1	1	3	1	3	1	120	1	2	7	1	086]
[52	1	1	1	1	2	1	014	1	1	10	2	104]
[53	1	1	3	3	3	1	140	1	1	41	15	051]
[53	1	2	2	1	2	1	035	1	1	14	1	064]
[60	3	1	2	1	1	1	023	1	1	13	3	074]
[62	1	2	4	2	2	1	140	1	1	9	8	089]

The classifications for the three methods obtained by running the three models are provided in Table 14. Note that row 1 in Table 14 represents the classification for S_Stage using NN, SVM, and RF methods for row 1 of Table 13, and so on.

B. S_Stage Classification Using Support Vector Machines

For this method, the actual and predicted values using the test data are given in Table 11 (columns 2 and 4). The predictions of unseen data could be found in Table 14, column 3. Here, only the code for fitting the model will be shown. The rest is similar to code of Section A above.

```
from sklearn import svm
from sklearn.svm import SVC
lm= svm.SVC()
lm.fit(X_train, y_train)
SVC(C=1.0, cache_size=200, coef0=0.0, degree=3,
    ↪ decision_function_shape=`ovo', kernel=`rbf
    ↪ ', max_iter=-1, shrinking=True,
tol=0.001, verbose=False)
```

TABLE 14. S_STAGE CLASSIFICATIONS FOR UNSEEN DATA

For Row #	NN	SVM	RF
1	5	3	5
2	3	2	2
3	1	1	1
4	2	2	2
5	3	3	3
6	1	1	1
7	5	3	5
8	2	2	2
9	2	2	2
10	3	3	4

TABLE 15. SVM CLASSIFICATION REPORT

Class	Precision	Recall	F1-Score	Support
1	0.93	0.81	0.87	381
2	0.84	0.73	0.78	336
3	0.49	0.86	0.62	326
4	0	0	0	22
5	1	0.01	0.01	140

The ac curacies of SVM classifier on training and testing sets are 1.0 and 0.69, respectively. The Confusion Matrix, and the classification report are listed below. Class 5 has only 1 correct classification (TP=1) and 139 incorrectly classified (FP=139).

$$
\begin{array}{c} \\ \mathbf{1} \\ \mathbf{2} \\ \mathbf{3} \\ \mathbf{4} \\ \mathbf{5} \end{array}
\begin{array}{c} \begin{array}{ccccc} \mathbf{1} & \mathbf{2} & \mathbf{3} & \mathbf{4} & \mathbf{5} \end{array} \\
\begin{pmatrix} 309 & 12 & 60 & 0 & 0 \\ 53 & 244 & 83 & 0 & 0 \\ 1 & 30 & 281 & 0 & 0 \\ 0 & 3 & 19 & 0 & 0 \\ 0 & 3 & 136 & 0 & 0 \end{pmatrix} \end{array}
$$

C. S_Stage Classification Using Random Forest

Predictions for test data, and predictions for new data (Table 13) are depicted in Table 11 (column 5), and Table 14 (column 4) ,respectively. The Python code is given below. The accuracy of RF classifier on training and testing sets are 1.0 and 1.0 ,respectively.

```
# Fitting Random Forest to the Training set
from sklearn.ensemble import
    ↪ RandomForestClassifier
lm=RandomForestClassifier(n_estimators=1000,
    ↪ max_depth=10,
random_state=0)
lm.fit(X_train, y_train)
```

The Confusion Matrix is demonstrated below. Table 16 shows the Random forest Classification Report. Here, Class 5 has TP=140 with no FN and FP.

$$
\begin{array}{c} \\ \mathbf{1} \\ \mathbf{2} \\ \mathbf{3} \\ \mathbf{4} \\ \mathbf{5} \end{array}
\begin{array}{c} \begin{array}{ccccc} \mathbf{1} & \mathbf{2} & \mathbf{3} & \mathbf{4} & \mathbf{5} \end{array} \\
\begin{pmatrix} 381 & 0 & 0 & 0 & 0 \\ 0 & 336 & 0 & 0 & 0 \\ 0 & 0 & 326 & 0 & 0 \\ 0 & 0 & 0 & 22 & 0 \\ 0 & 0 & 0 & 0 & 140 \end{pmatrix} \end{array}
$$

TABLE 16. RANDOM FOREST CLASSIFICATION REPORT

Class	Precision	Recall	F1-Score	Support
1	1	1	1	381
2	1	1	1	336
3	1	1	1	326
4	1	1	1	22
5	1	1	1	140

IV. CLASSIFICATION WITH WEKA

The same Breast Cancer dataset is used for classification using Weka. Neural Networks (Multi-Layer Perceptron), Support Vector Machines (SMOreg), and Random Forest algorithms are adopted. The dataset was split into 70% for training and 30% for testing as was the case in Section III above. The values of S_Stage were converted from numeric to nominal using *NumbericToNominal* filter to get the Confusion Matrix and the classification report for both Neural Networks and

Random Forest. This was not allowed with SVM (SMOreg). The same data of Table 13 is used by the models to predict unseen examples. The Weka tables that are equivalent to Tables 11 and 14 are Tables 17 and 18 ,respectively and are given below. Some of the results of SMOreg are rounded to get whole numbers. The statistics for each model are presented in their respective subsections (A-C).

TABLE 17. ACTUAL AND PREDICTED VALUES OF S_STAGE

Row #	Actual	NN-Pred	SVM_Pred	RF_Pred
1	1	1	1	1
4	3	3	1	3
7	3	3	2	3
8	1	1	1	1
10	2	2	2	2
21	2	2	2	2
22	1	1	1	1
23	2	2	2	2
24	5	5	6	5
25	5	5	3	5

TABLE 18. S_STAGE CLASSIFICATIONS FOR UNSEEN DATA

For Row #	NN	SVM	RF
1	5	6	5
2	2	2	2
3	1	1	1
4	2	2	2
5	3	3	3
6	1	1	1
7	5	5	5
8	2	2	2
9	2	2	2
10	4	5	4

A. *Neural Network Saistic Using Weka*

The accuracy of NN on the testing set is 1.0. The classification report, Confusion Matrix and further statistics produced by Weka for NN are as below. Note that the *Mean Absolute Error* measures the average of the absolute errors in a set of predictions, *Root Mean Squared Error* is the square root of the average of squared differences between predictions and actual observations, *Relative Absolute Error* is the sum of the absolute differences between the predictions and actual observations divided by the sum of the absolute differences between the average of the observation and the observations, and *Root Relative Squared Error* is the square root of the sum of the squared differences between the predictions and actual observations divided by the sum of the squared differences between the average of the observations and the observations.

$$
\begin{array}{c c}
 & \begin{array}{ccccc} \mathbf{1} & \mathbf{2} & \mathbf{3} & \mathbf{4} & \mathbf{5} \end{array} \\
\begin{array}{c} \mathbf{1} \\ \mathbf{2} \\ \mathbf{3} \\ \mathbf{4} \\ \mathbf{5} \end{array} &
\begin{pmatrix} 321 & 0 & 0 & 0 & 0 \\ 0 & 335 & 0 & 0 & 0 \\ 0 & 0 & 326 & 0 & 0 \\ 0 & 0 & 0 & 18 & 0 \\ 0 & 0 & 0 & 0 & 143 \end{pmatrix}
\end{array}
$$

TABLE 19. NN CLASSIFICATION REPORT FROM WEKA

Class	Precision	Recall	F1-Score	Support
1	1.00	1.00	1.00	382
2	1.00	1.00	1.00	335
3	1.00	1.00	1.00	326
4	1.00	1.00	1.00	18
5	1.00	1.00	1.00	143

Mean Absolute Error 0.0018
Root Mean Squared Error 0.0038
Relative Absolute Error 0.6114%
Root Relative Squared Error 0.9792%

B. *Support Vector Machine Statistics Using Weka*

Weka provided the following statistics for SMOreg. It did not allow producing the Confusion Matrix and the classification report.

Mean Absolute Error 0.1938
Root Mean Squared Error 0.4630
Relative Absolute Error 18.744%
Root Relative Squared Error 36.5768%

C. *Random Forest Statistics Using Weka*

The statistics and classification report provided by Weka for Random Forest are illustrated below.

$$
\begin{array}{c c}
 & \begin{array}{ccccc} \mathbf{1} & \mathbf{2} & \mathbf{3} & \mathbf{4} & \mathbf{5} \end{array} \\
\begin{array}{c} \mathbf{1} \\ \mathbf{2} \\ \mathbf{3} \\ \mathbf{4} \\ \mathbf{5} \end{array} &
\begin{pmatrix} 382 & 0 & 0 & 0 & 0 \\ 0 & 335 & 0 & 0 & 0 \\ 0 & 0 & 326 & 0 & 0 \\ 0 & 0 & 0 & 18 & 0 \\ 0 & 0 & 0 & 0 & 143 \end{pmatrix}
\end{array}
$$

TABLE 20. RF CLASSIFICATION REPORT FROM WEKA

Class	Precision	Recall	F1-Score	Support
1	1.00	1.00	1.00	382
2	1.00	1.00	1.00	335
3	1.00	1.00	1.00	326
4	1.00	1.00	1.00	018
5	1.00	1.00	1.00	143

Mean Absolute Error 0.0057
Root Mean Squared Error 0.0289
Relative Absolute Error 1.9552%
Root Relative Squared Error 37.5397%

V. BREAST CANCER DATASET PREDICTIONS

An attempt has been made to perform some predictions on the SEER Breast Cancer Dataset. These included predicting Survival Months and Tumor Size. Linear Regression resulted in a very high Mean Squared Error (372.01). This forced the normalization of all attributes' values to make them between 0 and 1. However, the results are also discouraging as can be seen in the tables below. Although, the errors look very small, but because the values of the attributes are very small, these errors are still large. Moreover, the comparison of actual and predicted values for both S_Months and Tumor_Size revealed large difference.

TABLE 21. MEAN SQUARED ERROR

Method	Mean Squared Error
Linear Regression	0.032551797301851120
Bayesian Ridge	0.032272116790858174
Support Vector Machine	0.032785887677874580

TABLE 22. MEAN SQUARED ERROR FOR SURVIVAL MONTHS

Method	Mean Squared Error
Linear Regression	0.005817131
Bayesian Ridge	0.005812664
Support Vector Machine	0.006662543

VI. CLASSIFICATION OUTCOME DISCUSSION

A. *Discussion Based on Python Results*

- For the classification using the test set (Table 11), SVM has four incorrect classifications, and NN has just two with one nearer to the actual value than SVM. Here, RF was the best followed by NN. SVM did not perform well enough.
- As mentioned above, the actual classes that were hidden from the three models are: 5, 2, 1, 2, 3, 1, 5, 2, 2, 4. Table 14 reveals that RF was able to get them all, NN missed two, and SVM missed three actual classes.
- By comparing the three confusion matrices for NN, SVM, and RF, it is obvious that RF has the highest TPs for class 1 (381) followed by NN (336). For class 2, RF was superior (336) and SVM followed with TP=224. RF is leading with TP=326 and then NN with TP=301. Both NN and SVM failed to grant any class 4 as TP, but RF got a TP count of 22. Remember, there are only 66 rows for class 4 in the dataset. Once more, RF leads for class 5. SVM correctly classified only one class 5.
- By comparing Tables 12, 15, and 16, it is perceived that RF is superior with regards to Precision, Recall, and F1-Score. NN and SVM did not perform well with class 4, but NN scored better with class 5.

B. *Discussion Based on Weka Results*

- The predicted values for SVM in Table 17 missed classifying four classes compared to the actual values during testing. Even worse, SVM produced a class value equal to 6, which does not exist in the dataset. Both NN and RF matched all the actual values.
- For the unseen dataset (Table 18), both NN and RF achieved all the values of the classes. However, SVM missed two values and supplied the value 6 for class 5, and 5 for class 4.
- By observing the confusion metrices for NN and RF, it is clear they both performed very well. They have equal TPs for all the classes without any FP, TN, and FN. Note that confusion matrices and classification reports are only issued by Weka when classifying Nominal attributes. SVM did not allow classification on nominal S_Stage, but only numeric S_Stage attribute. This should explain why they were not included in this discussion.
- The same applies to the classification reports of NN and RF. Precision, Recall, and F1-Score are all perfect.
- The Mean absolute Error and the Root Mean Squared Error for NN (0.0018 and 0.0038, respectively) are the smallest, and SVM has the highest errors of 0.1938 and 0.4630, respectively.

C. *Discussion Based on Python and Weka Results*

- For SVM, the Python program produced both the Confusion Matrix and classification report. This was not allowed in Weka.
- From Tables 11 and 17, SVM missed four classifications and introduced the value 6 which is not a valid class in the database. RF performed equally well using both Python and Weka. NN performed better with Weka.
- For the unseen data (Tables 14 and 18), SVM missed the most values (correct classes) using both Weka and Python program. However, it missed more classes with Weka. Class 6, which never exist was introduced in Weka but not with the Python Program. RF got the classification correct for both approaches, while NN missed two classes using the program and none with Weka.
- Using the confusion matrices, both NN and RF were able to get all TP values with no FP, FN, and TN values. However, with the Python program, RF almost achieved the same counts for all classes as in Weka with a slight difference not exceeding 3 with no FP, FN, and TN values.
- In Weka, NN performed well with all the classes, but it had an issue with class 4 using Python. RF performed equally well in both.

VII. CONCLUSION

Based on the discussion above, it can be concluded that Random Forest technique is the best for classification of the underlying Breast Cancer Dataset. However, more data and attributes are needed to provide even better classification. The analysis also revealed that Weka outperformed the Python program with regards to Neural Networks. It is further concluded that SVM did not perform as good as the other two techniques using this dataset and the selected attribute. Furthermore, further classification work could be carried out using other attributes including T_Stage, N_Stage, Grade, and A_Stage.

The results of applying prediction to Tumor Size and Survival Months were misleading and characterized by high prediction errors. However, analytics using prediction could be pursued if further data and attributes are added with the possibility of removing some of the nominal attributes.

REFERENCES

[1] "What is breast cancer? breast cancer definition," accessed on August 2020. [Online]. Available: https://www.cancer.org/cancer/breast-cancer/about/what-is-breast-cancer.html

[2] H.-B. Lee and W. Han, "Unique features of young age breast cancer and its management," vol. 17, no. 4, pp. 301–307. [Online]. Available: https://www.ncbi.nlm.nih.gov/pmc/articles/PMC4278047/

[3] M. T. Groot, R. Baltussen, C. A. Uyl-de Groot, B. O. Anderson, and G. N. Hortobagyi, "Costs and health effects of breast cancer interventions in epidemiologically different regions of africa, north america, and asia," vol. 12, pp. S81–S90. [Online]. Available: http://doi.wiley.com/10.1111/j.1075-122X.2006.00206.x

[4] K. L. Kashyap, M. K. Bajpai, and P. Khanna, "Breast cancer detection in digital mammograms," in 2015 IEEE International Conference on Imaging Systems and Techniques (IST). IEEE, pp. 1–6. [Online]. Available: http://ieeexplore.ieee.org/document/7294523/

[5] Hanung Adi Nugroho, Faisal N, Indah Soesanti, and Lina Choridah, "Analysis of digital mammograms for detection of breast cancer," in in Proc. the 2014 International Conference on Computer, Control, Informatics and Its Applications (IC3INA), 2014, pp. 25–29.

[6] R. Sangeetha and K. S. Murthy, "A novel approach for detection of breast cancer at an early stage using digital image processing techniques," in 2017 International Conference on Inventive Systems and Control (ICISC). IEEE, pp. 1–4. [Online]. Available: http://ieeexplore.ieee.org/document/8068625/

[7] N. El Atlas, M. El Aroussi, and M. Wahbi, "Computer-aided breast cancer detection using mammograms: A review," in 2014 Second World Conference on Complex Systems (WCCS). IEEE, pp. 626–631. [Online]. Available: http://ieeexplore.ieee.org/document/7060995/

[8] B. Hela, M. Hela, H. Kamel, B. Sana, and M. Najla, "Breast cancer detection: A review on mammograms analysis techniques," in 10th International Multi-Conferences on Systems, Signals & Devices 2013 (SSD13). IEEE, pp. 1–6. [Online]. Available: http://ieeexplore.ieee.org/document/6563999/

[9] T. Cahoon, M. Sutton, and J. Bezdek, "Breast cancer detection using image processing techniques," in Ninth IEEE International Conference on Fuzzy Systems. FUZZ- IEEE 2000 (Cat. No.00CH37063), vol. 2. IEEE, pp. 973–976. [Online]. Available: http://ieeexplore.ieee.org/document/839171/

[10] L. Wang, "Microwave sensors for breast cancer detection," vol. 18, no. 2, p. 655. [Online]. Available: http://www.mdpi.com/1424-8220/18/2/655

[11] M. Gupta and B. Gupta, "A comparative study of breast cancer diagnosis using supervised machine learning techniques," in 2018 Second International Conference on Computing Methodologies and Communication (ICCMC). IEEE, pp. 997–1002. [Online]. Available: https://ieeexplore.ieee.org/document/8487537/

[12] A. F. M. Agarap, "On breast cancer detection: an application of machine learning algorithms on the wisconsin diagnostic dataset," in Proceedings of the 2nd International Conference on Machine Learning and Soft Computing - ICMLSC '18. ACM Press, pp. 5–9. [Online]. Available: http://dl.acm.org/citation.cfm?doid=3184066.3184080

[13] M. Amrane, S. Oukid, I. Gagaoua, and T. Ensari, "Breast cancer classification using machine learning," in 2018 Electric Electronics, Computer Science, Biomedical Engineerings' Meeting (EBBT). IEEE, pp. 1–4. [Online]. Available: https://ieeexplore.ieee.org/document/8391453/

[14] D. Bazazeh and R. Shubair, "Comparative study of machine learning algorithms for breast cancer detection and diagnosis," in 2016 5th International Conference on Electronic Devices, Systems and Applications (ICEDSA). IEEE, pp. 1–4. [Online]. Available: http://ieeexplore.ieee.org/document/7818560/

[15] D. Mittal, D. Gaurav, and S. Sekhar Roy, "An effective hybridized classifier for breast cancer diagnosis," in 2015 IEEE International Conference on Advanced Intelligent Mechatronics (AIM). IEEE, pp. 1026–1031. [Online]. Available: http://ieeexplore.ieee.org/document/7222674/

[16] M. R. Al-Hadidi, A. Alarabeyyat, and M. Alhanahnah, "Breast cancer detection using k-nearest neighbor machine learning algorithm," in 2016 9th International Conference on Developments in eSystems Engineering (DeSE). IEEE, pp. 35–39. [Online]. Available: http://ieeexplore.ieee.org/document/7930620/

[17] A. Osareh and B. Shadgar, "Machine learning techniques to diagnose breast cancer," in 2010 5th International Symposium on Health Informatics and Bioinformatics. IEEE, pp. 114–120. [Online]. Available: http://ieeexplore.ieee.org/document/5478895/

[18] K. Kourou, T. P. Exarchos, K. P. Exarchos, M. V. Karamouzis, and D. I. Fotiadis, "Machine learning applications in cancer prognosis and prediction," vol. 13, pp. 8–17. [Online]. Available: http://www.sciencedirect.com/science/article/pii/S2001037014000464

[19] I. I. Esener, S. Ergin, and T. Yuksel, "A new ensemble of features for breast cancer diagnosis," in 2015 38th International Convention on Information and Communication Technology, Electronics and Microelectronics (MIPRO). IEEE, pp. 1168–1173. [Online]. Available: http://ieeexplore.ieee.org/document/7160452/

[20] P. S. Pawar and D. R. Patil, "Breast cancer detection using neural network models," in 2013 International Conference on Communication Systems and Network Technologies. IEEE, pp. 568–572. [Online]. Available: http://ieeexplore.ieee.org/document/6524463/

[21] S. Charan, M. J. Khan, and K. Khurshid, "Breast cancer detection in mammograms using convolutional neural network," in 2018 International Conference on Computing, Mathematics and Engineering Technologies (iCoMET). IEEE, pp. 1–5. [Online]. Available: https://ieeexplore.ieee.org/document/8346384/

[22] D. Bardou, K. Zhang, and S. M. Ahmad, "Classification of breast cancer based on histology images using convolutional neural networks," vol. 6, pp. 24 680–24 693. [Online]. Available: https://ieeexplore.ieee.org/document/8353225/

[23] D. A. Ragab, M. Sharkas, S. Marshall, and J. Ren, "Breast cancer detection using deep convolutional neural networks and support vector machines," vol. 7, p. e6201.

[24] M. H.-M. Khan, "Automated breast cancer diagnosis using artificial neural network (ANN)," in 2017 3rd Iranian Conference on Intelligent Systems and Signal Processing (ICSPIS). IEEE, pp. 54–58. [Online]. Available: http://ieeexplore.ieee.org/document/8311589/

[25] J. Teng, "SEER breast cancer data," accessed on August 2020. [Online]. Available: https://ieee-dataport.org/open-access/seer-breast-cancer-data

[26] Ian H. Witten, Eibe Frank, Mark A. Hall, and Christopher J. Pal, The WEKA Workbench. Online Appendix for "Data Mining: Practical Machine Learning Tools and Techniques, 4th ed. Morgan Kaufmann. [Online]. Available: https://www.cs.waikato.ac.nz/ml/weka/Witten_et_al_2016_appendix.pdf

[27] Stages of cancer. Accessed on August 2020. [Online]. Available: https://www.cancer.net/navigating-cancer-care/diagnosing-cancer/stages-cancer

A Data-Driven Approach for Eye Disease Classification in Relation to Demographic and Weather Factors Using Computational Intelligence Software

Amna Alalawi[1], Les Sztandera[2], Parth Lalakia[3], Anthony Vipin Das[4], Gumpili Sai Prashanthi[5]

[1]DMgmt in Strategic Leadership Program, Thomas Jefferson University, Philadelphia, PA, USA
Email: Amna.Alalawi@Jefferson.edu

[2]Kanbar College of Design, Engineering, and Commerce, Thomas Jefferson University, Philadelphia, PA, USA
Email: Les.Sztandera@Jefferson.edu

[3]Global Affairs, Thomas Jefferson University, Philadelphia, PA, USA
Email: Parth.Lalakia@jefferson.edu

[4] Department of EyeSmart EMR & AEye, Indian Health Outcomes Public Health and Economics Research Centre (IHOPE), LV Prasad Eye Institute, Hyderabad, Telangana, India
Email: vipin@lvpei.org

[5] Department of EyeSmart EMR & AEye, Indian Health Outcomes Public Health and Economics Research Centre (IHOPE), LV Prasad Eye Institute, Hyderabad, Telangana, India
Email: saiprashanthi.g@lvpei.org

***Abstract* – Big data is the new gold, especially in health care. Advances in collecting and processing Electronic Medical Records (EMR), coupled with increasing computer capabilities have resulted in an increased interest in the use of big data in health care. Big data promises more *personalized* and *precision* medicine for patients with improved accuracy and earlier diagnosis, and therapy geared to an individual's unique combination of genes, environmental risk, and precise disease phenotype. Ophthalmology has been an area of focus where results have shown to be promising. The objective of this study was to determine whether the EMR record in LV Prasad Eye Institute (LVPEI) in India can contribute to the management of patient care, through studying how climatic and socio-demographic factors relate to eye disorders and visual impairment in the State of Telangana. The study was designed by merging a dataset obtained from the Telangana State Development Society to an existing EMR of approximately 1 million patients, who presented themselves with different eye symptoms and were diagnosed with several diseases from the years (2011-2019). The dataset obtained included weather and climatic variables to be tested alongside eye disorders. Microsoft Power BI was used to analyze the data through prescriptive and descriptive data analysis techniques to read patterns that can dig deeper into high-risk climatic and socio-demographic factors that correlate to eye diseases. Our findings revealed that there is a high presence of Cataract in the state of Telangana, mostly in rural areas and throughout the different weather seasons in India. Men tend to be the most affected as per the number of visits to the clinic, while home makers make the most visit to the hospital, in addition to employees, students, and laborers. While cataract is most dominant in the older age population, diseases such as astigmatism and conjunctivitis are more present in the younger age population. The study appeared useful for taking preventive measures in the future to manage the treatment of patients who present themselves with eye disorders in Telangana. In addition, this research created a pathway for new methods in the study of how EMRs contribute to new knowledge in ophthalmology.**

Keywords* –big data; ophthalmology; ocular diseases; artificial intelligence.

I. INTRODUCTION

India is home to over 8.3 million people with Vision Impairment (VI), the highest in the world [3]. Even though, in 1976, India became the first country in the world to start a national program for control of blindness for the goal to reduce blindness prevalence to 0.3 percent by 2020, the prevalence of blindness still stands at 1.99 percent, according to the National Blindness and Visual Impairment Survey, released in October 2019 [1] by the Union Ministry of Health and Family. The prevalence of blindness and visual impairment is one of the highest in Telangana, a state in Southern India, as inferred from survey [1]. The significant reasons indicated in the survey were due to cataract and refractive error [2].

All surveys in the country have shown that cataract is the most common cause of blindness and all prevention of blindness programs have been "cataract-oriented." However, it has recently been recognized that the visual outcome of the cataract surgeries as well as the training of ophthalmologists has been less than ideal.

This study uses Artificial Intelligence (AI) and machine learning techniques to explore a dataset containing information on 873,448 patients who visited LV Prasad Eye Institute (LVPEI), a multi-tier ophthalmology hospital network, based in Hyderabad. The data was extracted from EyeSmart, the hospital's Electronic Medical Record (EMR) and health management system, and then merged with climatic factors to test the correlation between climatic variables and ocular diseases presented by the patients [3]. Studying risk factors, primarily associated with climate and the environment can lead to a better understanding of the causes, diagnosis and treatment of several eye diseases [5].

In healthcare, ophthalmology deals with the diagnosis and treatment of eye disorders. Some known diseases in ophthalmology are cataracts, retinal disorders, macular degeneration, and others. The relatively rapid and recent adoption of EMRs in ophthalmology has been associated with the promise that the accumulation of large volumes of clinical data would facilitate quality improvement and help answer a variety of research questions. Given that EMRs are relatively new in most practices and that clinical data are inherently more complex than other fields that have been altered by the digital revolution, these proposed benefits have yet to be realized [4].

With the rise of big data, it has now become easier to study how culture, race, climate, and other socio-demographic factors correlate to the spread of ocular diseases. This has shed light on recent research in medicine and ophthalmology. An investigation has been conducted with an aim for the application of artificial intelligence (AI)-based hierarchical clustering as a tool to optimize the in total excellence, values, and the security for the Adult Spinal Deformity Surgery (ADS) [16]. It has been observed that prior to this the ADS classification was based on certain radiographic parameters which have been correlated with the patient related outcomes. But the problems faced immensely by the researchers is to separate out the patients and the patterns manually that is in turn was based on hundreds of data parameters and the process was considered to be practically not feasible. Therefore, as a methodological approach for every probable cluster of patient (N) done on the basis of (M) surgery were normalized for two year enhancement and the massive rate of complication were computed. Thus, this particular study has therefore, highlighted that unsubstantiated hierarchical clustering of the patterns of findings that helps to initiate the prior operative judgment making by formulating a two year risk benefit grid. In this way the novel AI-ASD pattern of classification and identification have helped to diminish the risk and overall improvement [16]. It should be mentioned that smaller cities faces a lot of difficulties to maintain the sustainable welfare of countries in amalgamation with notable standards of living [17]. In another investigation, the emergency bases of hospitalization along with the all driven causes of mortality were utilized as the replacements of frailty. The researchers used to two different models to assign the deteriorating risk score to every subjects of the elderly population residing within the Municipality of Bologna, Italy [17]. The study design was a cohort study with of 58 789 subjects as sample size for overall six years with four year monitoring period. The study findings reported excellent power of discrimination along with calibration that demonstrated an excellent anticipating ability of the models utilized [17]. In this respect another study could also be illustrated that had utilized the application of health administrative databases along with authenticated algorithms to show a correlation in between the residential proximity towards foremost roadways along with the prevalence of three major neurological diseases like dementia, multiple sclerosis, and Parkinson's disease [18]. This particular study design was also a cohort study based on two different populations having the age group in the range of 20–50 years with sample size of 4.4 million suffering from multiple sclerosis and the matured adult groups having the age range of 55–85 years with sample population size of 2·2 million suffering from dementia or other Parkinson's disease. The researchers of the study estimated the associations among the following parameters such as the traffic proximity, incidence of dementia, Parkinson's disease, and the multiple sclerosis using the model of Cox proportional hazards which would also take into consideration of certain individualistic contextual parameters such as any injury to brain, diabetes, and the local income [18]. The study demonstrated the successful application of the health record databases along with the specialized analytical tool for the categorization of patterns of large or big data [18]. In today's world the relationship based on function in between the ncRNAs and the varied types of human diseases is considered to be a central task within the field of modern research for the formulation of eryeffective therapeutic approaches.

In Section 2 of this paper, we discuss and highlight different statistical tools and methods used to investigate the study of several demographic and climatic factors that impact upon the individuals in Telangana. While Section 3 focuses on providing a thorough analysis of the data findings, Section 4 highlights key findings and trends, and Section 5 includes conclusion and recommendations pertaining to the use of big data and data merging in EMR to reveal new insights in the study of visual impairment and eye disorders in Telangana. Visual impairment has continually exhibited an escalating trend in underdeveloped countries over the past years, and in India, the burden of visual impairment is high in urban and rural areas. Eye-care services should be accessible and affordable to individuals in need. This study intends to discover how socio-demographic and climatic factors correlate to the number of individuals affected using Artificial Intelligence tools. It is extremely important to mention that hardly any investigation had been conducted with the application of AI tools to categorize the huge data based on parameters like demographics and the weather in the field of ophthalmology. So it can be considered that this scientific article is considered to be a significant contribution in terms of novelty or originality and also considered to be a significant progress in the field of scientific research as the approach is unconventional and a novel one with successful outcomes.

II. Methodology

To gain insight into the climatic and socio-demographic factors that correlate to the risk of ocular diseases in the State of Telangana, we used multiple approaches utilizing AI and statistical software and programming languages, including Microsoft Power BI and Python to explore the dataset, which contained information on 873,448 patients complaining of eye disorder symptoms across multiple categories of ocular diseases. Publicly available climatic variables were obtained and aligned to the dataset through a process called column mutation, and then examined by Microsoft Power BI, which heavily relies on visual illustrations and statistical storytelling to present findings and new insights. It should be noted that Power BI is considered to be an assortment of software or apps which all together works in amalgamation to transform the unrelated sources of data into a visually pattern oriented, continuous and dynamic insights. Column mutation, which is the merging of datasets, was done through Python, an interpreted, object-oriented programming, that codes the columns in a language called Syntax. It works out on the principle of logical and arithmetic computation. This tool has an advantage to handle large and complex datasets. The process was however timely given the large volume of patients. The process was repeated more than once to ensure minimal error in the merging process. Microsoft Power BI was then used to model the data in order to obtain the visualizations and insights.

The master dataset or the big data, which was explored and analyzed, covered clinical visits are from the year 2011-2019, and included demographic information of the patient, including age, gender, profession, data of visit, district of resident, and symptoms and diagnosis of the patient in relation to eye disease. To look further into this issue, we merged climate variables to the dataset to explore the relationship with eye disorders. The AI approach can be of varied types namely conventional symbolic AI, Computational intelligence, and statistical tools or the combination of all of the above. Here in the present assignment the Computational intelligence approach has been adopted for the analytical purpose [22].

The climate variables we examined were average temperature, minimum temperature, maximum temperature, humidity, rainfall, and solar radiation. This data was retrieved from the Telangana State Development Planning Society in the state of Telangana. The findings that relate to temperature and its effect on Cataract in older age was consistent in high and low temperatures.

III. Analysis

It has proven valuable to first observe which diseases are the most prevalent in the different areas of Telangana, and what age and gender are most affected to get a full understanding of the criticality of the eye disorder epidemic and to provide a baseline against which to compare the climate and patient demographic variables examined.

The use of EMRs in generating new insights has been an increasing trend in the area of ophthalmology. Research in ophthalmology has benefited greatly from the use of EMRs in expanding the breadth of knowledge in areas such as disease surveillance, health services utilizations and outcomes. In addition, the quantity of data available has increased, that it is now highly recommended to work on data linkage systems in eye research, as such data can offer insights into advantages and limitations for future direction in eye research [5].

The timespan of this dataset is between 2011-2019, a total of 8 years. There has been consistency to already known information through the analysis, specifically on gender and age-related eye conditions. Creative featuring techniques have been used to shed the light on the most critical variables through trial and error of testing for relationship in accordance to eye disease.

IV. Findings and Trends

This section highlights key findings of the study, as well as trends in relation to the subject matter as per the demographic and climatic variables tested.

A. *Gender and Eye Disorders*

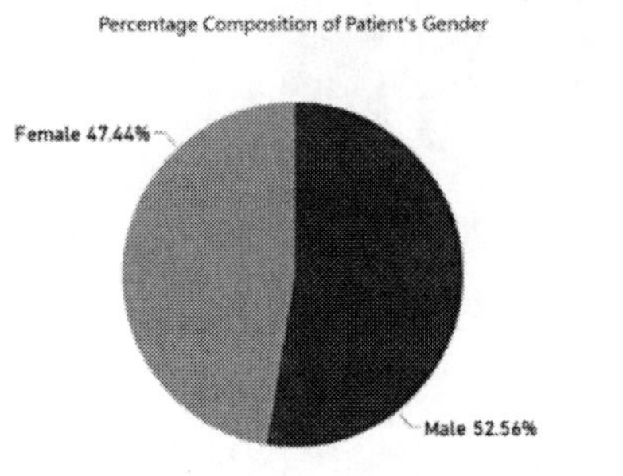

Figure 1. Clinical Visits by Gender (2011-2019)

Figure 1 indicates that between the years 2011-2019, 53% of the patients were male patients who were seen for eye disorders, and 47% were female patients. This finding is in line with the gender study that was conducted on 2.3 million patients of all those who presented to LV Prasad Institute from the years 2011-2019 [3]. Globally, one of the social determinants of health that has been universally identified is gender. In India, health inequalities between men and women have played a pivotal role in disease development, including eye disorders. With respect to eye care, women have been generally cited to have higher rates of blindness in India and are less likely to access appropriate eye services [6][7]. However, as we can see from the study which was focused on Telangana, this is not the case, as male patients exceeded female patients, and this could be for the reason that Telangana has been ranked as one of the top ten innovative and developed states in India according to the India Innovation Index 2019 [15] where access to healthcare is available and appreciated by both male and female.

India has been one of the countries where efforts to strengthen the evidence-base for blindness control has received significant attention from policy planners and program managers. Over the past four decades, a series of population-based blindness and visual impairment surveys have been undertaken in India, using different survey methods. This included detailed eye examination surveys, as well as rapid assessments [8].

B. Occupation and Clinical Visits

Percentage of Clinical Visits by Occupation

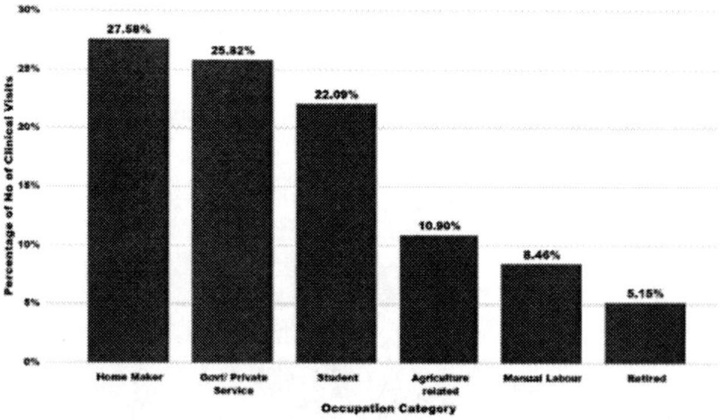

Figure 2. Clinical Visits by Profession (2011-2019)

In addition, when studying the correlation between profession and clinical visits, it appeared that home makers, employees in the government and private sectors, and students make the top three categories of those are who most affected. Figure 2 depicts this analysis and portrays the top six professions taken from the analysis. We can also see that workers in Agriculture and manual laborers tend to present themselves with eye disorders as well, and that could be to the nature of the job, in which they are exposed to certain chemicals, dust, and usually work in heated environments. Recent estimates from the World Health Organization indicate that 90 per cent of all those affected by visual impairment live in the poorest countries of the world [9]. India is home to one-fifth of the world's visually impaired people and therefore, any strategies to combat avoidable blindness must take into account the socio-economic conditions within which people live [9].

Home-makers could also translate to housewives, who are at higher-risk of visual disorders, and this is in line with a study that was conducted in 2009 on women in Indian culture, where it showed that housewives are more likely to suffer from heart diseases than working women, and that is due to lack of education, lifestyle that is based on obesity and cultural myths that do not focus on women's health. Having a similar study related to eye disorders and visual impairment, as per the study based on the sample of the population from Telangana, the same pattern can be seen and it can potentially be from these similar reasons [10].

C. Location and Eye Disorders in Older Age (41-70)

Number of Visits by Location (Age 41-70)

Location	Number_of_visits
Paloncha	5471
Kothagudam	2930
Kothagudem Bazar	2684
Manuguru	2380
Bhadrachalam	2287
Yellandu	1867
Adilabad	1634
Tekulapalli	1432
Burgampahad	1309
Madhapur	1126

Figure 3. Location and Eye Disorders in Older Age Population

Figure 3 shows the locations that people with eye disorders come from and is focused on the older age population. Cataract seemed to be the most disease that has affected older age in Telangana, which is the clouding of the natural human lens. Cataract is a condition known to affect older age, and this study revalidates the information.

D. Location and Eye Disorders in Younger Age (11-20)

Number of Visits by Location (Age 11-20)

Location	Number_of_visits
Paloncha	601
Madhapur	325
Adilabad	256
Bhadrachalam	226
Kothagudam	177
Kothagudem Bazar	168
Nagarkurnool	132
Manuguru	128
Gachibowli	127
Kondapur	116
Yellandu	116

Figure 4. Location and Eye Disorders in Younger Age Population

Figure 4 shows the location that people with eye disorders come from and is focused on the younger age population. Astigmatism, which is an irregularity of the shape of the cornea was present in younger age population. Astigmatism has been linked to being a hereditary condition in ophthalmology.

In both contexts, it appeared to be that eye disorders are mostly concentrated in residents from the district of Paloncha, and even though this district has a higher literacy rate than state average is 77%, 10% higher than that of the state average which is at 67%, it has been reported that it has been hit with pollution and contaminated water in 2015. The state-run thermal power plant installed in 2015 caused pollution and health disorders including eye disorders [11]. Residents complained of gray water, and doctors in Paloncha confirmed that the prolonged exposure to air and water pollution has led to higher incidences of respiratory diseases, tuberculosis, skin diseases, blurring of vision and irritation in the eyes, such as Cataract, Cornea, Anterior Segment, Retina, and Glaucoma [11].

E. Consistent Prevalence of Cataract in Rainfall

Number of Visits for Right-Eye Diseases by Cumulative Rainfall

Right-eye Diseases	Cummlative Rainfall	Number of Visits
CATARACT, SENILE, OTHER AND COMBINED FORMS	2.11	4126
Compound Myopic Astigmatism	2.11	8058
EMMETROPIA	2.10	15253
INTRAOCULAR LENS, PSEUDOPHAKOS	2.12	5837
Presbyopia	2.15	5820
Senile cataract	2.05	8134
Senile cataract,INTRAOCULAR LENS, PSEUDOPHAKOS	2.03	3146
Simple Hypermetropia,Presbyopia	2.13	4164
Simple Myopia	2.12	7686
Simple Myopic Astigmatism	2.12	4172

Figure 5. Right Eye Diseases in Relation to Rainfall

Figure 5 shows the diseases that affect the right eye the most when tested alongside rainfall. Globally, cataract is the single most important cause of blindness, and the second most common cause of moderate and severe vision impairment (MSVI) according to the Global Burden of Disease, Injuries and Risk Factors Study, and it is most predominant in Southeast Asia. Cataract contributed to a worldwide 33.4% of all blindness and 18.4% of all MSVI. Translating the same into actual numbers, cataract caused blindness in 10.8 million of overall 32.4 million blind and visual impairment in 35.1 million of 191 million visually impaired individuals [13].

The close relationship between climate, environment and the development of Cataract is crucial to understand for future preventative measures. In Telangana, it shows that Cataract is the disease most prevalent in rainfall.

F. Consistent Prevalence of Pterygium in Relation to Global Radiation

Right-Eye Diseases as Influenced by Global Radiation

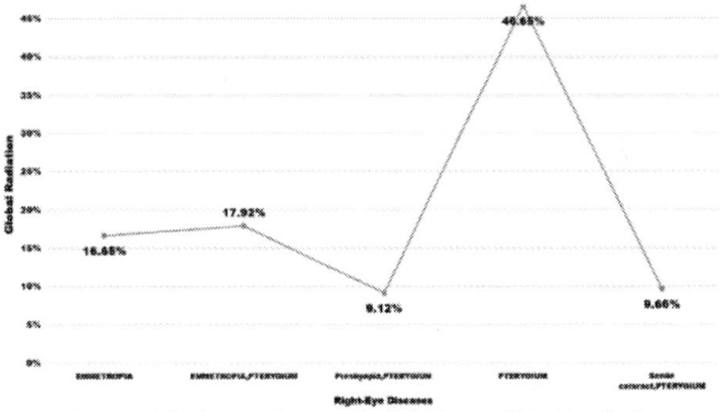

Figure 6. Right Eye Diseases in Relation to Global Radiation

Figure 6 shows the diseases that affect the right eye the most when tested alongside global radiation. We analyzed patients who presented with degeneration symptoms, and correlated the diagnosis to climatic factors, such as humidity, rainfall, temperature and global radiation. The above analysis shows the top 5 most prevalent degeneration right-eye diseases as impacted by global radiation. Pterygium shows to be most prevalent at over 46% of the total global radiation value. The analysis was done on a patient basis and not a disease basis, as the data showed that one patient can develop more than one disease.

G. Consistent Prevalence of Pterygium in Relation to Windspeed

Right-Eye Diseases as Influenced by Windspeed

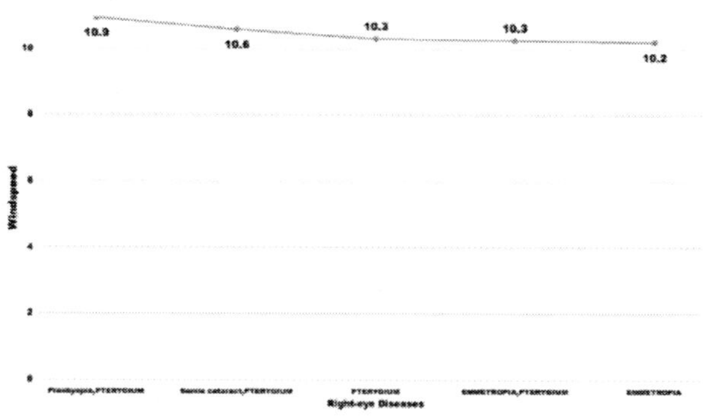

Figure 5. Right Eye Diseases in Relation to Windspeed

Figure 5 shows the diseases that affect the right eye when tested alongside windspeed. The analysis above shows the top 5 most prevalent right-eye diseases with degeneration as a symptom and how the diseases are influenced by maximum windspeed. Pterygium was also the most present among patients and concentrated at average maximum windspeed of between 10.2 and 10.9.

V. CONCLUSION

This data analytics study provides an expanded exploration of how socio-demographic and climatic factors affect the prevalence of visual impairment and eye disorders in Telangana. Applying several statistical techniques, including pattern recognition, and generating other data visualizations, we were able to validate previously identified findings about gender's relation to eye disorders in Telangana. We found the tools we used to be very useful for a discovery research to better understand the sample set of patients and to generate informative and understandable visuals.

Big data can serve to boost the applicability of clinical research studies into real-world scenarios, where population, race, and climate create a challenge. It equally provides the opportunity to enable effective and precision medicine by performing patient stratification. This is indeed a key task toward personalized healthcare. A better use of medical resources by means of personalization can lead to well-managed health services that can overcome the challenges of a diverse population where poverty is high. Thus, creative featuring and data merging for health management of EMRs can have an impact on future clinical research.

From a systems perspective, we observe that a patient is influenced by several co-factors that result in the development of eye disorders, and that is significant in studying patient care from a holistic standpoint. AI tools create the pathway to merging publicly available data and aligning multiple variables as part of the overall influence. This technique is widely applied in decision-making and outcome assessment for an enhanced healthcare experience, in which modeling knowledge and expert experience are studied more thoroughly for new pattern recognition. However, variables must be minimized in order to capture the underlying knowledge, or otherwise patterns will be harder to spot. Thus, we attempt to apply this in the future with less variables to overcome the challenges in the first phase or data merging.

We recommend that the authorities spend more time and funds on creating awareness to educate individuals and families about the visual impairment crisis in Telangana. Creation of awareness is one of the most comprehensive approaches to sensitize communities concerning the consequences of eye disorders, but also one of the avenues to equip individuals with knowledge, skills and correct attitudes towards a healthier lifestyle.

Besides creation of awareness, this study also recommends ophthalmologists' understanding of all factors that influence a disease other than medical history, and to look at each patient uniquely in terms of social income, cultural upbringing and offer a more individualistic approach in educating a patient from the criticality of self-care, to help patients deviate away from high risk situations that can cause eye disorders, and to find ways from an earlier age for more effective preventative results that can reduce the number of affected individuals with vision impairment in Telangana.

REFERENCES

[1] G. Rao, N. Khanna, and A. Payal, "The global burden of cataract," *Current Opinion in Ophthalmology, 22* no. 1, pp. 4-9, 2011.

[2] A. Das, P. Kammari, and S. Ranganath Vadapalli, "Big data and the eyeSmart electronic medical record system-An 8-year experience from a three-tier eye care network in India," *Indian Journal of Ophthalmology, 68* no. 3, pp. 427, 2020.

[3] S. Marmamula, R. Khanna, and G. Rao, "Unilateral visual impairment in rural south India–Andhra Pradesh Eye Disease Study (APEDS)", *International Journal of Ophthalmology, 9* no.5, pp.763, 2016.

[4] M. V. Boland, "Big data, big challenges," Ophthalmology, *123* no.1, pp. 7-8, 2016.

[5] A. Clark, J. Ng, N. Morlet, and J. Semmens, "Big data and ophthalmic research," *Survey of Ophthalmology, 61* no.4, pp. 443-465, 2016.

[6] E.M. Messmer, "The pathophysiology, diagnosis, and treatment of dry eye disease," *Deutsches Ärzteblatt International, 112* no.5, pp. 71, 2015.

[7] D. Matthews, "How gender influences health inequalities," *Nursing Times, 111* no.43, pp. 21-23, 2015.

[8] N. Diaz-Granados, K. B Pitzul, L. Dorado, F. Wang, S. McDermott, M.B. Rondon, and D. Stewart, "Monitoring gender equity in health using gender-sensitive indicators: a cross-national study," *Journal of Women's Health, 20* no.1 pp. 145-153, 2011.

[9] G.V.S Murthy, S.K. Gupta, D. Bachani, R. Jose, and N. John, "Current estimates of blindness in India," *British Journal of Ophthalmology, 89* no.3, pp.257-260, 2005.

[10] S.K Angra, G.V. Murthy, S.K. Gupta, and V. Angra, "Cataract related blindness in India and its social implications," *The Indian Journal of Medical Research, 106*, pp. 312-324, 1997.

[11] A. Janati, H. Matlabi, H. Allahverdipour, M. Gholizadeh, and L. Abdollahi, "Socioeconomic status and coronary heart disease," *Health Promotion Perspectives, 1* no.2, pp. 105, 2011.

[12] S. Kumar, "National security environment," *India's National Security*, pp. 25-236, Routledge India, 2016.

[13] S.G. Honavar, "Eliminating cataract blindness: Are we on target?" *Indian Journal of Ophthalmology, 65* no.12, pp. 1271, 2017.

[14] G. Bakshy https://www.jagranjosh.com/current-affairs/india-innovation-index-2019-karnataka-tops-the-list-followed-by-tamil-nadu-and-maharashtra-1571375106-1, 2019, (Accessed on 07.09.2020).

[15] C.P. Ames, J. Smith, F. Pellisé, M. Kelly, A. Alanay, E. Acaroglu, and Jr. C. Shaffrey, "Artificial intelligence based hierarchical clustering of patient types and intervention categories in adult spinal deformity surgery: towards a new classification scheme that predicts quality and value," *Spine, 44* no.13, pp. 915-926, 2019.

[16] F. Bertini, G. Bergami, D. Montesi, G. Veronese, G. Marchesini, and P. Pandolfi, "Predicting frailty condition in elderly using multidimensional socioclinical databases," *Proceedings of the IEEE, 106*(4), 723-737, 2018.

[17] H. Chen, J. Kwong, R. Copes, P.J. Villeneuve, A. Van Donkelaar, and A.S. Wilton, "Living near major roads and the incidence of dementia, Parkinson's disease, and multiple sclerosis: a population-based cohort study," *The Lancet, 389*(10070), pp. 718-726, 2017.

[18] E.P. Barracchia, G. Pio, D. D'Elia, and M. Ceci, "Prediction of new associations between ncRNAs and diseases exploiting multi-type hierarchical clustering," *BMC bioinformatics, 21* no.1, pp. 1-24, 2020.

[19] B. Familiar and J. Barnes, "Data Visualizations, Alerts, and Notifications with Power BI. In Business in Real-Time Using Azure IoT and Cortana Intelligence Suite," pp. 397-473, *Apress*, Berkeley, CA, 2017.

[20] M. Lutz, "Programming Python: powerful object-oriented programming," *O'Reilly Media*, 2010.

[21] G. Marcus and E. Davis, "Rebooting AI: Building artificial intelligence we can trust," *Pantheon*, 2019.

Comparing Variable Importance in Prediction of Silence Behaviours between Random Forest and Conditional Inference Forest Models

Stephen Barrett, Geraldine Gray
School of Informatics
Technological University Dublin
Dublin, Ireland
S.Barrett@live.ie, Geraldine.Gray@tudublin.ie

Colm McGuinness
School of Business
Technological University Dublin
Dublin, Ireland
Colm.McGuinness@tudublin.ie

Michael Knoll
Dept. of Work & Organizational Psychology
University of Leipzig
Leipzig, Germany
Michael.Knoll@uni-leipzig.de

***Abstract*—This paper explores variable importance metrics of Conditional Inference Trees (CIT) and classical Classification And Regression Trees (CART) based Random Forests. The paper compares both algorithms variable importance rankings and highlights why CIT should be used when dealing with data with different levels of aggregation. The models analysed explored the role of cultural factors at individual and societal level when predicting Organisational Silence behaviours.**

***Index Terms*—Random Forest; Variable Importance; Bias; PDP; Survey Data; Culture; GLOBE; Organisational Silence.**

Research indicates that there are many individual reasons why people do not speak up when confronted with situations that may concern them within their working environment. This phenomenon is referred to as Organisational Silence, and is considered both an individual and collective level behaviour [1]. Employees do not call attention to problems that make their life uncomfortable within an organisation, resulting in self-censorship and trivialisation of problems [2]. The end result is that employees make a decision to stay silent [3].

Organisational Silence impacts both an organisation's ability to adapt to change and individuals who experience it [4]. Companies are now becoming more global in their outlook, necessitating research into how culture may play a role in developing bespoke feedback mechanisms. In 1999, foreign sales by multi-national businesses exceeded $7 trillion dollars a year and had a growth rate of over 20% more than traditional exports [5]. This highlights a need for managers with a global mindset, of which a shortage exists among the fortune 500 companies [6].

Organisational Silence had been explored previously with respect to societal culture in a tangential manner but not as the core focus of research papers. During the literature review for this paper, it was found that several papers focused on facets of *organisational* culture and how they predicted sub domains of Silence [7]. At the time of writing no research was found that modelled the probability of engaging in Silence based on *societal* differences across cultures. The previous studies did not focus on cultural and organisational attributes that contribute to classify if a person engaged in Silence behaviours. It has been hypothesised that a manager's leadership type could moderate the effect of Silence behaviours as a result of culture [8], however there was no analytic work applied to the topic.

The aim of this study is to explore patterns found by models that predict an employee's propensity to engage in Silence. Variable importance measures are examined to understand why two models differed in their rankings of importance. *Partial Dependency Plots* (PDP) are used to explore the impact of changes in the predictors on Silence behaviours. This study involves the analysis of data collected from three countries representing three different cultures (Germany, Italy and Poland).

Section I describes the two ensemble models used in analysing the survey data and highlights two methods for examining the role of predictors in predicting Silence behaviours. Section II describes the survey instrument used to collect the data for this study. Section III describes the analysis done, and the results of data modelling. We conclude this work in section IV.

I. Ensemble Modelling

An ensemble mechanism takes more than one model and trains it on a particular problem. Each model - especially if they are highly variable models like Decision Trees - takes advantage of the model's tendency to overfit the data [9]. To use an analogy, each model is an expert in its particular area, for example a specific attribute in the data set. When all the models are fit to the data, their expert opinions are combined to make a final decision. In modelling, this can be implemented as the mode across all model outputs in a classification problem. These methods use simpler base models as their constituent parts, where voting or aggregation of the results can produce extremely accurate classifiers. It has been pointed out in the context of bioinformatics that ensembles of Data Mining classifiers have the ability to reduce model bias and model overfitting, especially in datasets with class imbalance problems [10]. This study utilises two ensemble techniques, discussed next.

A. Random Forest

Random Forest can be used with any modelling technique to attempt to improve its accuracy. However it is generally associated with Decision Trees or Regression Trees. For this study, one base learner was the CART model [11]. The user can specify the number of trees to be included in the Random Forest. Each tree is allowed to grow fully without being pruned back, producing many overfit trees. However, the algorithm introduces randomisation into the process by applying bootstrap sampling with replacement to the dataset. A second randomisation step only allows the model to split on a random selection of attributes at each node for each tree, decorelating the trees [12]. By necessitating that only a random sample of predictors is used at each split, the trees can focus on less predictive predictors that would have been overshadowed by more powerful predictors in the dataset. The two randomisation steps result in different trees overfitting different sections of the dataset. Classification is based on a majority vote amongst all trees.

CART uses the Gini Index as the impurity measure, as it forces the splits to be binary. The Gini index score is calculated for the data pre-split and post-split, with the lowest Gini score deciding the split point. However CART has several disadvantages, which are exacerbated by using it as a base learner for Random Forest. Trees are likely to select attributes with more variation in the predictor space [13]. This is especially prevalent in categorical data and variables with high levels of missing values. Consequently, this distorts variable importance measures. Some of CARTs disadvantages have been addressed by introducing CITs [14].

CITs use a generalised statistical test of independence to combat against overfitting and the aforementioned variable bias tendency. The algorithm operates in two steps, the first is attribute selection where an association test between the attribute and the outcome of interest is calculated [15]. The null hypothesis is that the attribute X_i has no association with the outcome variable Y. Due to the multiple comparisons, a Bonferroni corrected p-value threshold can be used. If the attribute and the outcome are both numeric, then the test statistic is a correlation test. If both attributes are categorical in nature, dummy variables are created and a χ^2 test of association is performed. If one of the attributes is numeric and the other categorical then an ANOVA is performed [14]. Once the attribute has been identified, the second step involves selecting a split point in the attribute, which can be determined using normal splitting procedures for Random Forest (see 16 for more details). Pruning is not used by default, as a stopping criteria can be set based on a cutoff (1 - p-value) pre-specified, which should produce an optimal predictive tree and can be tuned using cross validation [12]. CITs remove the bias that is inherent in CART, providing splits that are more reliable in interpretation of variable importance.

B. Variable Importance

In this study, permutation was used to determine a variable's importance. The predictor in question is shuffled so that the values in the dataset are basically random and any links with that predictor to the patterns in the rest of the dataset are broken [17]. The difference in accuracy is recorded per tree and aggregated across all the trees in the forest [12]. The importance is scaled per predictor based on the accuracy drop, and ranked. The method is referred to as Permutation Importance.

Permutation importance can be problematic when used with Random Forest if variables are correlated [18]. It has been shown that highly correlated data have a tendency to inflate the importance of non informative predictors as long as those predictors were correlated with predictive attributes [19]. Permutation should be done for groups of items that are highly correlated with each other. In the case of the silence attributes, the mean correlation was extremely high, which would mean that all silence attributes should be permuted together. This would produce a variable importance score where all the silence constructs in theory would be very important in comparison to other non correlated variables. However this method results in the loss of nuance on how the variables in isolation help in the prediction. Therefore a variation of this method was utilised in this study via the `party` package (version 1.3-1) in R. Variable importance ranking involved permutation of attributes within a group of attributes where the correlation among the variables was at a minimum of 0.2 [19]. The method is conceptually similar in spirit to partial correlation [18]. A conditioning grid is created based on the partition of feature space by individual trees within the Random Forest framework resulting in a discretised feature space. Then the variable is shuffled within this newly created grid and the Out Of Bag (OOB) error is recorded. The difference is then taken between the non-permutated and the permutated Random Forest OOB. Research suggested that using CITs as a basis for Random Forest to produce variable importance scores "*appear to strike a good balance between identification of significant variables and avoiding unnecessary flagging of correlated variables*" [20]. Interested readers are directed to [18] for an accessible version or [19] for a more in-depth treatment.

While the procedures described above tend to converge on their recommendations for what the most important variables are for predictions, they generally do not show if the variables positively or negatively impact the probability of the predictions.

C. Partial Dependancy Plots

Ensembles of models are more difficult to interpret due to the multiple models used in their construction. One method of model interpretation for classification models is the use of PDPs. On a conceptual level a PDP is used in conjunction with a model to plot model predictions when one or more of the independent variables is varied [21]. The average of the predicted value across all participants is taken and plotted against the varying probability of engaging in Silence as the predictor changes. All other variables are held either at their mean or their median [22]. For example, take a hypothetical dataset with 20 predictors ($x_1..x_{20}$) and 2000 rows, with each row representing a participant in a survey and each predictor representing a factor that has been measured. A model M is generated to predict y_i. If the range of values that needs to be tested is 100 for x_i, then 100 datasets are created with the value of x_i being the only change for each copy. The PDP value is then calculated by using each of the datasets to generate a value y_i from the model M. The mean value y_i is then taken to give an average value for the model at that value x_i. This becomes computationally expensive when the number of copies becomes unmanageable so the median or mean for the values of x_i not being varied is a computational short cut. The result can then be plotted to show the changes in X producing a change in Y [9].

One of the advantages of the technique is the ability to see the relationship type (linear, non linear) between the independent variable and the object being predicted [23, Section 5.1]. A number of studies utilised PDPs to tease out the relationships in models [24]–[26]. The technique does have some problems when used in conjunction with correlated data where some combinations of correlated values are not reasonable [23, Section 5.1]. PDPs were used in this study to interrogate constructs where such a pattern was permissible and interpretable. It is recommended to use rug plots as part of any PDP plot to limit interpretation to within the range of the training set, thus avoiding models extrapolating beyond the data range [27].

II. Survey Instrument

The survey consisted of 136 questions and was designed by Organisational Silence researchers under the administration of the fourth author of this paper. All questions pertaining to this survey were taken from previously published research papers or added by the researchers based on their expertise in the area of organisational silence research. All scales were translated into their local languages and then translated back to English to confirm there was nothing lost in the translation. Inconsistencies were resolved by communication with the project administrator. Construct's names start with a capital letter.

The survey included questions on demographic information such as age, gender, country, industry worked and type of contract the participant was on. Cultural aspects of silence were measured using 13 constructs from the *Global Leadership and Organisational Behaviour Effectiveness* (GLOBE) questionnaire [28]. The constructs measured both societal and organisational practices related to: (1) Power Distance (collective response to power; acronym ends with "_pd"); (2) Uncertainty Avoidance Practices (effort undertaken by the collective to avoid uncertainty in their lives; acronym ends with "_ua"); (3) Future Orientation Practices (the process by which a group plans and is rewarded for future orientated behaviour; acronym ends with "_fo"); (4) Institutional Collectivism (propensity of people to act as a collective; acronym ends with "_c"); (5) Humane Orientation (propensity to promote and reward humane behaviour; acronym ends with "_ho"); (6) Performance Orientation (attitude to high standards and performance improvement; acronym ends with "_po") and finally (7) Gender Egalitarianism (collectives attempts to maximise or minimise the differences between men and women; acronym ends with "_g"). The constructs were generated from questions where the participants were queried about both their organisation and society. The constructs were aggregated to individual and societal level for the GLOBE societal constructs and individual and industry level for the GLOBE organisational constructs. Satisfaction With Life was measured by adjusting *"The Satisfaction with Life Scale"*. It originally consisted of 5 statements where the respondents answered on a 7 point Likert scale [29]. This study adapted the structure of the original questions to ask if respondents were satisfied (Satisfaction) with their health, their jobs, their life and their ability to do their jobs. The four questions were treated as separate constructs.

Additional constructs relating to the individual were included in the survey. These included Organisational Citizenship Behaviour (7 questions inspired by [30]); Mental Health (5 questions taken from [31]); and Health (16 questions taken from [32]). Individual perceptions of Climate For Authenticity (indv_cfa_calc) was covered using a 6 question construct inspired by [33]. It measured if participants could be true to themselves and express themselves in a manner that was consistent with their feelings irrespective of outside influences. Psychological Safety Climate (ind_psc_calc, 7 questions taken from [34]) measured if the climate within an organisation was amenable to employees taking personal risks. They were included to measure perceived office environments. Expectation of remaining in the same job (from [35]) was extended to expectation of remaining in the same organisation, and profession, until retirement.

Six silence constructs were added to the survey including: (1) Acquiescent (employees feel their opinion does not matter and it will not change anything; indv_sil_as); (2) Quiescent (fear of the consequences either from their management or from their co-workers because they do not agree with the group; indv_sil_qs); (3) Prosocial (to protect co-workers or the company; indv_sil_ps); (4) Opportunistic (to gain advantages for themselves; indv_sil_os); Diffident (silence due to lack of confidence; indv_sil_di) and Disengaged Silence (due to the individual being disengaged from their role within the organisation; indv_sil_de) [36], [37]. Relationship To Organisation was measured using three questions asking how much a participant identified with their colleagues, line manager and company [38]. Finally, the question *how often did you express concerns or opinions to someone who is able to change the situation* comprised of four possible answers but was binned into a binary identifying those participants who engaged in Silence. This was the label predicted by the two Random Forest models used in the study.

III. Data Analysis

A. Data Manipulation

All variables were standardised. Dummy binary variables were created for all character variables. Validity was determined using Confirmatory Factor Analysis. Reliability analysis was carried out using McDonald's Omega as described in [39]. Only valid and reliable constructs were interpreted. In total, there were 774 (Italy = 191, Germany = 450, Poland = 133) records with 91 columns. There was a class imbalance in the dataset for those that engaged in Silence (yes = 596, no = 178). Research suggests upsampling/downsampling methods could be used to balance the data leading to improved predictive accuracy. However, this idea was discarded as some research suggests it could result in loss of information or overfitting the model [40]. The *Receiver Operator Curve* (ROC) metric is resilient against the effects of unbalanced datasets [12].

The mean was taken for each participant for every question related to each construct. For example the construct Acquiescent Silence was generated by the equation $\bar{AS} = (sil_9 + sil_{10} + sil_{12})/n$. All constructs aggregated to individual level are prefixed with "indv_". The GLOBE country level scores were generated by taking the average score for all the individuals per country, producing one score per construct per country. They are pre-fixed with "grp_". Similarly the organisational constructs were aggregated to industry level by taking the average score for all individuals per industry and producing a single score per industry. These are prefixed in the data with "ind_"

B. Modelling

The Random Forest using CART as a base learner was tuned by varying *mtry* from 2 to 80 and minimum node size from 2 to 20 in increments of five. The optimal values used in the final models were 17 for *mtry*, and 2 for node size. The Conditional Inference Forest model was tuned across the same *mtry* range where the optimal *mtry* value was found to be 57. All other tuning parameters were left at their defaults.

All tuned models were run on a ten fold cross validated dataset and repeated ten times, to get an average *Area Under The Curve* (AUC) performance. The CART based Random Forest model had an $AUC_{\mu} = 0.65$ and a standard deviation of $AUC_{sd} = 0.08$ ($Kappa_{\mu} = 0.1$, $Kappa_{sd} = 0.09$). Conditional Inference Forests produced a result of $AUC_{\mu} = 0.65$ with a standard deviation of $AUC_{sd} = 0.08$ ($Kappa_{\mu} = 0.13$, $Kappa_{sd} = 0.11$). Figure 1 shows confusion matrices for both models where opacity indicates number of classifications, with blue indicating the majority of classifications. Both models had problems with identifying people who did not engage in Silence. The high precision for both models in predicting those that engage in Silence contrasts a low precision for those that did not engage in Silence.

Variable importance results can be seen in Table I, along with the number of distinct values per attribute. Uncertainty Avoidance Societal Practices (grp_gls_ua) was the most important predictor for Conditional Inference Forests but the

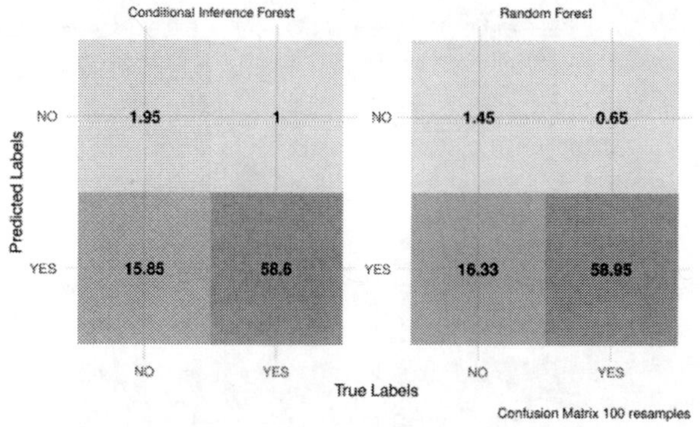

Fig. 1. Average values for Confusion Matrices for all models across 100 samples.

Random Forest suggested it was the 36th most important predictor. Models were in relative agreement when ranking the importance of the next four predictors (within 3 places), each had a relatively high number of distinct values. In contrast, ind_calc_education, qual_level_second_level and qual_calc_degree all have large disparities between rankings illustrating CART Random Forest's bias towards attributes with a larger number of distinct values.

TABLE I
Top 10 Variable Importance Ranking of Conditional Inference Forest With corresponding CART Random Forest Ranking

Feature Code	Distinct Values	CIF Rank	CRF Rank
grp_gls_ua	3	1	36
indv_sil_as	19	2	2
indv_sil_qs	19	3	3
indv_gls_pd	29	4	1
indv_cfa_calc	35	5	6
ind_calc_education	2	6	65
indv_gls_ho	24	7	5
indv_sil_de	19	8	14
indv_glo_ua	19	9	7
indv_sil_os	18	10	22
indv_sil_di	19	11	15
present	5	12	40
qual_level_second_level	2	13	59
indv_sil_ps	19	14	8
qual_calc_degree	2	15	56

[a] CIF = Conditional Inference Forest; CRF = CART Random Forest

PDPs were generated in Figure 2 for the top 5 predictors for Conditional Inference Forests. Jitter was added to the rug plot to show where the models may be extrapolating beyond their bounds. Figure 2 shows that the silence predictors Acquiescent Silence (indv_sil_as) and Quiescent Silence (indv_sil_qs) had an expected positive relationship to the probability of someone engaging in Silence. Panel D highlights that as Individual Power Distance Societal Practices increases the probability of engaging in Silence increases. In several studies, high power distance societies tended not to openly express their anger or dissatisfaction with their superiors compared with low power

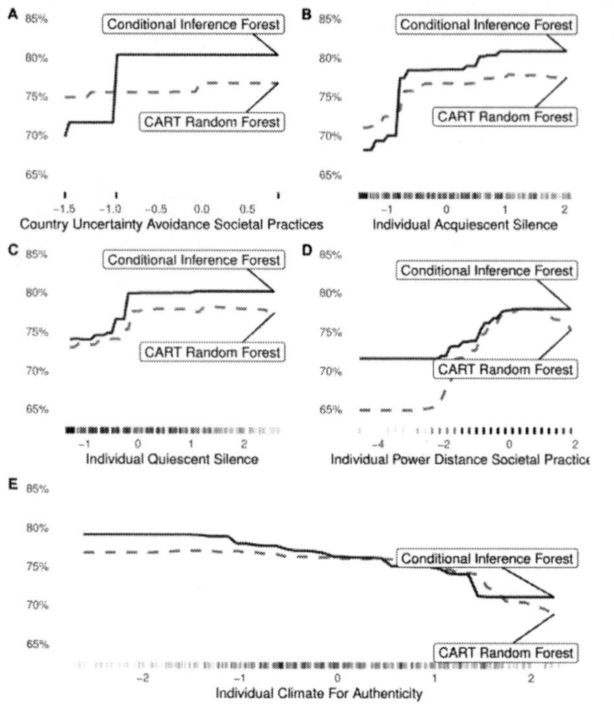

Fig. 2. Partial Dependancy Plots for top Predictors for Conditional Inference Forests.

distance nations [41]. Panel E indicates that as a Climate for Authenticity increases, the probability of participants engaging in Silence decreases. In previous research, it was found that Climate for Authenticity was found to have a positive relationship with voice, while a negative relationship to Quiescent Silence, Pro-Social Silence, Opportunistic Silence, and Quiescent Silence [42]. Panels B, C, D and E modelled expected patterns based on existing research, reinforcing the external validity of the model [36].

It is apparent from both Conditional Inference Forest and Random Forest, that as Uncertainty Avoidance Societal Practices (grp_gls_ua) increased, the probability of engaging in Silence also increased. This was a previously unknown pattern, although several components of Uncertainty Avoidance that may promote Silence behaviours had been documented previously. For example, societies having a highly formalised management structure, an inclination towards hierarchical structures and exhibit a strong resistance to change [43] [44]. This suggests that people in high Uncertainty Avoidance societies may engage in Silence behaviours because they feel any feedback they give would result in no changes in the status quo, in essence Acquiescent Silence.

IV. Conclusions and Future Work

This paper shows how Random Forests in conjunction with PDPs can be used with variable importance measures to highlight non linear relationships between predictors and target variables. However, a CART based random forest showed a bias for predictors with more values. A CIT based forest did not have the same bias. For example, Uncertainty Avoidance Societal Practices was the number one predictor for the Conditional Inference Forest, but was not even in the top 20 predictors for the CART based Random Forest. It is also worth noting that while the pattern plotted for the construct in Panel A of Figure 2 highlights that both Random Forests are in agreement with the relationship between the predictor and the outcome, the pattern is far more pronounced in the Conditional Inference Forest.

Based on these findings, it is suggested where the predictor space has varying number of distinct values per predictor, and model interpretation is the goal of the analysis, that Conditional Inference Forest is better than Random Forest for exploring variable importance. This finding is particularly pertinent for researchers who wish to use tree based modelling for survey data where the questions pertaining to the constructs have a different number of available options.

A weakness in the study was average predictive accuracy of the models. However, moderate AUC scores are common when analysing psychometric survey data. For example, a study that applied a Generalized Additive Model to predict the frequency participants would take cocaine reported an AUC of 0.567 [45]. Another example used an online questionnaire to record several constructs to identify features that would highlight individuals social support needs for "*Online Health Social Networks*" . The resulting mean AUC performance was 0.8. Finally a third study ran several machine learning algorithms to try to predict major depressive disorders from self reported surveys. The study attempted to predict five such disorders with an average AUC of 0.71 (0.71, 0.63, 0.73, 0.74, 0.76) [46].

Modelling in this study highlighted how culture plays a role in whether someone will engage in Silence or not. The models appeared to suggest that people in environments with high Authenticity are less likely to engage in Silence behaviours. It also highlights that the higher the power distance within a society, the more likely someone will engage in Silence. Both of these findings have already been previously explored in the Silence literature. However, the patterns related to uncertainty avoidance were not previously known, and indicate that the higher the value in this construct, the more inclined someone is to engage in Silence behaviours. The results of this analysis suggests that, within this data, culture plays a role in silence engagement both at local and country level. This is demonstrated in Figure 2 for both Societal level uncertainty avoidance and the local Climate for Authenticity. Panels A-D show that the four main constructs level off, suggesting interactions may play a role in mediating the role of each construct in influencing Silence. Data from more countries is needed to confirm the pattern is not an artifice of having too little data.

Partial dependency plots suffer when applied to highly correlated data because they condition on the marginal distribution (See [23, Section 2.1.1]). Other methods exist that are not so readily impacted by correlation such as *Accumulated*

Local Effects (ALE) plots which condition on the conditional distribution while averaging over the differences in the predictions, as opposed to the average of the predictions [47]. ALE plots could be investigated to see if the same patterns highlighted in Figure 2 remain consistent with a larger dataset.

ACKNOWLEDGEMENT

The Italian data sample was collected by Paola Gatti and Chiara Ghislieri (Universit degli Studi di Torino, Italia), the Polish sample by Sylwiusz Retowski (SWPS University of Social Sciences and Humanities) and the German sample by Rolf van Dick (Goethe Universitt Frankfurt, Germany).

All analysis and exploration of data was carried out in `R` [48]. This paper was produced using `bookdown` (version 0.16) and `rticles` (version 0.14) packages [49], [50]. Scale validity and reliability was undertaken using the `lavaan` package (version 0.6-5) [51]. Data manipulation and plotting of PDPs were undertaken using `tidyverse` (version 1.2.1), `pdp` (version 0.7.0), `ggrepel` (version 0.8.0) and `cowplot` (version 0.9.3) packages [27], [52]–[54]. Modelling was applied using `tidymodels` (version 0.02) and `caret` (version 6.0-80) packages [55], [56]. The CART Random Forest model as well as permutated variable importance was generated via the `randomForest` package (version 4.6-14) [57]. The Conditional Inference Forest Model and variable importance of the same model was applied using the `party` package (version 1.3-1) [58].

REFERENCES

[1] E. W. Morrison, "Employee Voice and Silence," *Annual Review of Organizational Psychology and Organizational Behavior*, vol. 1, no. 1, pp. 173–197, 2014, doi: https://doi.org/10.1146/annurev-orgpsych-031413-091328.

[2] M. L. DeVault, *Liberating method: Feminism and social research*. Temple University Press, 1999.

[3] F. Tahmasebi, S. M. Sobhanipour, and M. Aghaziarati, "Burnout ; Explaining the Role of Organizational Silence and Its Influence (Case study : Selected Executive Organizations of Qom Province)," vol. 3, no. 8, pp. 272–282, 2013.

[4] A. Edmondson, "Psychological safety and learning behavior in work teams," *Administrative science quarterly*, vol. 44, no. 2, pp. 350–383, 1999, doi: https://doi.org/10/b9rmv3.

[5] R. J. House, P. J. Hanges, S. A. Ruiz-Quintanilla, P. W. Dorfman, M. Javidan, and M. V. Dickson, "Cultural influences on leadership: Project GLOBE," *Advances in Global Leadership*, vol. 1, pp. 171–233, 1999, doi: https://doi.org/8042818.

[6] M. M. Javidan, P. W. Dorfman, M. S. de Luque, R. J. House, M. S. De Luque, and R. J. House, "In the Eye of the Beholder: Cross Cultural Lessons in Leadership from Project GLOBE," *Academy of Management Perspectives*, vol. 20, no. 1, pp. 67–90, 2006, doi: https://doi.org/10/b9ds7b.

[7] J. Wynen, B. Kleizen, K. Verhoest, P. Lgreid, and V. Rolland, "Just keep silent… Defensive silence as a reaction to successive structural reforms," *Public Management Review*, pp. 1–29, 2019.

[8] R. Bogosian, "The intersection of national cultural values and organizational cultures of silence and voice, and the moderating effect of leadership," *AIB Insights*, vol. 18, no. 2, pp. 16–20, 2018.

[9] T. Hastie, R. Tibshirani, and J. Friedman, "The Elements of Statistical Learning," *Bayesian Forecasting and Dynamic Models*, vol. 1, pp. 1–694, 2009, doi: https://doi.org/10/cw7rjn.

[10] T. M. Khoshgoftaar, D. J. Dittman, R. Wald, and W. Awada, "A review of ensemble classification for dna microarrays data," in *2013 IEEE 25th International Conference on Tools with Artificial Intelligence*, 2013, pp. 381–389, doi: https://doi.org/10/gf5hbg.

[11] L. Breiman, J. H. Friedman, R. A. Olshen, and C. J. Stone, *Classification and Regression Trees*. CRC press, 1984.

[12] M. Kuhn and K. Johnson, *Applied Predictive Modeling*. Springer, 2013.

[13] A. P. White and W. Z. Liu, "Technical Note: Bias in Information-Based Measures in Decision Tree Induction," *Machine Learning*, vol. 15, no. 3, pp. 321–329, 1994, doi: https://doi.org/10/dbhwp2.

[14] T. Hothorn, K. Hornik, and A. Zeileis, "Unbiased recursive partitioning: A conditional inference framework," *Journal of Computational and Graphical Statistics*, vol. 15, no. 3, pp. 651–674, 2006, doi: https://doi.org/10/d47hbq.

[15] A. Venkatasubramaniam, J. Wolfson, N. Mitchell, T. Barnes, M. Jaka, and S. French, "Decision trees in epidemiological research," *Emerging Themes in Epidemiology*, vol. 14, no. 1, pp. 1–12, 2017, doi: https://doi.org/10/gf5g96.

[16] T. Hothorn, K. Hornik, and A. Zeileis, "Ctree: Conditional inference trees," *The Comprehensive R Archive Network*, vol. 8, 2015.

[17] S. Nembrini, I. R. Knig, and M. N. Wright, "The revival of the Gini importance?" *Bioinformatics*, vol. 34, no. 21, pp. 3711–3718, 2018, doi: https://doi.org/10/gdkz3q.

[18] C. Strobl, T. Hothorn, and A. Zeileis, "Party on! A new, conditional variable importance measure available in the party package," 2009, Accessed: Aug. 20, 2020. [Online]. Available: https://cran.r-project.org/web/packages/party/index.html.

[19] C. Strobl, A.-L. Boulesteix, T. Kneib, T. Augustin, and A. Zeileis, "Conditional Variable Importance for Random Forests," *BMC Bioinformatics*, vol. 9, no. 307, 2008, Accessed: Aug. 20, 2020. [Online]. Available: http://www.biomedcentral.com/1471-2105/9/307.

[20] L. Auret and C. Aldrich, "Empirical comparison of tree ensemble variable importance measures," *Chemometrics and Intelligent Laboratory Systems*, 2011, doi: https://doi.org/10/chrsv7.

[21] J. H. Friedman, "Greedy function approximation: A gradient boosting machine," *Annals of statistics*, pp. 1189–1232, 2001, doi: https://doi.org/10/fbgj35.

[22] A. Natekin and A. Knoll, "Gradient boosting machines, a tutorial," *Frontiers in Neurorobotics*, vol. 7, no. DEC, 2013, doi: https://doi.org/10/gfts5q.

[23] C. Molnar, *Interpretable machine learning*. lulu.com, 2020.

[24] D. P. Green and H. L. Kern, "Modeling heterogeneous treatment effects in large-scale experiments using Bayesian Additive Regression Trees," in *The annual summer meeting of the society of political methodology*, 2010.

[25] R. A. Berk and J. Bleich, "Statistical procedures for forecasting criminal behavior: A comparative assessment," *Criminology & Pub. Pol'y*, vol. 12, p. 513, 2013.

[26] J. Elith, J. R. Leathwick, and T. Hastie, "A working guide to boosted regression trees," *Journal of Animal Ecology*, vol. 77, no. 4, pp. 802–813, 2008, doi: https://doi.org/10/fn6m6v.

[27] B. M. Greenwell, "Pdp: An R Package for constructing partial dependence plots," *R J*, vol. 9, no. 1, p. 421, 2017, Accessed: Jul. 01, 2020. [Online]. Available: https://cran.r-project.org/web/packages/pdp/index.html.

[28] R. J. House, P. W. Dorfman, M. Javidan, and P. J. Hanges, *Strategic Leadership across Cultures: The GLOBE Study of CEO Leadership Behavior and Effectiveness in 24 Countries*. 55 City Road, London, 2019.

[29] E. Diener, R. A. Emmons, R. J. Larsen, and S. Griffin, "The Satisfaction with Life Scale," *Journal of Personality Assessment*, vol. 49, no. 1, pp. 71–75, 1985, doi: https://doi.org/10/fqqbmr.

[30] R. Van Dick, M. W. Grojean, O. Christ, and J. Wieseke, "Identity and the extra mile: Relationships between organizational identification and organizational citizenship behaviour," *British Journal of Management*, vol. 17, no. 4, pp. 283–301, 2006, doi: https://doi.org/10/fjv4dk.

[31] J. E. Ware, "SF-36 health survey update," *Spine*, vol. 25, no. 24, pp. 3130–3139, 2000, doi: https://doi.org/10/fv3fbd.

[32] L. R. Derogatis, R. S. Lipman, K. Rickels, E. H. Uhlenhuth, and L. Covi, "The Hopkins Symptom Checklist (HSCL): A self?report symptom inventory," *Behavioral Science*, vol. 19, no. 1, pp. 1–15, 1974, doi: https://doi.org/10/fn39gn.

[33] A. Grandey, S. C. Foo, M. Groth, and R. E. Goodwin, "Free to be you and me: A climate of authenticity alleviates burnout from emotional labor," *Journal of Occupational Health Psychology*, vol. 17, no. 1, pp. 1–14, 2012, doi: https://doi.org/10/fpps98.

[34] M. Baer and M. Frese, "Innovation is not enough: Climates for initiative and psychological safety, process innovations, and firm performance,"

Journal of Organizational Behavior, vol. 24, no. 1, pp. 45–68, 2003, doi: https://doi.org/10/fvkggk.

[35] S. C. Liebermann, J. Wegge, and A. Mller, "Drivers of the Expectation of Remaining in the Same Job until Retirement Age: A Working Life Span Demands-Resources Model," *European Journal of Work and Organizational Psychology*, vol. 22, no. 3, pp. 347–361, 2013, doi: https://doi.org/10.1080/1359432X.2012.753878.

[36] M. Knoll and R. van Dick, "Do I Hear the Whistle...? A First Attempt to Measure Four Forms of Employee Silence and Their Correlates," *Journal of Business Ethics*, vol. 113, no. 2, pp. 349–362, Apr. 2013, doi: https://doi.org/10/r67.

[37] C. T. Brinsfield, "Employee silence motives: Investigation of dimensionality and development of measures," *Journal of Organizational Behavior*, vol. 34, no. 5, pp. 671–697, 2013, doi: https://doi.org/10/r66.

[38] T. Postmes, S. A. Haslam, and L. Jans, "A single-item measure of social identification: Reliability, validity, and utility," *British Journal of Social Psychology*, vol. 52, no. 4, pp. 597–617, 2013, doi: https://doi.org/10/gddc6w.

[39] K. A. Bollen, "Issues in the comparative measurement of political democracy," *American Sociological Review*, pp. 370–390, 1980.

[40] G. M. Weiss, K. McCarthy, and B. Zabar, "Cost-sensitive learning vs. Sampling: Which is best for handling unbalanced classes with unequal error costs?" *Dmin*, vol. 7, nos. 35-41, p. 24, 2007.

[41] X. Huang, E. V. de Vliert, G. V. der Vegt, E. V. D. Vliert, and G. V. D. Vegt, "Breaking the silence culture: Stimulation of participation and employee opinion withholding cross-nationally," *Management and Organization Review*, vol. 1, no. 3, pp. 459–482, 2005, doi: https://doi.org/10/fn4hfr.

[42] M. Knoll and R. van Dick, "Authenticity, employee silence, prohibitive voice, and the moderating effect of organizational identification," *The Journal of Positive Psychology*, vol. 8, no. 4, pp. 346–360, 2013, doi: https://doi.org/10/gfbzbr.

[43] G. Oliver, *Organisational Culture for Information Managers*. Elsevier, 2011.

[44] C. N. Grove, "Introduction to the GLOBE research project on leadership worldwide," *Professional Knowledge Center, GROVEWELL LLC. Retrieved July*, 2005. https://www.grovewell.com/wp-content/uploads/pub-GLOBE-intro.pdf (accessed Nov. 29, 2017).

[45] R. Suchting, J. N. Vincent, S. D. Lane, C. E. Green, J. M. Schmitz, and M. C. Wardle, "Using a Data Science Approach to Predict Cocaine Use Frequency from Depressive Symptoms," *Drug and alcohol dependence*, vol. 194, pp. 310–317, 2019.

[46] R. C. Kessler *et al.*, "Testing a Machine-Learning Algorithm to Predict the Persistence and Severity of Major Depressive Disorder from Baseline Self-Reports," *Molecular psychiatry*, vol. 21, no. 10, p. 1366, 2016.

[47] D. W. Apley and J. Zhu, "Visualizing the effects of predictor variables in black box supervised learning models," *arXiv preprint arXiv:1612.08468*, 2016.

[48] R Core Team, *R: A language and environment for statistical computing*. Vienna, Austria: R Foundation for Statistical Computing, 2018.

[49] Y. Xie, *Bookdown: Authoring Books and Technical Documents with R Markdown*. Chapman and Hall/CRC, 2016.

[50] J. Allaire *et al.*, "Rticles: Article formats for r markdown," 2020, Accessed: Aug. 15, 2020. [Online]. Available: https://CRAN.R-project.org/package=rticles.

[51] Y. Rosseel, "Lavaan: An R Package for Structural Equation Modeling," *Journal of Statistical Software*, vol. 48, no. 2, pp. 1–36, 2012, Accessed: Apr. 13, 2020. [Online]. Available: https://cran.r-project.org/web/packages/lavaan/index.html.

[52] C. O. Wilke, "Cowplot: Streamlined plot theme and plot annotations for 'ggplot2'," 2018, Accessed: Mar. 16, 2020. [Online]. Available: https://CRAN.R-project.org/package=cowplot.

[53] K. Slowikowski, "Ggrepel: Automatically Position Non-Overlapping Text Labels with 'ggplot2'," 2018, Accessed: May 19, 2020. [Online]. Available: https://cran.r-project.org/web/packages/ggrepel/index.html.

[54] H. Wickham, "Tidyverse: Easily install and load the 'tidyverse'," 2017, Accessed: Jul. 01, 2020. [Online]. Available: https://CRAN.R-project.org/package=tidyverse.html.

[55] K. Max and H. Wickham, "Tidymodels: Easily install and load the 'tidymodels' packages," 2018, Accessed: Apr. 20, 2020. [Online]. Available: https://CRAN.R-project.org/package=tidymodels.html.

[56] Max Kuhn *et al.*, "Caret: Classification and regression training," 2018, Accessed: Apr. 20, 2020. [Online]. Available: https://CRAN.R-project.org/package=caret.

[57] A. Liaw and M. Wiener, "Classification and regression by randomForest," *R News*, vol. 2, no. 3, pp. 18–22, 2002, Accessed: Jun. 11, 2020. [Online]. Available: https://cran.r-project.org/web/packages/randomForest/index.html.

[58] C. Strobl, A. L. Boulesteix, A. Zeileis, and T. Hothorn, "Bias in random forest variable importance measures: Illustrations, sources and a solution," *BMC Bioinformatics*, 2007, Accessed: Aug. 20, 2020. [Online]. Available: https://cran.r-project.org/web/packages/party/index.html.

Detecting Users from Website Sessions: A Simulation Study

Corné de Ruijt

Faculty of Science
Vrije Universiteit Amsterdam
Amsterdam, the Netherlands
Email: c.a.m.de.ruijt@vu.nl

Sandjai Bhulai

Faculty of Science
Vrije Universiteit Amsterdam
Amsterdam, the Netherlands
Email: s.bhulai@vu.nl

***Abstract*—In real click data sets, the user initiating a web session may be censored, as unique users are commonly determined by cookies. One way to study the effect of this censoring on various website metrics, and to study the effectiveness of algorithms trying to undo this censoring, is by simulation. We therefore propose a click simulation model, which is capable of simulating user censoring due to cookie churn or the usage of multiple devices, but for which we still keep the uncensored ground truth. To recover unique users from session data, we compare several (H)DBSCAN*-type (Hierarchical Density-based Spatial Clustering of Applications with Noise) algorithms, where we assume that all sessions in a cluster likely originate from the same user. From this comparison, we find that even though the best (H)DBSCAN*-type algorithm does significantly outperform other benchmark clustering methods, it performs considerably worse than when using the observed cookie clusters. I.e., websites for which the assumptions of our simulation model hold, our results suggest that uncovering users from their session data using clustering algorithms may lead to considerably larger errors in terms of user related websites metrics, compared to using cookies to uncover users.**

Keywords–Click models; Session clustering; HDBSCAN*

I. INTRODUCTION

The current Internet environment heavily relies on cookies for the enhancement of our Internet browsing experience. These cookies play a crucial role in session management, the personalization of websites and ads, and user tracking. However, the usage of multiple devices, multiple browsers, and the focus on cookie management, have made the problem of identifying single users over multiple sessions more complex. One study reports that as much as 20% of all Internet users delete their cookies at least once a week, whereas this percentage increases to approximately 30% when considering cookie churn on a monthly basis [1].

Not being able to track Internet users may lead to suboptimal behavior of search engines and online ads, as these have less information about the previous search and click behavior to infer the user's preference for certain items. As cookie churn and the usage of multiple devices cause the user to be censored, we relate to this by the term user censoring.

The problem of unrevealing which session(s) originate(s) from which user has been considered in previous literature, which to our knowledge all have been using real-world data sets to test their algorithms on. Although these real-world data sets have the advantage of capturing much of the complexity of users' click decisions, they also have two clear disadvantages. First, as users are only identified by cookies, we can conclude that two sessions having the same cookie originate from the same user. However, the opposite is not always true: two sessions having different cookies are not per definition different users. The user's cookie might have churned, or the user might have initiated a session from a different device, creating another cookie. Hence, the ground truth is only partially observed in these data sets. Second, using real-world data sets limits the possibility of studying the sensitivity of an algorithm on the underlying click data set: most real-world data sets come from large search engines, which may not always be representative for all websites.

Therefore, we propose a click simulation model, and use realizations of this model to study the effectiveness of several (H)DBSCAN*-type clustering algorithms on uncovering users from their sessions. To measure the effectiveness of these algorithms, we not only consider the error in terms of typical supervised clustering error measures such the adjusted Rand index, but also in terms of the error in estimating overall web statistics, such as the number of unique users, distribution of the number of sessions per user, and the user conversion distribution.

To avoid making the simulation model overly complex, we decided to model user interactions with a search engine. This has two main advantages: first, there exists quite extensive literature on what type of parametric models are accurate for modeling user behavior on search engines [2]. Second, apart from dedicated search engines, a search tool is also a common feature on websites serving other purposes [3]. Another measure against complexity is that we assume all users push homogeneous queries, that is, although we allow users to have different preferences for items returned by the search engine, we do assume all users push the same query.

This paper has the following structure. Section II discusses relevant literature related to session clustering. Section III discusses the simulation model, adaptions of (H)DBSCAN*, and the experimental setup. Section IV discusses the results, whereas Section V discusses the implications of these results and ideas for further research.

II. RELATED WORK

Simulating click behavior is not a new concept: Chucklin et al. [2][pp. 75-77] suggest using pre-fitted click models for this purpose, where the model is pre-fitted to public click data sets. One risk of using pre-fitted models is an availability bias: can the characteristics of public click data sets, commonly provided by large search engines, easily be generalized over all search engines? Also, these data sets do not always provide the type of information one is interested in, such as the device used to initiate a session.

Fleder and Hosanagar [4] provide a generative approach for modeling user preferences, which we will discuss in more depth in Section III-A. This model can be used as an alternative to model user preferences. Pre-fitted and generative models do have a trade-off in terms of accuracy vs interpretability. I.e., pre-fitted models may have an accurate estimate of user item preferences, but provide little understanding in why this preference over different items has a certain shape, whereas generative models do explain why a user has a certain item preference, but these models might be less accurate.

Several authors have studied how cookie censoring occurs. For example, [1][5][6] consider cookie censoring due to cookie churn, whereas [7] considers cookie censoring due to using multiple devices. Results from these studies can be used to model cookie churn dynamics in a simulation model.

Identifying unique users from sessions can be seen as a specific case of the entity/identity resolution problem [8]. Though what makes this problem special is the nature of the data set. This typically consists of a large number of sessions, for which clicks and web page meta-data (such as the URL) are logged. Because of these characteristics, entity resolution algorithms that do not account for these characteristics are likely to fail in their objective. Karakaya et al. [9] give a survey of the literature on cross-device matching, i.e., where it is assumed that user censoring occurs as users use multiple devices. However, many of the approaches listed can also be applied to more general settings.

The problem of uncovering users from their sessions obtained considerable scientific attention following the 2015 ICDM and 2016 CIKM machine learning challenges [9]–[11]. Interestingly, although at a first glance much of the literature seems to relate to the same problem, the context of the data, and how the problem is interpreted seems to vary greatly. The 2015 ICDM and 2016 CIKM challenges consider the problem from the perspective of an online advertiser, where data is gathered from multiple websites. Others consider the problem from a single website perspective [1][8][12]. Although the underlying problem may be the same from both perspectives, the solution may not. E.g., since in the advertisement case the data set contains a variety of URLs from different websites, these solutions rely more on natural language processing techniques than in the single website case.

There also seems to be ambiguity in whether the solution should allow for overlapping session clusters. Most commonly (like in the 2015 ICDM and 2016 CIKM challenges), the problem is modeled as a binary classification problem, predicting whether pairs of sessions originate from the same user [9]. As a result, this interpretation of the problem does allow for overlapping session clusters. Other approaches restrict themselves to non-overlapping clusters, but do however have other disadvantages, like computational feasibility for large data sets [13], or additional assumptions about user behavior [1].

III. Methods

A. Simulating click data with cookie-churn

We will describe the simulation model in three parts. The first part models how users navigate through a single Search Engine Result Page (SERP), for which we use a click model. The second part models how user preferences over different items are determined, while the third part models how a session's underlying user is censored due to cookie churn or the usage of multiple devices.

To describe the simulation model, the following notation will be used. Let $i \in \{1,\ldots,n\}$ be a query-session, which produces a SERP of unique items $\mathcal{L}_i \subseteq \mathcal{V}$, with $\mathcal{V} = \{1,\ldots,V\}$ the set of all items, indexed by v. A (query-)session consists of a sequence of interactions with a single SERP, and these interactions are completely defined by the click model. Let $u_i \in \mathcal{U}$ denote the user initiating query-session i, with $\mathcal{U} = \{1,\ldots,U\}$ the set of all users. The user index u is used instead of u_i in case the precise query-session i is irrelevant.

1) Simulating SERP interactions: To simulate clicks on a search engine, we employ the Simplified Dynamic Bayesian Network model (SDBN) [14]. The main reason for choosing SDBN is that, though the model is simple, it seems to perform reasonably well in comparison to other parametric click models when predicting clicks [2]. The two main variables in this model are, for all $u \in \mathcal{U}$, $v \in \mathcal{V}$, the probability of attraction $\phi_{u,v}^{(A)}$ (probability of user u clicking item v, given that v is evaluated), and the probability of satisfaction $\phi_{u,v}^{(S)}$ (probability of user u evaluating an item at position $l+1$ in the SERP, given that item v at position l was just clicked). SDBN assumes that the first item in a SERP is always evaluated.

2) User item preferences: To come up with reasonable values for $\phi_{u,v}^{(A)}$ and $\phi_{u,v}^{(S)}$, we use the same approach as in [4], which we will refer to as Fleder-Hosanagar's model. That is, each user $u \in \mathcal{U}$ and each item $v \in \mathcal{V}$ is represented by the vectors $\boldsymbol{\eta}_u = \left(\eta_1^{(u)}, \eta_2^{(u)}\right)$, and $\boldsymbol{\psi}_v = \left(\psi_1^{(v)}, \psi_2^{(v)}\right)$ respectively, where both are drawn i.i.d. from a standard bivariate normal distribution. The probabilities $\phi_{u,v}^{(A)}$, and $\phi_{u,v}^{(S)}$ are then determined by the multinomial logit:

$$\phi_{u,v}^{(X)} = \frac{e^{\omega_{u,v}+\nu^{(X)}}}{\sum_{v' \in \mathcal{V}\setminus\{v\}} e^{\omega_{u,v'}} + e^{\omega_{u,v}+\nu^{(X)}}}, \tag{1}$$

with $\omega_{u,v} = -q \log \delta(\boldsymbol{\eta}_u, \boldsymbol{\psi}_v)$, and $X \in \{A, S\}$. Here δ is some distance function, in our case Euclidean distance. $q \in \mathbb{R}^+$ is some constant value that models the user preference towards nearby products, and $\nu^{(A)}$, $\nu^{(S)}$ are salience parameters for attraction and satisfaction, respectively.

3) User censoring: User censoring is incorporated in the simulation model in two ways: by letting cookies churn after some random time T, and by switching from device d to some other device $d^{'}$. First, we consider the cookie lifetime $T_{u,o,d}^{\text{cookie}}$ for the o-th cookie of user u on device d, and the user lifetime T_u^{user}. Whenever the cookie lifetime of cookie o ends, but the current user lifetime is strictly smaller than T_u^{user}, a new cookie $o^{'}$ is created, for which the lifetime is drawn from the cookie lifetime distribution F^{cookie}. For a period of $T_{u,o^{'},d}^{\text{cookie}}$, all click behavior of user u on device d will now be registered under cookie $o^{'}$.

Second, after each query-session, a user may switch from device d to $d^{'}$, which happens according to transition matrix P. Whenever a user switches devices, we consider whether the user has used this device before. If not, a new cookie $o^{'}$ is created, and we draw a new cookie lifetime from F^{cookie}.

However, the cookie lifetime $T^{\text{cookie}}_{u,o,d}$ does not end prematurely when the user switches from device d to d'. If later on the user switches back to device d while the cookie lifetime $T^{\text{cookie}}_{u,o,d}$ has not ended, the behavior of user u is again tracked via cookie o until another device switch occurs or cookie o churns.

Putting this censoring into practice requires us to provide five distributions: 1) a distribution F^{abs} for the time between query-sessions, which following [6] we will refer to as the *absence time*, 2) a distribution for the cookie lifetime (F^{cookie}), 3) a distribution for the user lifetime (F^{user}), 4) the device transition matrix P, and 5) the initial device probability π. All distributions were adopted from previous literature, which is summarized in Table I.

TABLE I. DISTRIBUTIONS REGULATING COOKIE CHURN.

Variable	Description	Distribution
$T^{\text{cookie}}_{u,o,d}$	Cookie lifetime o-th cookie of user u on device d	Hyper-exponential [1]
$T^{\text{abs}}_{u,i}$	Time between sessions i and $i+1$ of user u	Pareto-I, fitted using data from [6]
T^{user}_{u}	Lifetime of user u	Sum of N_u hyper-exponentials [1], $N_u \sim geom(\rho)$
P, π	Device transition matrix and initial transition probabilities	From [7], removing the game console device from the state space

4) Summary of the simulation procedure: By combining the three simulation modules, we obtain the full simulation procedure. In short, we first simulate attraction and satisfaction parameters $\phi^{(A)}_{u,v}$, $\phi^{(S)}_{u,v}$ for all (u, v) pairs using Fleder-Hosanagar's model. Second, we simulate clicks for a set of $\mathcal{U}_{\text{warm-up}}$ users (where $\mathcal{U}_{\text{warm-up}} \cap \mathcal{U} = \emptyset$) using SDBN, where the item order for each query-session is determined uniformly at random. Third, we again run SDBN, now incorporating user censoring, over the set $\mathcal{U}$. The item order in each query-session is now draw i.i.d. from a multinomial distribution (without replacement), where the probabilities are proportional to the overall item popularity found during the warm-up phase. The simulation's source code is available via Github [15].

Although so far we assumed all users arrive at $t = 0$, we shift all times after the simulation to obtain click behavior spread out over time. Here, we assume a Poisson arrival process with rate γ. I.e., the first query-session of user u starts some exponentially distributed time after the initial query-session of user $u - 1$. Note that these inter-first session times only depend on the time of the first session of the previous user, not on any other subsequent behavior of that user.

B. Session clustering

1) Introducing maximum cluster sizes to HDBSCAN and DBSCAN*:* Due to space limitations, we will refer to [16][17] and [18] for details on how the DBSCAN* and HDBSCAN* algorithms work. What we will use, is that both algorithms initially represent the data in a dendogram. The dendogram is obtained by computing a Minimum Spanning Tree (MST) over the complete weighted graph of pairwise distances between data points (in our case sessions), which causes a considerable speed improvement compared to many other hierarchical clustering methods.

As the data is represented in a dendogram, all data points are at the leaves of this binary tree. This tree has the property that if the shortest path between two leave nodes has to use an edge closer to the root node, then these two data points are further apart. This implies that, if we perform a horizontal cut on the tree, this cut relates to some maximum distance ϵ, and all branches below this cut share the property that all data points connected in this branch are at most ϵ apart. Leaf nodes above the ϵ-cut are labeled as noise, and obtain their own cluster.

To impose a maximum cluster size, we employ three strategies, which we name MS-DBSCAN*, MS-HDBSCAN*$^-$ and MS-HDBSCAN*$^+$ (the abbreviation 'MS' stands for 'Maximum Size'). In MS-DBSCAN*, we first make the ϵ-cut to obtain branches $\mathcal{T} = \{\tau_1, \ldots, \tau_m\}$. Next, if some branch τ_j contains more than β data points, we split the branch again at the root node: considering the branches at the left and right child of the root of τ_j as potential clusters. This splitting is continued until all branches have fewer than β data points, after which we assign all data points in one branch to the same cluster.

Both MS-HDBSCAN*$^-$ and MS-HDBSCAN*$^+$ first perform HDBSCAN* using the relative excess of mass to split the dendogram into different branches. Next, we apply the same strategy as in MS-DBSCAN*, where we continue splitting the branches until all branches have fewer than β data points. As a last step, we rerun HDBSCAN* separately on the individual branches, which may again split a branch into smaller branches if that improves the relative excess of mass over all resulting clusters. The only difference between MS-HDBSCAN*$^-$ and MS-HDBSCAN*$^+$ occurs when some found branch (in other words, cluster) does not make any splits for which the left and right child have at least M data points, for some given $M \in \mathbb{N}$. In MS-HDBSCAN*$^+$, we consider all points in this branch to be contained in the same cluster, whereas MS-HDBSCAN*$^-$ assumes all data points in this branch are noise points.

2) Session cluster re-evaluation: As one might have noticed, insofar we have not used any information from the cookies. I.e., knowing which sessions have the same cookie could provide valuable information about the underlying user. In particular, we wish to train a model that can function as an alternative to the standard distance measure δ in (H)DBSCAN*, such as Euclidean or Manhattan distance, which we then again can plug into the adapted (H)DBSCAN* algorithms.

Obtaining session clusters with re-evaluation is done as follows. Assume we have a trained classifier $\hat{f}(X_i, X_{i'})$, which returns the probability of sessions X_i and $X_{i'}$ originating from the same user. First, like in [19], we find for each point X_i the K nearest neighbors, which gives us a set $\mathcal{X}$ of all nearest neighbor session pairs. Second, we compute $-\log(\hat{f}(X_i, X_{i'}))$ for all $(X_i, X_{i'}) \in \mathcal{X}$, and fill this into a (sparse) $n \times n$ distance matrix W. For all pairs $(X_i, X_{i'}) \notin \mathcal{X}$, we assume the distance is some large value $\delta_{\max}$, which allows us to store W efficiently, and greatly speeds up computations compared to evaluating all pairwise same user probabilities. Distance matrix W can subsequently be used as distance measure δ in the algorithms discussed in Section III-B to obtain new session clusters.

We use a logistic regression model for $\hat{f}$, which we train by undersampling from a set $\mathcal{X}_{\text{clust}} \cup \mathcal{X}_{\text{cookie}}$, where $\mathcal{X}_{\text{cookie}}$ contains all pairwise sessions sharing the same cookie cluster, and $\mathcal{X}_{\text{clust}}$ is a set of all pairwise sessions sharing the same computed cluster. These computed clusters are obtained by running a (H)DBSCAN*-type algorithm using Euclidean distances.

3) DBSCAN with random clusters:* To benchmark the clustering approaches just discussed, we consider the following benchmark. We first cluster the sessions using the ordinary DBSCAN* algorithm, in which way we obtain initial clusters $\mathcal{B}_1^0, \ldots, \mathcal{B}_m^0$. Next, for each cluster $\mathcal{B}_j^h$ ($h \in \mathbb{N}_0$, with initially $h = 0$), if $|\mathcal{B}_j^h| > \beta$, we iteratively select $\min\{s_{j,h}, |\mathcal{B}_j^h|, \beta\}$ points uniformly at random from $\mathcal{B}_j$ to form a new cluster $\widetilde{\mathcal{B}}$, and update $\mathcal{B}_j^{h+1} \leftarrow \mathcal{B}_j^h \setminus \widetilde{\mathcal{B}}$. Here, $s_{j,h}$, $j = 1, \ldots, m$; $h = 0, 1, \ldots$; are drawn from a geometric distribution with $p = 0.5$. This process continues until for all $j \in \{1, \ldots, m\}$: $|\mathcal{B}_j^h| \leq \beta$ for some h, at which the remaining points in $\mathcal{B}_j^h$ are labeled as one cluster.

Intuitively, we select this benchmark as it captures the higher-level hierarchy clustering of DBSCAN*, but not the low-level clusters (as these clusters are picked at random). Therefore, comparing the previous methods with this random clustering approach allows us to assess whether the smaller size clusters reveal more information than the larger ones.

C. Experimental setup

1) Simulation parameters: Our experimental design consists of two steps. First, we consider a simulation base case on which we evaluate the clustering approaches discussed in Section III-B. In this base case, the users' first query arrival follows a Poisson process with rate $\gamma = 0.2$ (minutes), after which subsequent behavior over time of a particular user is modeled according to F^{abs}, F^{cookie}, F^{user}, F^{device}, P, and π, of which the parameters were already given in Section III-A3. We use $U = 20,000$ users and $U_{\text{warm-up}} = 2,000$ warm-up users.

Furthermore, we remove the first 250 sessions (not part of the first $U_{\text{warm-up}}$ users, who are only used to estimate the overall item popularity), as these are likely to all be first sessions from newly arriving users, and therefore including them may lead to a bias in the data. Likewise, we remove all observations after $43,200$ minutes (30 days) to avoid the opposite bias: not having any new users. Users could pick from $V = 100$ items, and we choose as maximum list size $L = 10$.

For parameters that could not be adopted from the literature, we tried several parameter values. We find that $q = 1$ (user preference for nearby products), $\rho = 0.5$ (geometric parameter for the number of user lifetime phases N_u), and salience parameters $\nu^{(A)} = \nu^{(S)} = 5$ are reasonable for our base case. In the second step of the experimental design, we make adjustments to the latter parameters, that is, those not adapted from the literature.

2) Features and MS-(H)DBSCAN hyper-parameter settings:* The simulated data set is split into a training and test set according to a 70/30 split over the users. For each session, we use the session's *start time*, *observed session count* (as observed by the cookie), *number of clicks*, and whether the session's *SERP has at least one click* as features. Furthermore, to obtain a vector representation of the items and interactions with the SERP, we first compute a bin-count table. This table contains per item the *total number of clicks*, *skips (no click)*, and the *log-odds ratio between clicks and skips* over 30 percent of all training sessions, which combined are used as item vector representations. For each SERP, we subsequently concatenate the item vector representations based on their position in the SERP, and multiply this vector with the vector of clicks, vector of skips (=no click), and a hot vector of the last clicked item. The resulting three vectors are, together with the features mentioned earlier, concatenated to obtain the final session vector.

For each method, we experiment with (H)DBSCAN's k-NN parameter, for which we tried $k \in \{1, 3, 5\}$. For DBSCAN*-like algorithms, we try

$$\epsilon \in \left\{ \left(q_{\max} \left(q_{\min}/q_{\max} \right)^{\ell/N} \right) | \ell \in \{1, \ldots, N\} \right\}, \quad (2)$$

with $N = 9$ and $q_{\min}$, $q_{\max}$ the minimum and maximum Euclidean distance between all session pairs of 1,000 sampled sessions. For HDBSCAN*-type algorithms, we set the minimum cluster size to $M = 2$. To train classifier $\hat{f}$, we first run MS-DBSCAN* with the best found values for k and ϵ from earlier validation of MS-DBSCAN* on the training set to, together with the cookie clusters, obtain $\mathcal{X}_{\text{train}}$. Next, we compute the Manhattan and Euclidean distances, and infinity norm between the session vectors of each pair $(i, i') \in \mathcal{X}_{\text{train}}$, which are used as feature vector to train a logistic regression model. We select for each point the $K = 1,000$ nearest neighbors to evaluate the classifier $\hat{f}$ on. All non-evaluated pairs receive distance $\delta_{\max} = -\log\left(10^{-6}\right)$. Next, the MS-(H)DBSCAN* algorithms are evaluated using the new distance matrix W, where we experiment again with $k \in \{1, 3, 5\}$, and

$$\epsilon \in \left\{ q_{\min} + \frac{\ell(q_{\max} - q_{\min})}{N_{\text{re-eval}}} | \ell \in \{1, \ldots, N_{\text{re-eval}}\}, \right\}, \quad (3)$$

using $N_{\text{re-eval}} = 5$.

3) Error metrics: We considered error metrics from two perspectives. First, we consider error measures with respect to the overall website performance. More precisely, given some final clustering $\{\mathcal{B}_1^{\text{final}}, \ldots, \mathcal{B}_m^{\text{final}}\}$, the following error measures are computed. 1) We compute the APE (absolute percentage error) between the real and estimated number of unique users (the latter being equal to m), 2) the Kullback-Leibler divergence (KL-divergence) between the real and estimated user session count distribution (the latter being equal to the cluster size distribution), and 3) the KL-divergence between the real and estimated user conversion distribution. Here, user conversion is defined as the fraction of items clicked per user over all shown (but not necessarily evaluated) items.

The second perspective is on the level of the clusters themselves, where we consider two error measures. To determine the quality of the clusters, we computed the adjusted Rand index (ARI) [20] between computed and real session clusters. Besides ARI, we also measure how well the model distinguishes whether each new session originates from an existing or already observed user, which is measured using the accuracy score. Since ARI measures the overlap between the computed and real session clusters, we consider ARI to be our main error measure.

IV. Results

A. Results on the base simulation case

Table II shows how the different models perform in terms of several error measures on both the train and test set. For each method, the shown results are the best results obtained under the different hyper-parameters tried for that method under that data set. I.e., in theory the hyper-parameters might be slightly different between training and test, though in practice we found this was rarely the case.

TABLE II. RESULTS ON THE BASE CASE.

Model	Data set	ARI	KL-div. session count	KL-div. conversion	APE unique user	New user accuracy
MS-DBSCAN*	train	0.0012	**0.55**	0.13	15	**0.56**
MS-DBSCAN*$_p$	train	**0.14**	0.74	**0.092**	77	0.5
DBSCAN*-RAND	train	0.0002	1	0.096	**0.011**	0.42
MS-HDBSCAN*$^+$	train	0.0007	0.75	0.15	10	0.52
MS-HDBSCAN*$^-$	train	0.0007	0.75	0.15	10	0.52
MS-HDBSCAN*$_p^+$	train	0.092	0.9	0.11	**0.011**	0.46
MS-HDBSCAN*$_p^-$	train	0.1	0.9	0.11	**0.011**	0.46
OBS	*train*	*0.91*	*0.017*	*0.0032*	*15*	*0.95*
MS-DBSCAN*	test	**0.0022**	**0.11**	**0.0026**	60	**0.56**
MS-DBSCAN*$_p$	test	0.0015	1.4	0.13	**6.8**	0.4
DBSCAN*-RAND	test	0.0004	0.32	0.015	40	0.5
MS-HDBSCAN*$^+$	test	0.002	0.16	0.0042	53	0.55
MS-HDBSCAN*$^-$	test	0.002	0.16	0.0042	53	0.55
MS-HDBSCAN*$_p^+$	test	0.0015	1.4	0.13	7.2	0.4
MS-HDBSCAN*$_p^-$	test	0.0015	1.4	0.13	7.2	0.4
OBS	*test*	*0.91*	*0.1*	*0.0076*	*51*	*0.95*

The *OBS* model in the table are the scores one would obtain if the observed cookies would be used as clusters. Models using the classifier as distance measure are indicated using subscript p. What immediately becomes apparent is that, compared to these observed cookie clusters, all methods perform considerably worse. Hence, in the scenario we consider: a single query where the true location η_u is only revealed by clicked and skipped item locations, our approaches do not come near what one would obtain if one would simply take the observed cookies.

However, the scores do reveal some interesting patterns. First, approaches using a probabilistic distance measure seem to overfit the data: they perform relatively well (compared to the other approaches) on various measures on the training set, but on the test set these results are mitigated: here MS-DBSCAN* seems to work best when considering multiple error measures. Looking at the results from different hyper-parameter settings for MS-DBSCAN*, we observe that selecting $k = 1$ performed best. Furthermore, due to our maximum size constraint, the clusters did not alter for $\ell \geq 4$ (corresponding to $\epsilon \geq 6.33$).

Furthermore, methods without a probabilistic distance measure do outperform the DBSCAN*-RAND method on most measures. I.e., they perform better at picking sessions originating from the same user given high-level clusters, than if we would pick session pairs at random from these high-level clusters. Although it is difficult to draw a firm conclusion, these findings might be an indication that the same user signal we try to infer from the click data is somewhat weak: if our methods would not pick up a signal at all, we would expect them to have the same result as the DBSCAN*-RAND method.

B. Results on multiple simulation scenarios

In order to judge the sensitivity of our findings on the parameter settings of the simulation model, we permute the simulation settings to see if this alters our results. As re-running all models on all simulation settings would be computationally rather expensive, we only re-evaluate the best performing models on the simulation cases. Since in our base case we found that the parameters $k = 1$, and $\epsilon = \left(q_{\max}\left(q_{\min}/q_{\max}\right)^{2/3}\right)$ work reasonably well, these parameters are used for MS-DBSCAN* and DBSCAN*-RAND. The maximum cluster size remains the same as in the base case.

Fig. 1 shows how the models perform over the different simulation settings in terms of ARI, which is our main response variable. The figure suggests that all cluster models do stochastically dominate DBSCAN*-RAND. Furthermore, MS-DBSCAN* seems to outperform the other clustering methods in terms of ARI. As assumptions like homogeneity of variance or normality do not hold in this case, we used a Kruskall-Wallis test, which rejects in this case that all median ARI scores over the different methods are the same for any reasonable significance level (e.g., $\alpha = .01$, $p < 10^{-4}$). Pairwise one-sided Wilcoxon signed rank tests between MS-DBSCAN* and all other methods also indicate that MS-DBSCAN* performs significantly better than the other methods (all p-values are smaller than 10^{-4}).

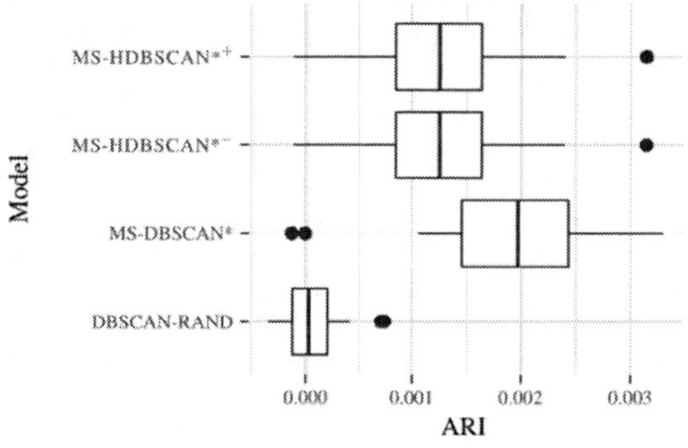

Figure 1. Scores over all simulations.

Considering the variance in the ARI scores, we noticed that strengthening the signal, that is, increasing click probabilities, leads to some improvement in ARI. The most obvious way to do so is by decreasing the number of items (which, as we use bin-counting, ensures each item has sufficient data for bin-counting). However, these improvements remain small. Also interesting is that, when correlating the different error scores over all simulation cases, ARI seems to be weakly correlated with most other error measures, with the sign being in the desired direction (i.e., decrease in KL-divergence for both session count and conversion, but an increase in the new user accuracy). However, improved APE for the number of unique users seems to lead to worse performance in terms of ARI and new user accuracy (Pearson correlations 0.38, and 0.95 resp.).

V. Conclusion and Discussion

In this paper, we presented a homogeneous query click simulation model, and illustrated its usage to the problem of uncovering users from their web sessions. The simulation model is composed of several parametric models, of which previous literature suggests that these models work well in explaining typical patterns observed in click data, while remaining relatively simple. Such patterns include the position bias, cookie censoring, and user preference over multiple products.

Furthermore, we illustrated the simulation model on the problem of (partially observed) session clustering, that is, identifying unique users from their query-sessions. To solve this problem, we tested several mutations of (H)DBSCAN*, where these mutations differ from HDBSCAN* or DBSCAN* as they allow for incorporating a maximum cluster size. From comparing these (H)DBSCAN*-type algorithms, we found that the accuracy of using cookies largely outperform that of not or partially using cookie data. This considerable difference seems to be due to two reasons. 1) The simulated censored cookies turned out to be rather accurate, implying that, assuming the parameters used for cookie censoring adapted from previous literature are accurate, censoring in cookie data does not impose that much of a problem in accurately measuring the metrics studied in this paper. 2) As we only considered a homogeneous query, the user preferences are only revealed from the items users clicked, a signal the various (H)DBSCAN*-type algorithms found difficult to detect. Strengthening this signal, e.g., by increasing the number of clicks, led to a small improvement in ARI.

Other interesting observations include the difference between using Euclidean distance and a probability distance measure in the (H)DBSCAN*-type algorithms, the latter being obtained from training a classifier on detecting whether session pairs originate from the same user. The results suggest that the probabilistic classifier tends to overfit. Also interesting is that, when considering the correlations between the various error metrics considered in this paper, we observed that some error measures show contradictory correlations. In particular, the positive correlation between cluster ARI and average percentage error in the number of unique users (.38), and between the accuracy in estimating whether the next session originates from a new user and the new user average percentage error (.95), indicate that optimizing for one of these error measures may lead to decreased performance in the other.

Although our findings suggest that the practicality of session clustering from single query click data is limited, the usage of the simulation model did allow for studying the sensitivity of the clustering algorithms on different click behavior, something that would not easily have been possible with real click data. It also allowed us to study the effects of user censoring caused by cookie churn or the usage of multiple devices, which showed that if we adopt models of cookie churn behavior found in the literature, this censoring only has a small negative effect on the accuracy of the website metrics discussed in this paper, with an exception for estimating the number of unique users.

Given our findings, a number of questions remain. First, it would be interesting to extend the simulation model to allow for multiple queries. As the solutions to the (multi-query) CIKM 2016 and ICDM 2015 cross-device matching competitions were quite successful, a logical hypothesis would be that incorporating multiple queries into the simulation model would improve the results obtained from (H)DBSCAN*-type algorithms. Second, in this study, we only used a logistic regression model to approximate the probability of two sessions originating from the same user. Given the limited success of this approach so far, it would be interesting to consider other approaches. As the limited results seem to be due to overfitting, including regularization or using bootstrap aggregation approaches could lead to better results. Third, there is still limited knowledge on how cookie censoring occurs. Currently, multiple models exist in the literature, but most models only consider a specific type of censoring, from which one cannot infer how these different types of censoring interact.

REFERENCES

[1] A. Dasgupta, M. Gurevich, L. Zhang, B. Tseng, and A. O. Thomas, "Overcoming browser cookie churn with clustering," in Proceedings of the fifth ACM international conference on Web search and data mining. ACM, 2012, pp. 83–92.

[2] A. Chuklin, I. Markov, and M. d. Rijke, Click models for web search. Morgan & Claypool Publishers, 2015.

[3] C. Luna-Nevarez and M. R. Hyman, "Common practices in destination website design," Journal of destination marketing & management, vol. 1, no. 1-2, 2012, pp. 94–106.

[4] D. Fleder and K. Hosanagar, "Blockbuster culture's next rise or fall: The impact of recommender systems on sales diversity," Management science, vol. 55, no. 5, 2009, pp. 697–712.

[5] D. Coey and M. Bailey, "People and cookies: Imperfect treatment assignment in online experiments," in Proceedings of the 25th International Conference on World Wide Web. ACM, 2016, pp. 1103–1111.

[6] G. Dupret and M. Lalmas, "Absence time and user engagement: evaluating ranking functions," in Proceedings of the sixth ACM international conference on Web search and data mining. ACM, 2013, pp. 173–182.

[7] G. D. Montanez, R. W. White, and X. Huang, "Cross-device search," in Proceedings of the 23rd ACM International Conference on Information and Knowledge Management. ACM, 2014, pp. 1669–1678.

[8] D. Jin, M. Heimann, R. Rossi, and D. Koutra, "node2bits: Compact time-and attribute-aware node representations," in ECML/PKDD European Conference on Principles and Practice of Knowledge Discovery in Databases, Proceedings, Part 1, 2019, pp. 483–506.

[9] C. Karakaya, H. Toğuç, R. S. Kuzu, and A. H. Büyüklü, "Survey of cross device matching approaches with a case study on a novel database," in 2018 3rd International Conference on Computer Science and Engineering (UBMK), 2018, pp. 139–144.

[10] ICDM, ICDM 2015: Drawbridge Cross-Device Connections, 2015, https://www.kaggle.com/c/icdm-2015-drawbridge-cross-device-connections, retrieved: August, 2020.

[11] CIKM, CIKM Cup 2016 Track 1: Cross-Device Entity Linking Challenge, 2016, https://competitions.codalab.org/competitions/11171, retrieved: August, 2020.

[12] S. Kim, N. Kini, J. Pujara, E. Koh, and L. Getoor, "Probabilistic visitor stitching on cross-device web logs," in Proceedings of the 26th International Conference on World Wide Web. ACM, 2017, pp. 1581–1589.

[13] F. M. Naini, J. Unnikrishnan, P. Thiran, and M. Vetterli, "Where you are is who you are: User identification by matching statistics," IEEE Transactions on Information Forensics and Security, vol. 11, no. 2, 2016, pp. 358–372.

[14] O. Chapelle and Y. Zhang, "A dynamic bayesian network click model for web search ranking," in Proceedings of the 18th international conference on World wide web. ACM, 2009, pp. 1–10.

[15] C. de Ruijt and S. Bhulai, SDBNSimulator, 2020, https://github.com/cornederuijtnw/SDBNSimulator, retrieved: August, 2020.

[16] R. J. Campello, D. Moulavi, and J. Sander, "Density-based clustering based on hierarchical density estimates," in Pacific-Asia Conference on Knowledge Discovery and Data Mining. Springer, 2013, pp. 160–172.

[17] R. J. Campello, D. Moulavi, A. Zimek, and J. Sander, "Hierarchical density estimates for data clustering, visualization, and outlier detection," ACM Transactions on Knowledge Discovery from Data (TKDD), vol. 10, no. 1, 2015, pp. 1–51.

[18] L. McInnes and J. Healy, "Accelerated hierarchical density clustering," arXiv preprint arXiv:1705.07321, 2017.

[19] M. C. Phan, Y. Tay, and T.-A. N. Pham, "Cross device matching for online advertising with neural feature ensembles: First place solution at CIKM cup 2016," arXiv preprint arXiv:1610.07119, 2016.

[20] L. Hubert and P. Arabie, "Comparing partitions," Journal of classification, vol. 2, no. 1, 1985, pp. 193–218.

Online Feature Selection for Semantic Image Segmentation

Rishav Rajendra
Canizaro Livingston Gulf States
Center for Environmental Informatics,
New Orleans, USA
email: rrajendr@uno.edu

Michael Christopher
Naval Research Laboratory
Center Geospatial Sciences
Stennis Space Center
Mississippi, United States
email: chris.michael@nrlssc.navy.mil

Elias Ioup
Naval Research Laboratory
Center Geospatial Sciences
Stennis Space Center
Mississippi, United States
email: elias.ioup@nrlssc.navy.mil

Md Tamjidul Hoque
Canizaro Livingston Gulf States Center for Environmental Informatics,
New Orleans, USA
email: thoque@uno.edu

Mahdi Abdelguerfi
Canizaro Livingston Gulf States Center for Environmental Informatics,
New Orleans, USA
email: mabdelgu@uno.edu

***Abstract*— In this project, we classify each pixel from the incoming stream of aerial imagery of water bodies as either "land" or "water" in real-time. Traditional batch feature processing techniques can be too slow to adapt to real-time changes. This paper proposes an online distributed framework for Semantic Segmentation using conditional independence to discard irrelevant and redundant features to train a fast and lightweight but accurate machine learning model. Through extensive experimental results using aerial imagery of water bodies, we demonstrate that our approach is faster than existing online feature selection methods while maintaining high accuracy.**

Keywords - machine learning; semantic segmentation; streaming images; feature selection.

I. INTRODUCTION

Traditional feature selection algorithms require all data-points to be available and presented before the feature selection process starts [6]. After all the features have been collected, the feature selection process begins. This is not always possible in the real world because we do not always know where the end-point is. In this work, we aim to solve this problem in terms of streaming aerial images of water bodies. As images arrive, we generate candidate features dynamically one at a time. We believe generating features one at a time provides a greater practical advantage over traditional feature selection. For example, in this research, we classify each pixel in an aerial image of water bodies into two classes: land and water. A single channel from the smallest image in our dataset contains 468,784 pixels (706 weight × 664 height). The images we use have four channels per image. As a result, the computational cost of generating features from these images is high. We believe waiting for the feature extracting process to complete before the learning begins is not practical for a real-time use case. It is preferable to generate features one at a time [10]. Online feature selection seeks to select the minimal set of features from the incoming features as they arrive while maintaining a high overall model accuracy. Online feature selection stores all the incoming data in two primary data structures: streaming data structure and streaming features structure.

A preliminary distinction is needed between streaming data structure and streaming features structures. For streaming data structure, the number of features selected remains the same throughout the entire feature selection process. Still, the number of data instances increases over time. However, in streaming features structure, the number of data instances per feature is fixed, but the number of features increases over time.

Lets us assume an algorithm chooses five features for both streaming data structure and streaming features structure after the first image. Assuming the number of features remains constant for streaming data structure but increases by one for every subsequent image in streaming features, even if the total number of features selected remains the same with streaming data structure, the total number of data instances across all five features will always increase after every image. However, for streaming features structure, even if we select five features after the first image and an additional feature with every new image, we will have significantly fewer data instances over time. Streaming features structure will only be a problem if our feature selection algorithm selects a very high number of features from every image. Ideally, our feature selection algorithm will choose only a small number of features giving streaming feature structure a significant advantage.

Two notable research efforts have greatly contributed to addressing the problem of online feature selection using a streaming feature structure. Zhou *et al.* presented Alpha-investing [15] for streaming feature selection. With Alpha-investing, Zhou *et al.* mainly focused on controlling the threshold during feature selection. Alpha-investing uses a p-value from linear and logistic regression to dynamically adjust the threshold while selecting new features. Alpha being "invested" increases the wealth and threshold to allow for a slight increase in the inclusion of incorrect features. However, for every instance when a feature from the dynamically generated stream is tested to be insignificant, wealth is "spent" which reduces the threshold. Alpha-investing can handle an infinite number of features, but only evaluates each new candidate feature exactly once without considering the redundancy of the selected features. On highly redundant datasets like the one we are using, Alpha-investing provides a very low and unstable prediction accuracy.

Koller *et al.* proposed a classification of input features F with respect to their relevance to a target T in terms of conditional independence [5][6]. They propose a learner-independent paradigm for feature subset selection, viewing an induction algorithm as a biased method for approximating the probability distribution of class labels given features and transforming this distribution of class labels that the induction algorithm attempts to approximate. They also classify elements into three disjoint categories belonging to X input features and their importance in C target class: (1) strongly relevant, (2) weakly relevant, and (3) irrelevant. Yu and Liu [13] improved this categorization by proposing a definition of feature redundancy, therefore, creating a path for efficient elimination of redundant features. For the following definitions, let F be a full set of features, F_i denotes the ith input feature, C denotes the target, and $S = F - \{F_i\}$ represent all input features excluding F_i.

Definition 1 (Conditional Independence) In a feature set F, two features F_i and F_j are conditionally independent given the set of features Z, if and only if

$$P(F_i|F_j,Z) = P(F_i|Z), \text{ denoted as Independent}(F_i,F_j|Z).$$

Definition 2 (Strong relevance) Feature F_i is strongly relevant to C if and only if

$$P(C|F_i S_i) \neq P(C|S_i).$$

Definition 3 (Weak relevance) Feature F_i is weakly relevant to C if and only if

$$P(C|F_i,S_i) = P(C|S_i), \text{ and } \exists S_i \subset S_i, \text{ such that}$$
$$P(C|F_i, S_i) \neq P(C|S_i).$$

A feature with weak relevance is not always in the final, optimal feature subset, but ideally, it would be included.

Definition 4 (Irrelevance) Feature F_i is irrelevant to C if and only if

$$\forall S \subseteq S_i, P(C|F_i,S_i) = P(C|S_i).$$

Yu and Liu [13] proposed dividing features into necessary and unnecessary features. In their definition derived from the Markov blanket, redundant features provide no additional information than features already selected, and irrelevant features provide no useful information in the final model.

Definition 5 (Markov blanket) Given a feature F_i, let $M_i \subset F(F_i \notin M_i)$, M_i is said to be a Markov blanket for F_i if and only if

$$P(F - M_i - \{F_i\}, C|F_i, M_i) = P(F - M_i - \{F_i\}, C|M_i).$$

where C is the Markov blanket. We can eliminate conditionally independent features from the selected candidate feature set using the Markov blanket without increasing the distance from the desired distribution [8].

Definition 6 (Redundant feature) Let G be the current set of features. A feature is redundant and hence needs to be removed from G if and only if there is a weak relevance and has a Markov blanket M_i within G.

In another study, Wu *et al.* developed a new framework that used feature relevance and a new algorithm called Online Streaming Feature Selection (OSFS) [12]. OSFS uses a two-step approach to discard irrelevant and redundant features from the streaming features as they arrive. Based on the definitions above, the entire feature set is divided into four basic disjoint parts: (1) irrelevant features, (2) redundant features, (3) weakly relevant but non-redundant features, and (4) strongly relevant features. First, the framework conducts an online relevance analysis, Definition 4, which determines a new feature with respect to its relevance to the target T and removes irrelevant ones. After that, the online redundancy analysis, Definition 6, eliminates redundant features from the features selected so far. These two steps are repeated one after the other until a stopping criterion is satisfied.

In Section 2, we go through the dataset we used to test our proposed frameworks, image augmentation and feature extractions methods used, the online feature selection framework used in this paper and the performance evaluation metrics used to judge models. In Sections 3 and 4, we discuss the results of proposed frameworks and the conclusion respectively.

II. METHODS

In this section, we describe the approach for benchmark and independent test data preparation, feature extraction, performance evaluation metrics, and finally, the path we took to establish the feature selection framework for semantic image segmentation.

A. Dataset

The images used for this work are aerial imagery of water bodies acquired during the agricultural growing seasons in the continental US by the National Agriculture Imagery Program (NAIP). NAIP is administered by the USDA's Farm Service Agency (FSA) through the Aerial Photography Field Office in Salt Lake City. This "leaf-on" imagery is used as a base layer for GIS programs in FSA's county service centers and is used to maintain the Common Land Unit (CLU) boundaries.

NAIP imagery is acquired at a one-meter Ground Sample Distance (GSD) with a horizontal accuracy that matches within six meters of photo-identifiable ground control points, which are used during image inspection.

We have a total of eight images. All images are captured with four bands of data: red, green, blue, and near-infrared. Every picture complies with the specification of no more than 10 percent cloud cover per quarter quad tile, weather conditions permitting. All imagery is inspected for horizontal accuracy and tonal quality.

B. Image Augmentation

As we have a deficient number of images, eight, we used various image augmentation techniques to increase the size of the available dataset. A total of eight image augmentation methods were used on each image channel.

The following image augmentation methods were applied on each image channel in the dataset mentioned in 2.A:

a) Random Image Rotation Augmentation

b) Random Flip Augmentation

c) Random Shift Augmentation

d) Random Channel Shift Augmentation

e) Gray Scale

f) Random Brightness Adjustment

g) Random Contrast Adjustment

C. *Feature Extraction*

Feature extraction can provide new attributes. After each image arrives and image augmentation methods are applied, features are extracted dynamically from each augmented image. Extracted features are then sent to the online feature selection framework. We derive three main features from the images: Gabor Kernel Features, Canny Edge Detector, and Gaussian Blur.

a) Gabor Kernel Features: Gabor Kernel Features are special classes of bandpass filters, i.e., they allow a specific 'band' of frequencies and reject the others. Gabor kernel-based features have been successfully and widely applied to a broad range of image processing tasks like texture recognition and face recognition [11]. This is because the characteristics of the Gabor kernel, mainly the frequency and orientation representations, are similar to those of the human visual system [7]. We extracted the Gabor features based on five parameters: (1) λ - Wavelength of the sinusoidal component, (2) θ - The orientation of the normal to the parallel stripes of the Gabor function, (3) ψ - The phase offset of the sinusoidal function, (4) σ - The standard deviation of the Gaussian envelope and (5) γ - The spatial aspect ratio and specifies the ellipticity of the support of the Gabor function. These five parameters control the shape and size of the Gabor function.

b) Canny Edge Detector: Canny Edge Detection is widely used in computer vision to locate sharp intensity changes and to locate object boundaries in an image [3]. A Canny Edge Detector classifies a pixel as an edge if the gradient magnitude of the pixel is more significant than those of pixels at both sides in the direction of maximum intensity change. It is optimal, according to the three criteria of proper detection, sound localization, and a single response to an edge [3]. We extracted the features from Canny Edge Detection using the OpenCV's implementation of the Canny Edge Detection algorithm [1]. The feature extraction process goes through different stages like Noise Reduction, finding the intensity gradient of the image, Non-maximum suppression, and Hysteresis thresholding.

c) Gaussian Blur: Gaussian Blur reduces the noise and detail of the image. This algorithm is applied to provide our frameworks "bad" or distorted data to create a robust model that can be reliable and used in real-life environments.

D. *Online Feature Selection Framework*

For real-time semantic image segmentation, we propose a new framework that accepts an image stream, applies the image augmentation techniques, extracts features from the images, and discards irrelevant and redundant features automatically. Due to the highly redundant images in our dataset, we believe the online relevancy analysis and online redundancy analysis from the OSFS framework [12] will be able to select the least number of features from the entire feature set while maintaining high and stable accuracy.

From a cold-start, OSSF initializes an empty feature set. After an image is presented to the OSSF, all four channels in the image are augmented one by one. Upon completion of the augmentation, OSSF extracts the feature vectors from the augmented image. While all features from the augmented image have not processed, check if the feature is relevant or not. If the feature is relevant, conduct the redundancy analysis. If the relevant feature is not redundant with other selected features, add the feature to the feature set. Process the next feature from the augmented image. After all features of that augmented image have been processed one-by-one, move on to the next augmented image. After processing all the augmented images, move on to the next channel of the original image. After all, channels have been processed, move to the next image from the data source until there are no images, or a pre-set condition is reached.

Algorithm 1: Online Feature Selection for Semantic Image Segmentation

```
input : image_stream
output: Best candidate features (BCF)
BCF = [];
while image_stream do
    for channels in image do
        // Augment each incoming channel
        for augmented channel do
            while GetNextFeature do
                Fi ← GetNextFeature();
                // Online relevance analysis
                if Fi relevant then
                    BCF = BCF ∪ Fi
                    // Online redundancy analysis
                    for each feature Y ∈ BCF do
                        if ∃S ⊆ BCF \Y, s.t. Ind(Y,C | S) then
                            BCF = BCF - Y;
                        end
                    end
                end
            end
        end
    end
end
```

Figure 1. The Online Semantic Segmentation Framework (OSSF).

We implemented our proposed framework, Figure 1, in Python for testing. To determine a given features' conditional independence, we used SciPy's implementation of the chi-square test of independence. The chi-square of independence is used to determine if there is a significant relationship between the features. Null-hypothesis of the chi-square test is that there is no association between the features. For the hypothesis test for the chi-square test of independence, the test statistic is computed and compared to a critical value. The critical value of the chi-square statistic is determined by the level of significance, typically 0.05, and the degrees of freedom. If the chi-square test statistic is higher than the critical value, the null-hypothesis is rejected, and the features are classified as conditionally independent. In the redundancy analysis phase, we check if there is a subset of features from the features selected so far, which is conditionally independent of the class label. We again use SciPy's chi-square test implementation described above for this functionality. If it is independent, then those features are classified as redundant and discarded.

We believe our framework can be significantly improved using a distributed approach. In a distributed environment, data and jobs are divided across multiple clusters by a driver program. A cluster is a group of computers that work together essentially as a single system. In OSSF, after one image arrives, we need to process all four of its channels sequentially. Each channel produces multiple augmented channels, and each augmented channel produces many features. Until all the features of the augmented channel have been produced one-by-one, the entire framework is suspended before moving to the next augmented channel. Even if a new image has already been presented to the framework, it must wait for the previous image to finish processing. This is very inefficient if the data-source is sending images at a fast rate. To tackle this problem, we propose D-OSSF, a distributed version of our framework where images are processed as soon as they arrive concurrently.

For D-OSSF, we use a Kafka producer to send images to a Spark Streaming client. We designed the Kafka producer to submit a new image to the Spark Streaming client every two seconds. The Spark Streaming client loads in the images using Spark's built-in image source API into Resilient Distributed Datasets (RDD). As the images continue to come in, Spark Streaming client creates a continuous series of RDDs, also known as a DStream. Each RDD in a DStream contains images from certain intervals. The Spark engine then transforms the DStream based on our online feature selection framework [14]. The Spark engine handles the underlying distribution operations on the DStreams and provides a high-level API for convenience.

E. *Performance Evaluation*

To evaluate the performance of our framework, we adopted a widely used 10-fold Cross-Validation (CV) approach. In the process of 10-fold CV, the dataset is segmented into ten parts. When one fold is kept aside for testing, the remaining nine folds are used to train the classifier. This process of training and test is repeated until each fold has been kept aside once for testing, and consequently, the test accuracies of each fold are combined to compute the average [4]. AUC is the area under the Receiver Operating Characteristics (ROC) curve, which is used to evaluate how well a predictor separates two classes of information (land and water in images). We used all the performance evaluation metrics listed in Table 1 below, as well as ROC and AUC, to test the performance of the proposed framework and test it with the existing approaches.

TABLE I. NAME AND DEFINITION OF THE EVALUATION METRIC

Name of Metric	Definition	Formula
Accuracy (ACC)	The ratio of samples predicted correctly out of the total sample.	$\frac{TP+TN}{FP+TP+TN+FN}$
Balanced Accuracy (BACC)	Average of recall and specificity.	$\frac{1}{2}\left(\frac{TP}{TP+FN}+\frac{TN}{TN+FP}\right)$
Precision (PR)	The ability of the classifier to not label a negative sample positive.	$\frac{TP}{TP+FP}$
Average Precision (AP)	Combines recall and precision for ranked retrieval results.	$\sum_n (R_n - R_{n-1}) P_n$
Recall	Ability of the classifier classifying positive samples.	$\frac{TP}{TP+FN}$
F1 Score	Harmonic mean of Precision and Recall.	$\frac{2TP}{2TP+FP+FN}$

For all definitions in Table 1, let TP be the number of true positives, TN be the number of true negatives, FP be the number of false positives, FN is the number of false negatives, and P_n and R_n be the precision and recall at the nth threshold respectively.

To test our sequential framework, we use default Scikit-learn's implementation of Logistic Regression (LR), Random Forest (RF), and Decision Tree (DT) classifiers [9]. We also use the eXtreme Gradient Boosting (XGBC) classifier by the Distributed (Deep) Machine Learning Community (DMLC) group [2]. For our distributed framework, we used default Logistic Regression, Random Forest, and Decision Tree classifiers from Spark's MLlib machine learning library [14].

III. RESULTS

In this section, we demonstrate the results of our sequential and distributed frameworks. We also compare our frameworks with Alpha-investing as a benchmark. All experiments were conducted on a computer with two AMD Opteron™ Processor 4386 (3.1 GHz) and 62 GB RAM. All frameworks were given the same sequence of images to avoid any bias. All the experiments were run a total of five times and averaged to minimize inconsistencies.

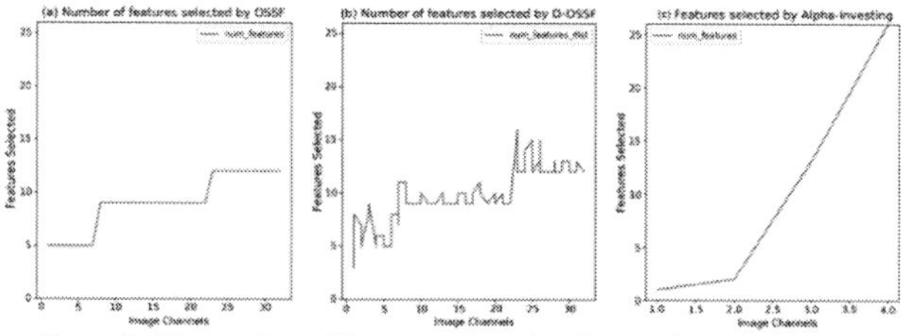

Figure 2. The number of features selected as image channels increase.

As seen in Figures 2a and 2b, both OSSF and D-OSSF end up picking twelve features after the feature selection process completed. We have eight images in our dataset and four channels per image. Every channel leads to nine augmented channels, and every augmented channel generates 32 features. So, both our frameworks, OSSF and D-OSSF, select a subset of 12 features out of 9,216 available features (8 images * 4 channels * 9 augmented channels * 32 features), thus discarding 99.87% of the incoming features. Figure 2a also shows that the number of features selected in the OSSF is exceedingly stable compared to D-OSSF in Figure 2b. OSSF is more stable because channels are processed one at a time. Features from a new channel are only processed after the current channel has been fully processed. So, the framework gets to run the online relevancy analysis and the online redundancy analysis before returning the selected feature set. In the distributed framework, channels are processed concurrently. Features than are passed to the online relevancy analysis in one of the executors of the Spark ecosystem are added into the candidate feature set and may not be able to go through the redundancy test before another executor returns the feature set. This is a classic example of concurrency where multiple operations are happening at once. But this is not a problem as the selected feature set goes through the redundancy analysis eventually and discard the redundant features. This is proved as the number of features selected at the end of the process across multiple runs in both algorithms is equal. However, the number of features chosen by Alpha-investing, Figure 2c, goes up rapidly as the number of image channels increases. This caused a memory overflow across multiple runs, and we could not process the entire dataset due to hardware limitations. The overflow in Alpha-investing usually occurs in highly redundant datasets like the one we are using as it does not conduct a redundancy analysis.

TABLE II. EVALUATION METRICS OF OSSF (IN %)

Model	ACC	PR	BACC	AP	Recall	F1 Score
DT	91.68	91.39	90.72	92.34	95.63	93.27
LR	91.71	91.39	90.73	92.16	95.72	93.30
RF	91.68	91.39	90.73	92.33	95.63	93.27
XGBC	91.71	91.39	90.72	92.34	95.63	93.27

The ACC of OSSF increases from 86.63% after the first channel to 91.68% at the end for DT, RF and XGBC, a 5.51% increase. Similarly, the ACC of LR increases from 83.23% to 91.91%, a 9.25% increase. Other metrics follow a similar trend. For DT, PR increases from 88.20% to 91.39%, BACC increases from 86.06% to 90.72%, AP increases from 89.54% to 92.34%, Recall improves from 89.36% to 95.63%, and F1 Score increases from 88.63% to 93.27%. We can see that the models learn and improve over time as they gets more data. The performance of Alpha-investing was very erractic with some models even reaching 0% for PR, AP and Recall. Overall, Alpha-investing the metrics for Alpha-investing started pretty high but sharply decreased as the number of image channels increased.

TABLE III. EVALUATION METRICS OF D-OSSF (IN %)

Model	ACC	PR	BACC	AP	Recall	F1 Score
DT	90.45	90.72	90.45	90.25	95.25	94.82
LR	91.39	90.93	91.39	90.27	93.97	93.22
RF	89.95	90.72	89.95	91.01	94.87	93.22
XGBC	91.38	90.72	91.38	92.35	93.51	94.82

Evaluation metrics of D-OSSF, Table 3, follow similar trends to OSSF results. The ACC of D-OSSF increases from 85.43%, 84.11%, 87.43%, and 86.49% to 90.67%, 91.23%, 89.73%, and 91.24% for DT, LR, RF and XGBC respectively. That is a 5.78%, 7.85%, 4.17%, and 5.20% increase respectively. For DT, PR increases from 88.73% to 90.72%, BACC increases from 85.39% to 90.45%, AP increases from 87.98% to 90.25%, Recall improves from 89.05% to 95.25%, and F1 Score increases from 86.63% to 94.82%. D-OSSF's distributed framework does not degrade the performance of models and follows the performance of OSSF very closely.

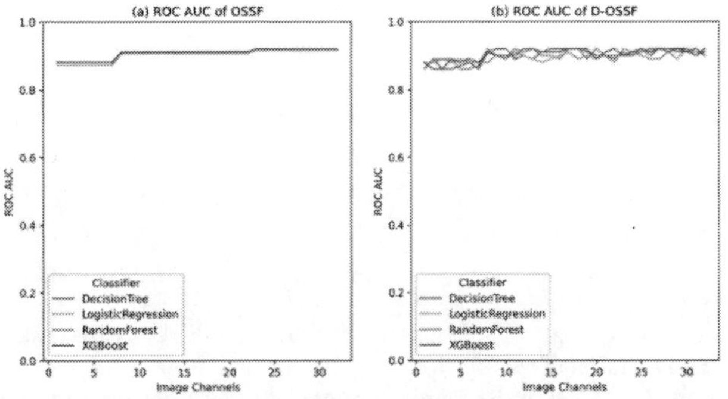

Figure 3. ROC AUC of all three frameworks.

From Figure 3a and 3b, we can see that both our sequential and distributed frameworks achieve comparable results. The AUC of ROC of OSSF, Figure 3a, goes from 0.88 after the first channel to 0.92 at the end for XGBoost, Random Forest, and Decision Tree classifiers, a 4.16% increase. The AUC of ROC of Logistic Regression goes from 0.87 after the first channel to 0.92 by the end, a 5.06% increase. Similarly, the ROC AUC of Decision Tree, Logistic Regression, Random Forest and XGBoost in D-OSSF, Figure 3b, go from 0.86, 0.88, 0.86, and 0.88 to 0.92, 0.91, 0.91 and 0.90 respectively.

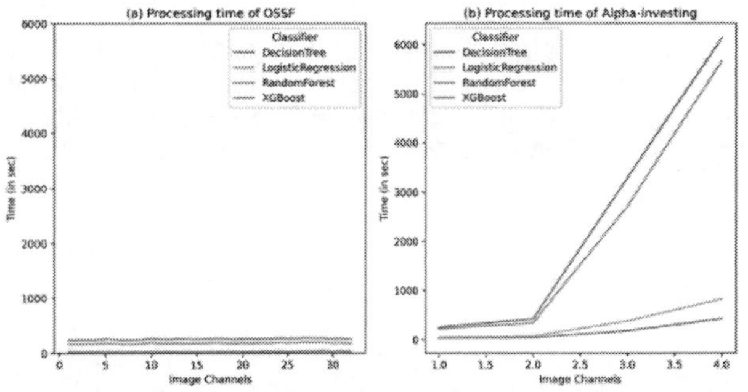

Figure 4. Comparison between the run-time of our OSSF and Alpha-investing.

From Figure 4b, we can see that the erratic nature of Alpha-investing finally ends with the time taken to process each channel going up rapidly before crashing on the fourth channel. The processing time of OSSF, Figure 4a, remains relatively constant as the number of channels increases.

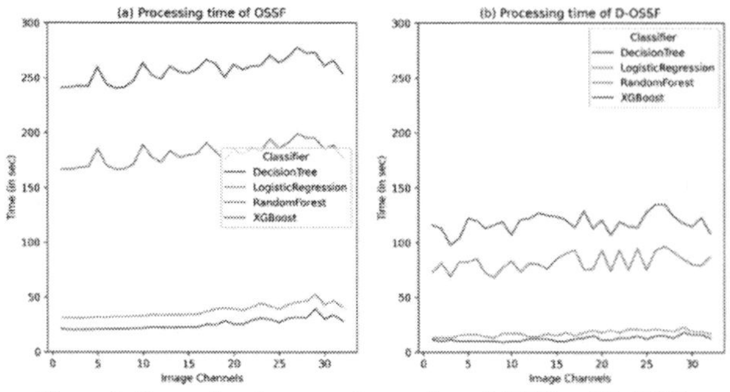

Figure 5. Comparison between the run-time of OSSF and D-OSSF.

From Figure 5a, we can see that for OSSF, on average, the Decision Tree classifier takes the least amount of time with 25.53 seconds. Logistic regression is next on the line with an average of 37.50 seconds. Random Forest takes 180.80 seconds, and XGBoost takes 257.00 seconds on average. From Figure 5b, we observe that for D-OSSF, the Decision Tree classifier again takes the least amount of time with just 12.13 seconds on average, and Logistic Regression takes 17.22 seconds. The Random Forest and XGBoost take 81.81 seconds and 118.34 seconds on average, respectively. D-OSSF, on average, decreases the overall time taken by almost 54% across all classifiers.

IV. CONCLUSIONS

Our aim with this project was to create a framework for Online Semantic Segmentation, which takes in images on the go, extracts, and selects a very low number of features while maintaining a high of model accuracy in real-time. These frameworks are especially important in unknown real-life environments where we do not have previous knowledge of the subject and images stream in as time progresses.

A. Summary

In this research work, two novel frameworks have been developed. These two frameworks are summarized below:

a) Sequential Online Feature Selection Framework: We developed a novel sequential framework for Online Semantic Segmentation that accepts images one at a time, extracts, and selects features on the go. This framework's final accuracy of 91.39% and average processing time per image channel of 25.53 seconds with Decision Tree classifier outperforms other online feature selection algorithms. The 5.51% increase in accuracy over time also proves that our framework can improve as the size of our dataset increases.

b) Distributed Online Feature Selection Framework: Using a distributed Spark ecosystem, we reduced the overall run-time of our framework by almost 54% across all classifiers. The distributed framework produces almost exactly the same performance metrics and selects the same number of features. With the final accuracy of 92.17% and average processing time per image channel of just 12.13 seconds with Decision Tree classifier, we believe our model can be used for real-time implementations.

B. Future Scopes

The frameworks proposed in this research are novel approaches to online Semantic Segmentation by extracting and selecting features on the go. As the size of datasets grows, the importance of online feature selection will grow. The methods used in this research work can also be applied to other fields of computer vision, which require fast training and deployment. We hope to inspire new research in the area of distributed online feature selection across diverse fields.

REFERENCES

[1] G. Bradski and A. Kaehler, "Learning OpenCV: Computer Vision With The OpenCV Library," O'Reilly Media, Inc, 2008.

[2] T. Chen and C. Guestrin, "XGBoost: A Scalable Tree Boosting System," Proceedings of the 22nd ACM Sigkdd International Conference on Knowledge Discovery and Data Mining, 2016, pp. 785-794.

[3] L. Ding and A. Goshtasby, "On The Canny Edge Detector," Pattern Recognition 2001, pp. 721-725.

[4] T. Hastie, R. Tibshirani, and J. Friedman, "The Elements of Statistical Learning," Springer Series in Statics, 2009.

[5] G. H. Jogn, R. Kohavi, and K. Pfleger, "Irrelevant Features and the Subset Selection Problem," Machine Learning Proceedings, 1994, pp. 121-129.

[6] D. Koller and M. Sahami, "Toward Optimal Feature Selection," Stanford InfoLab, 1996.

[7] C. Lee and S. Wang, "Fingerprint Feature Extraction Using Gabor Filters," Electronics Letters, 1999, pp. 288-290.

[8] J. Pearl, "Probabilistic Reasoning in Intelligent Systems", Networks of Plausible Inference, 2014.

[9] F. Pedregosa *et al.* "Scikit-learn: Machine Learning in Python," The Journal of Machine Learning Research 12, 2011, pp. 2825-2830.

[10] S. Perkings and J. Theiler, "Online Feature Selection Using Grafting," International Conference on Machine Learning, 2003, pp. 592-599.

[11] T. Weldon, W. Higgins, and D. Dunn, "Efficient Gabor Filter Design For Texture Segmentation," Pattern Recognition, 1996, pp. 2005-2015.

[12] X. Wu, K. Yu, H. Wang, and W. Ding, "Online Streaming Feature Selection," International Conference on Machine Learning, 2010, pp. 1159-1166.

[13] L. Yu and H. Liu. "Efficient Feature Selection Via Analysis Of Relevance And Redundancy," Journal of Machine Learning Research, 2004, pp. 1205-1224.

[14] M. Zaharia *et al.* "Apache Spark: A Unified Engine For Big Data Processing," Communications of the ACM, 2016, pp. 56-65.

[15] J. Zhou, D. Foster, R. Stine, and L. Ungar, "Streaming Feature Selection Using Alpha-Investing," Proceedings of the Eleventh ACM SIGKDD International Conference on Knowledge Discovery in Data Mining, 2005, pp. 384-393.

DCGAN-Based Data Augmentation for Enhanced Performance of Convolution Neural Networks

Christian Reser and Christoph Reich
Institute for Data Science, Cloud Computing and IT Security
Furtwangen University of Applied Science
Furtwangen, Germany
Email:{christian.reser, christoph.reich}@hs-furtwangen.de

***Abstract*—The quality of steel is essential for many products. Unfortunately, during the production process of steel, surface defects (scratches, inclusions, etc.) occur, resulting in financial losses for steel producers. Therefore, to find and classify surface damage at the earliest stage of the steel production process to take actions for mitigating quality is preferred. Recently, neural networks have shown the usefulness of image classification. Prerequisite is a large data set. But to collect a large data set often takes too long and is too expensive. This paper investigates how to handle smaller data sets, generate artificial data by augmentation and evaluate their efficiency. Of special interest is the augmentation of images by Deep Convolutional Generative Adversarial Networks (DCGANs). A detailed evaluation and comparision with other augmention techniques show that DCGAN augmentation outperformed other augmentations in accuracy and loss, but it is no replacement for a large data set.**

Keywords*—Convolutional Generative Adversarial Network; Steel Surface Damage; Augmentation; Image Classification; Neural Network; Industry 4.0.

I. Introduction

In the field of machine learning, image classification using convolutional neural networks is nowadays one of the most common approaches. Convolutional neural networks gained popularity because of their success in many image classification problems and the acceptable processing time through the availability of fair GPU (Graphics Processing Unit) prizes. Further, the training time has been cut down, by pre-trained deep convolutional neural networks, such as ResNet [1], which can classify thousands of images from the public available imagenet data set [2]. Mostly essential for a good performance of high accuracy and low loss of neural network results is a huge data set for the training. If there is no such huge data set, because of difficulties to collect (e.g., particle collisions), high expenses (e.g., deep water pictures), or high time consumption (e.g., seldom events), image augmentation can be the solution. This is often the case in the steel industry, as companies often do not find the time to collect enough images to create a good data set. This may require processes to be interrupted, which can lead to financial loss. Surface inspection would be so important for the industry, because it allows material defects to be detected early and sorted out before further processing. Typically, through augmentation, a data set can be expanded by flipping images (horizontally or vertically), apply random zoom, random rotation or random shear of images, for example. This method can make a machine learning model more robust, more accurate, and prevent it from overfitting, but only, if the data set itself has enough variations. Variations of images are: intra-class variation, scale variation, view-point variation, occlusion, illumination, background Clutter [3]. But often, the data set is too small and a model can become overfitted easily. To improve such small data set, a new approach is taken. The augmentation by Deep Convolutional Generative Adversarial Network (DCGANs) introduced by Radford et al. in [4]. DCGANs are a variation of the Generative Adversarial Networks introduced by Goodfellow in [5], especially for images.

In the next section (Section: II), related work is discussed. In Section III, the used steel image data is described and how the data is prepared for our experiments. Section IV will give information about the used augmentation methods of this work. Section V describes the used neural network architecture, the training method, and the evaluation method. The results of the experiments are shown in Section VI and in the last Section VII, a conclusion and an outlook are given.

II. Related Work

The work from Shorten and Khoshgoftaar in [6] deals with the problem of limited data in data sets. They focus on data augmentation to enhance the size and quality of image data sets to get better training results and prevent overfitting at the same time. They provide an overview of all the different augmentation techniques. In general, there are two main branches of augmentation techniques. Basic image manipulations and deep learning approaches. The basic image manipulations takes one original image and performs different manipulations on it, such as geometric transformations or color space transformations. With these techniques, multiple images can be generated out of one original image to enhance the data set. Advanced techniques, based on Deep learning augmentation make use of Generative Adversarial Networks (GANs). These augmentation techniques will be used in this work, especially for generating new images for the NEU-DET data set [7].

He et al. in [8] developed a defect detection system to precisely classify and locate the damage on a steel plate surface. They used the NEU-DET data set [7] which is used in this work too. A detailed explanation of the data set will be given in Section III. He et al. used deep learning methods and gained a very high classification accuracy of almost 99%. The difference to our work is the usage of a lightweight neural network for faster training and predictions. Furthermore, we only want to use a small part of the data set to simulate a small data set and evaluate the trained models on the whole. Our small data set will be enhanced by augmentation techniques explained by Tschuchnig in [9]. He describes the process of augmenting images of online accessible celebrity faces data set with DCGAN networks to improve the training results. Tschuchnig DCGAN network generates images of 64x64 pixels, which is not sufficient enough for the data set used in this paper. In this work the size of 128x128 images will be generated.

In [10], Perez and Wang compared traditional augmentation techniques with GAN augmentation on the tiny-imagenet-200 data set [2]. The difference to this work is that Perez and Wang used a GAN to do style transformations instead of generating new images. They came to the conclusion that it is not worth, because traditional augmentations performed better and had three times less computing time than the GAN style transformation.

In [11], Li et al. data set of six different steel surface damages is used. They also used a specialized You Only Look Once (YOLO) network. Their YOLO model can classify and localize the damage in the steel surface images. In this work, we try to classify similar defects with a smaller data set and with a smaller CNN (Convolutional Neural Network) architecture.

Other works of surface inspection deal not only with steel, but also with textile processing like Stübl et al. in his work [12] or with transparent materials like Satorres et al. in [13]. Zamuner and Jacot did it even with watch parts in [14].

III. Northeastern University Data Set

The data set we use for the augmentation experiments and evaluation is provided from the Northeastern University (NEU) and public available at [7]. The data set contains images with six different steel surface damages: Crazing, inclusion, patches, pitted surface, rolled inscale and scratches. Each of the six classes contain 300 samples, 1800 images in total. For doing the augmentation experiments we decreased the data set and removed three classes of the data set. So we only had to deal with the three classes, crazing, patches, inclusion, shown in Figure 1. Further, the data set of 300 images per steel surface image class is reduced to the range of 10 to 50 (3.3 to 15% of the original data set). This allows to generate 250 to 290 images by augmentation and evaluate the achievable classification accuracy, either by using the small data set complemented by augmented images or by using the original data set. Further detailed explanation about the augmentation of steel surface images can be found in Section IV.

IV. Augmentations

A common problem in machine learning with deep neural networks are data sets containing too few data samples. The success of deep learning models are highly dependent on the

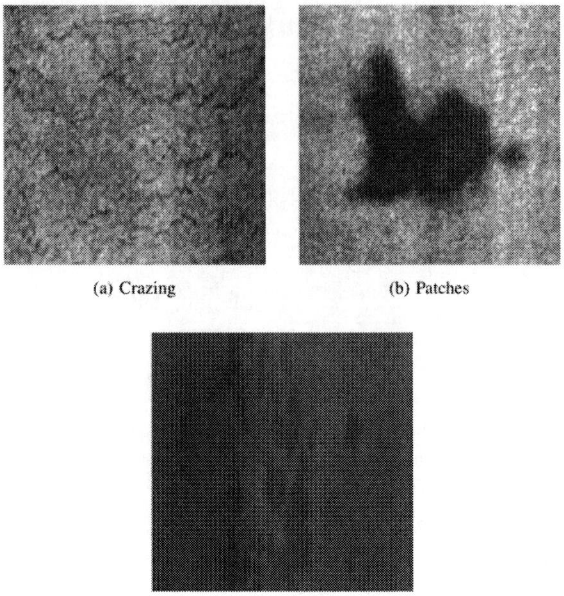

(a) Crazing (b) Patches

(c) Inclusion

Fig. 1. Steel Surface Image Classes

underlying data. Consistency, accuracy, and completeness of data sets are essential for the achievement of good classification results by neural networks. There are a couple of challenges to collect image samples for specific domains. In Roh et al. [15], the challenges are divided into data improvement of existing data, manual or weak labeling of data, and the data acquisition. All these challenges result very often in a weak data set, with too few numbers of samples. One approach to extend the data set is by using augmentation. Image augmentation is the technique to increase the size of the training set without acquiring new images. The basic augmentation technique is duplicating images with some kind of variation (e.g., flipping) so the model can learn from more examples. Ideally, we can augment the image in a way that the features of an original data set are preserved, but the changes within the image are enough to add some variation. Usually, images from the data set are inverted vertically or horizontally, randomly zoomed, stretched, rotated or noise is added to them. A newer method to extend a data set is by using DCGAN Networks to generate new samples. By giving the network many samples of one class, the network learns class-specific patterns in images and generate new images out of a noise vector to expand a given data set. When used correctly in industry, a lot of time can be saved when filling a huge data set, thus preventing financial losses.

A. Common Basic Augmentation

As explained in the introduction, a data set with little data can be expanded by augmentations. The most commonly used augmentations are image transformations. To do so, we used the Augmentor Python package available from [16]. With this technique, we can generate multiple images from every image in the original data set. For example, Figure 2 shows an original image from the class patches with the different augmentations we used in this work. We use random horizontal and vertical flipping, random zoom 0-20% and random rotation in a range from -180 degree to +180 degree. All of these augmentations are applied with a certain probability to every image, which means that sometimes all augmentations are applied and sometimes only a few. With basic augmentations, such as flipping and rotation, features from the original image still remain. With augmentation like random zoom, features get scaled. This is an obstructing factor when analysing the size of any preexisting damage. But, since it is not relevant in this case, random zoom is used in this work.

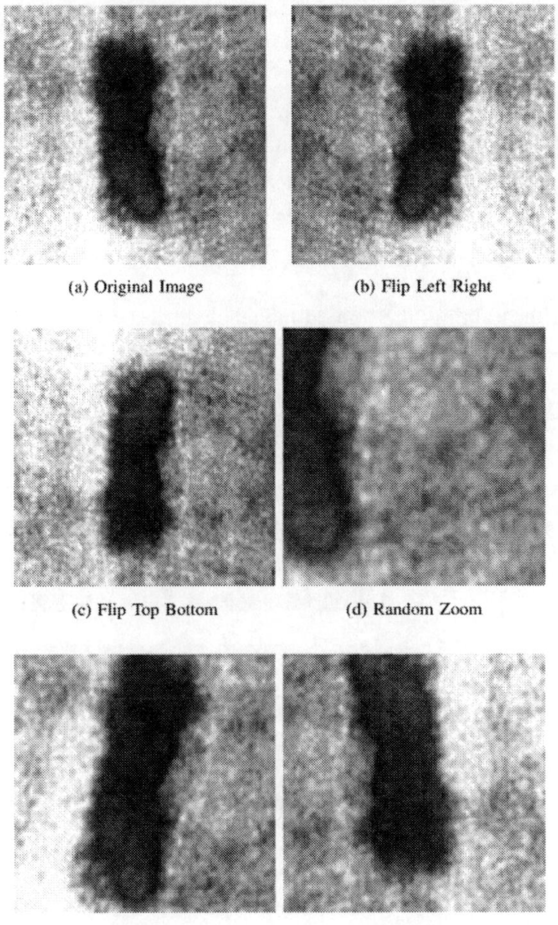

(a) Original Image (b) Flip Left Right

(c) Flip Top Bottom (d) Random Zoom

(e) Random Rotate (f) All Together

Fig. 2. Common Image Augmentations

B. *Augmentation with DCGANs*

This technique of augmentation can be used to generate real-looking samples for the data set preserving the features of the original images. The general architecture of a DCGAN network can be seen in Figure 3. A GAN consists of two concatenated models, the Generator and the Discriminator network. The Generator creates fake images out of an N-dimensional noise vector. The Discriminator gets real and fake images as input and determines whether an image is real or not. The adversarial loss is provided by the Discriminator to the Generator which then creates images, that are as close as possible to real images. [17]. The assumption is, that these new images are expected to be variations of the original image, preserving the features of the original image, but that has not been proven yet.

V. Experimental Setup Using DCGANs for Augmentation

In this section, we explain the neural network architecture, the training method and the evaluation method.

A. *Preparation of the Data Sets*

We want to show that a small data set enhanced with generated samples from a trained DCGAN model performs better than a model trained without the generated samples. To do so we took subsets of 10, 20, 30, 40, 50 samples per class from the full data set of 300 samples per class and trained DCGAN models for each subset. Each subset requires three models, one for each class. All models were trained for 3000 epochs. Checkpoints of the generator were saved after 600, 1200, 1800, 2400 epochs and the last. That makes a total number of 15 models, each on five different checkpoints. In Figure 4, we can see a generated image for each class from the best performing generator model. The full result of the models can be seen in Section VI.

B. *DCGAN Network Architecture*

A DCGAN consists of a generator and a discriminator. For both, the architecture of Shrestha was taken from his blog article in [18]. The dimension of the noise vector which is the input for the generator is 100 and it generates an image of 128x128 pixels. The generator has 24 layers. The discriminator has 22 layers and takes 128x128 pixel images as input. The output of the discriminator is a binary decision if the input image is a real image or a generated fake image from the generator.

C. *Convolutional Neural Network Description*

Since the used data set has been trained successfully on a deep convolutional neural network by He et al. in [8], the approach in this work is to train it on a lightweight convolutional neural network shown in Table I, to measure only the improvements with the different augmentation techniques.

TABLE I. Neural Network Architecture

LAYER	FILTERS	OUTPUT SHAPE	ACTIVATION
Input Layer	-	(128, 128, 3)	-
Conv2D	64	(128, 128, 64)	relu
MaxPooling2D	-	(64, 64, 64)	-
Flatten	-	262144	-
Dense	64	(64, 64, 64)	relu
Output Layer	-	3	softmax

It consists of an input layer that takes images of 128x128 pixels as input, only one convolutional layer with 64 filters

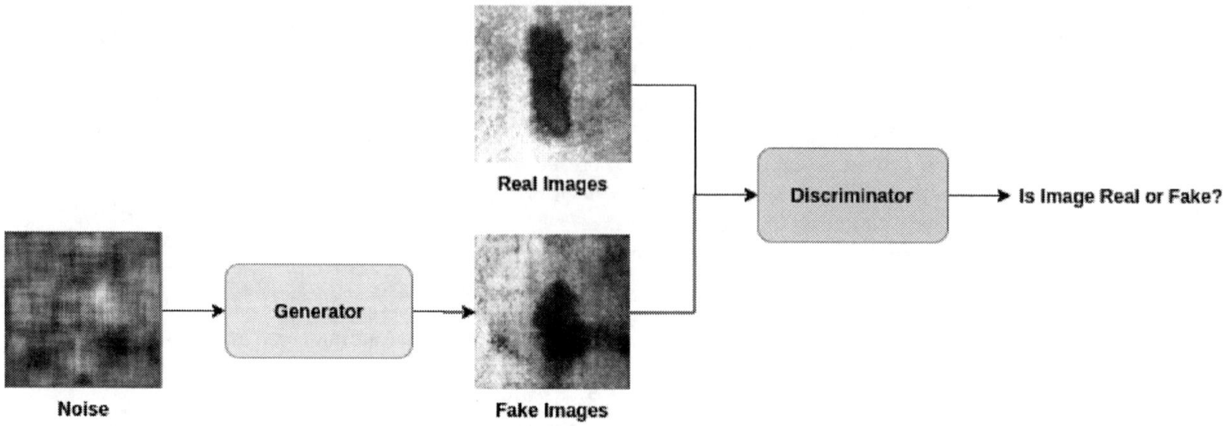

Fig. 3. Generative Adversarial Network

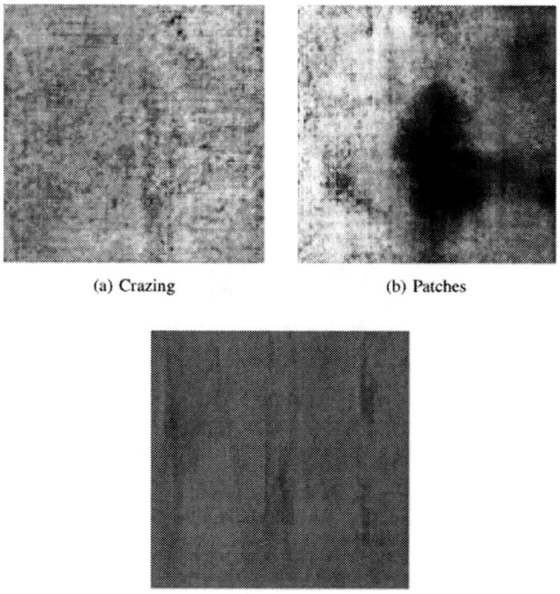

(a) Crazing

(b) Patches

(c) Inclusion

Fig. 4. Augmentation by DCGANs

and Rectified Linear Unit (ReLU) activation function, one maxpooling layer, one flattening layer, one dense layer with 64 units and ReLU activation function and the output layer with 3 neurons for class probabilities provided by the softmax activation function.

D. Training Setup

Every model was trained with the same hyperparameters as described in the Table I above to compare the results. The networks were trained with the architecture from I for 100 epochs on the different data sets. As optimizer we used Adam (short for Adaptive Moment Estimation) which has a learning rate of 0.001 initially. The loss function is categorical cross-entropy because multiclass classification is used. Each epoch took 120 images from the image generator for training and 30 for validation. While training, the models weights got saved every time the validation loss improved. If the model did not improve in at least every 7 epochs, the learning rate got decreased by the factor of 0.1 to enable fine-tuning of the weights.

E. Evaluation Setup

After training, the trained models loaded the weights of the best performing epoch and got evaluated on the whole original data set, consisting of 300 images per class. The results will be given in the next section.

VI. Experimental Results

A. Original Data Set

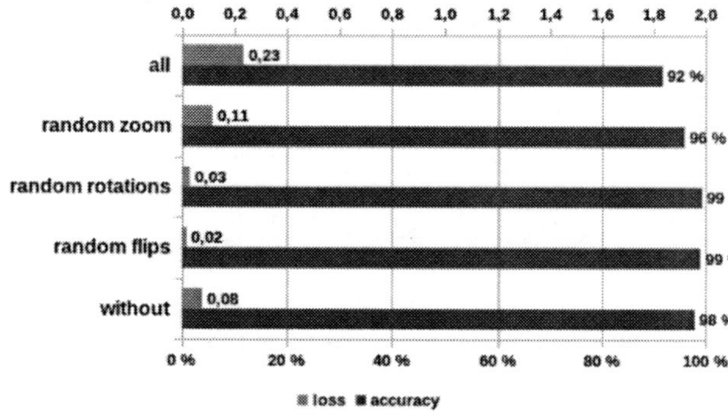

Fig. 5. Original data set

The results from the models trained on the original 300 samples per class data set are given in Figure 5. It can be see seen that the trained model performed quite well with an accuracy of 98.7% even without augmentations . Additional data samples of random flips and rotations improved the accuracy by 1% and the loss from 0.08 to 0.02 with flips and 0.03 with rotations. The model with random zoom augmentation did not improve. Most likely the features of the original image are not preserved by this augmentation method. The model that used all augmentations together wasn't as successful, adding image variations that are too far from the original images.

B. Neural Networks Trained with Reduced Data Set

The results from the neural network models trained on the reduced data sets are illustrated at Figures 6 to 10. As expected, it shows that these models perform much worse than those from the original data set. The models from 10 and 20 samples per class almost never reached a validation loss below 1. The different augmentations showed us that random flips and rotations always improve the validation accuracy but not the validation loss significantly. The best performing model from the reduced data set in terms of accuracy was the one with 40 samples per class, augmented with random rotations. It reached 90% validation accuracy but with a validation loss of 0.72. The best performing model in terms of validation loss was the one trained with 30 samples per class augmented with random rotations. It reached 0.37 validation loss and 85% validation accuracy. Combined it is a drawback to the original data set of 9% validation accuracy and 0.96 validation loss. Surprisingly, it was not the models trained with 50 samples per class. This might be connected to the images being selected randomly out of the original data set for every reduced data set, therefore the quality of the 40 was better than the quantity of the 50 images per class.

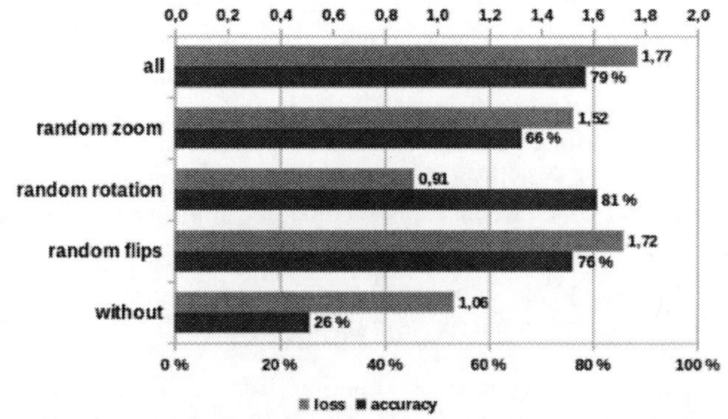

Fig. 6. 10 Samples per Image Class

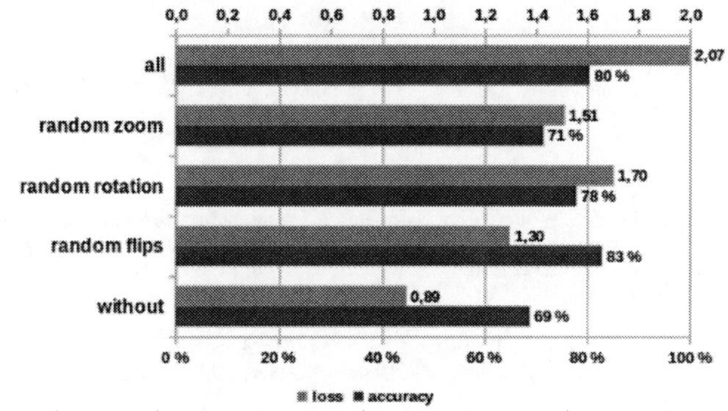

Fig. 7. 20 Samples per Image Class

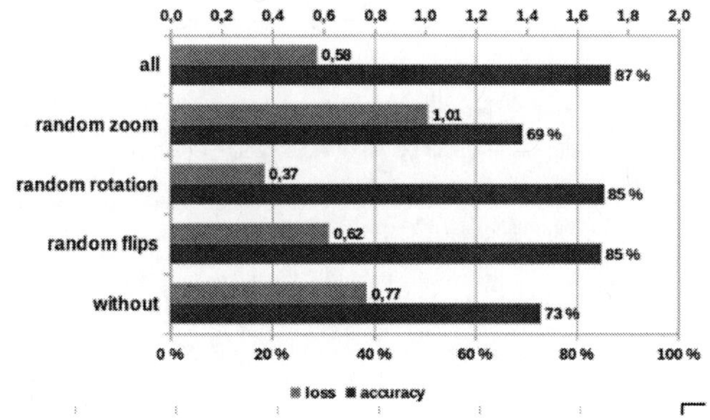

Fig. 8. 30 Samples per Image Class

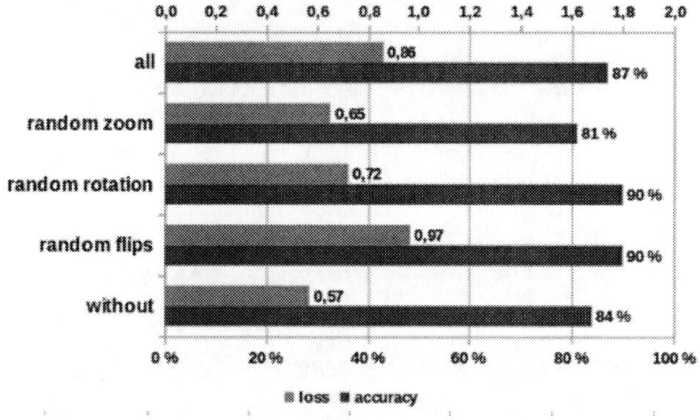

Fig. 9. 40 Samples per Image Class

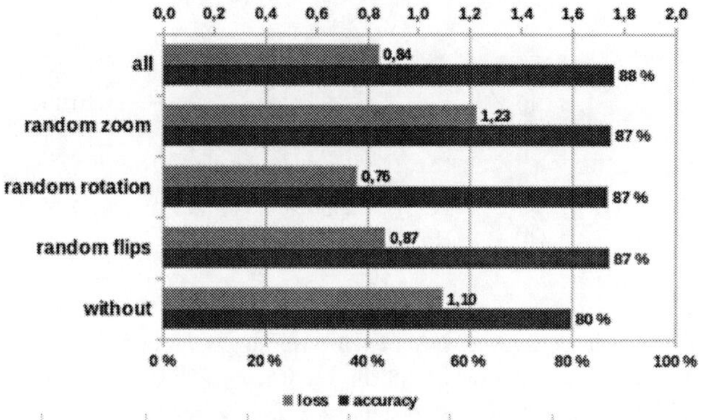

Fig. 10. 50 Samples per Image Class

C. Neural Networks Trained with DCGAN Generated Data Set

As described in Section V, the DCGAN models provided generated data sets for each subset. They are all listed in Table II. On these generated data sets, models were trained the same way as the original and reduced data sets were trained.

The results show that data sets from 10 and 20 samples per class lead to a very significant loss. Using 30 samples per class is more efficient, but the best results were achieved with 40 and 50 samples per class. These DCGAN augmented data sets outperformed other augmentations on the reduced data sets in loss and accuracy. The best model was trained on

TABLE II. RESULTS WITH GAN GENERATED DATA SETS

SAMPLES PER CLASS + 300 AUGMENTED	EPOCH	ACCURACY	LOSS
10	600	80%	0.87
10	1200	73%	1.13
10	1800	67%	2.13
10	2400	75%	1.12
10	3000	71%	2.19
20	600	78%	0.62
20	1200	74%	0.72
20	1800	61%	1.17
20	2400	74%	0.77
20	3000	71%	1.03
30	600	88%	0.49
30	1200	86%	0.38
30	1800	86%	0.47
30	2400	82%	0.61
30	3000	84%	0.56
40	600	88%	0.32
40	**1200**	**92%**	**0.23**
40	1800	88%	0.31
40	2400	89%	0.32
40	3000	88%	0.30
50	600	87%	0.47
50	1200	87%	0.55
50	1800	85%	0.35
50	2400	87%	0.40
50	3000	84%	0.56

a data set generated out of 40 samples per class after 1200 epochs. It reaches a validation accuracy of 92% and a loss of 0,23 which is in terms of accuracy 2% better and in terms of loss 0.14 better than the best models from the reduced data sets together. A full comparison of the best models with different techniques can be seen in Figure 11.

As expected the overall best model was trained on the original data set with a validation accuracy of 99% and a validation loss of 0.02. From the reduced data sets, the DCGAN augmented data set outperformed every other augmentation used in this work with an accuracy of 92% and a loss of 0.23. The best models with common augmentations reached an accuracy of only 90% and a loss of 0.37.

Through DCGAN augmentation we reached improvements of 2% accuracy and 0.14 loss towards common augmentation techniques. The trade-offs to the original data set were 8% accuracy and 0.21 loss.

VII. CONCLUSION AND OUTLOOK

The goal of this work was to enhance a shortened data set with DCGAN generated images and to train a model that performs better on the original data set than models from the shortened data set with common augmentation techniques. In the end, our results show that a well trained DCGAN network can generate images to improve a data set with limited image samples for such a use case in steel surface damages.

One drawback of this method is that all DCGAN models generated images from the same checkpoint. In this work, it is basically the average best models for each class. For further research DCGANs from different checkpoint epochs and classes could be used to improve the quality of the data set quality even more. One observation was that a good variety of generated samples is needed. To do so, the model should not train too few epochs and not too many. If the model trains too little, it likely generates more noise and if it trains too much, the model always generates the same image.

One other observation from the common augmentation techniques was that if you put all augmentations together, the model performs worse than with only one or without any augmentation. We assume that in this case there are too many variations possible within one picture, which weakens the model. This will be part of further investigation.

We can conclude that this method can improve the quality of a small data set, but it cannot replace the quality of a large data set.

ACKNOWLEDGEMENT

This work has received funding from EFRE (European Regional Development Fund) and the Ministries for Research of Baden-Wuerttemberg from the program: Innovation and Energy Transition.

REFERENCES

[1] K. He, X. Zhang, S. Ren, and J. Sun, "Deep residual learning for image recognition," *CoRR*, vol. abs/1512.03385, 2015. [Online]. Available: http://arxiv.org/abs/1512.03385

[2] J. Deng, W. Dong, R. Socher, L. Li, Kai Li, and Li Fei-Fei, "Imagenet: A large-scale hierarchical image database," in *2009 IEEE Conference on Computer Vision and Pattern Recognition*, 2009, pp. 248–255.

[3] R. Poppe, "A survey on vision-based human action recognition. image and vision computing 28(6), 976-990," *Image Vision Comput.*, vol. 28, pp. 976–990, 06 2010.

[4] A. Radford, L. Metz, and S. Chintala, "Unsupervised representation learning with deep convolutional generative adversarial networks," 2015.

[5] I. J. Goodfellow, J. Pouget-Abadie, M. Mirza, B. Xu, D. Warde-Farley, S. Ozair, A. Courville, and Y. Bengio, "Generative adversarial networks," 2014.

[6] C. Shorten and T. Khoshgoftaar, "A survey on image data augmentation for deep learning," *Journal of Big Data*, vol. 6, 12 2019.

[7] "Neu-det data set," available: http://faculty.neu.edu.cn/yunhyan/NEU_surface_defect_database.html.

[8] Y. He, K. Song, Q. Meng, and Y. Yan, "An end-to-end steel surface defect detection approach via fusing multiple hierarchical features," *IEEE Transactions on Instrumentation and Measurement*, vol. 69, no. 4, pp. 1493–1504, 2020.

[9] M. E. Tschuchnig, "Adversarial networks — a technology for image augmentation," in *Data Science – Analytics and Applications*, P. Haber, T. Lampoltshammer, and M. Mayr, Eds. Wiesbaden: Springer Fachmedien Wiesbaden, 2019, pp. 97–98.

[10] L. Perez and J. Wang, "The effectiveness of data augmentation in image classification using deep learning," 2017.

[11] J. Li, Z. Su, J. Geng, and Y. Yin, "Real-time detection of steel strip surface defects based on improved yolo detection network," *IFAC-PapersOnLine*, vol. 51, no. 21, pp. 76 – 81, 2018, 5th IFAC Workshop on Mining, Mineral and Metal Processing MMM 2018. [Online]. Available: http://www.sciencedirect.com/science/article/pii/S2405896318321001

[12] G. Stübl, B. Moser, and J. Scharinger, "On approximate nearest neighbour field algorithms in template matching for surface quality inspection," in *Computer Aided Systems Theory - EUROCAST 2013*, R. Moreno-Díaz, F. Pichler, and A. Quesada-Arencibia, Eds. Berlin, Heidelberg: Springer Berlin Heidelberg, 2013, pp. 79–86.

[13] S. Satorres, J. Ortega, J. Garcia, A. García, and E. Estevez, "An industrial vision system for surface quality inspection of transparent parts," *The International Journal of Advanced Manufacturing Technology*, vol. 68, pp. 1123–1136, 09 2013.

[14] G. Zamuner and J. Jacot, "A system for the quality inspection of surfaces of watch parts," in *Precision Assembly Technologies and Systems*, S. Ratchev, Ed. Berlin, Heidelberg: Springer Berlin Heidelberg, 2012, pp. 134–143.

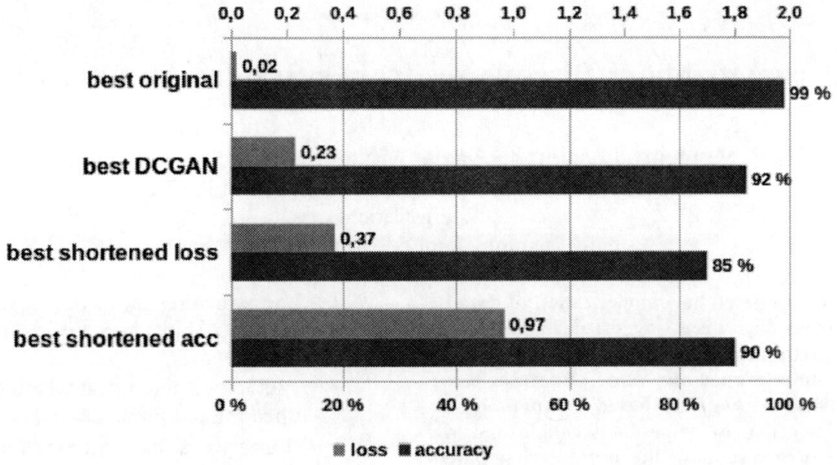

Fig. 11. Overview of the Best Results

[15] Y. Roh, G. Heo, and S. E. Whang, "A survey on data collection for machine learning: a big data - AI integration perspective," *CoRR*, vol. abs/1811.03402, 2018. [Online]. Available: http://arxiv.org/abs/1811.03402

[16] Mdbloice, "mdbloice/augmentor," Mar 2020. [Online]. Available: https://github.com/mdbloice/Augmentor

[17] M. Salvaris, D. Dean, and W. H. Tok, *Generative Adversarial Networks*. Berkeley, CA: Apress, 2018, pp. 187–208, available: https://doi.org/10.1007/978-1-4842-3679-6_8.

[18] A. Shrestha, "Generating modern art using generative adversarial network(gan) on spell," Jul 2020. [Online]. Available: https://towardsdatascience.com/generating-modern-arts-using-generative-adversarial-network-gan-on-spell-39f67f83c7b4

Big Data Monetization: Discoveries from a Systematic Literature Review

Domingos S. M. P. Monteiro, Luciano de Aguiar Monteiro, Felipe Silva Ferraz, Silvio R. L. Meira
Center of Advanced Studies and Systems of Recife
Recife, Brazil
E-mail: { dsmpm, lam, fsf, srlm}@cesar.school

Abstract— **This study investigated how monetization of data in a Big Data environment has been suggested in academic literature. Our goal was to find out what methods have been applied to determine the relevance and value of data in these environments and if these methods are based, in any way, on information theory. In order to come to a conclusion, we applied a formal process of systematic literature review based on the methodology suggested by Kitchenham. The results showed that, in spite of the progress made on the topics of Big Data and the application of analytical methodologies over the last decades, there is no method based on data that is widely used to determine the value of a datum in a Big Data environment. By observing the results, it is possible to conclude that little attention has been given to the dimension Value in academic studies related to Big Data when compared to searches directed to the other three classical dimensions (Volume, Velocity and Variety). More specifically, in terms of economic value, studies are even scarcer, and the existing ones do not share a common view on how to measure this value. If, on the one hand, monetization in Big Data environments is still a field that needs to be better explored in academic literature, on the other hand, these intangible assets, i.e., data, grow exponentially and are more and more present in the corporate world. It highlights the opportunity to develop studies in search of standards that can be widely accepted and used to this end.**

Keywords-Big Data; Big Data Monetization; Analytical Techniques; Artificial Intelligence; Systematic Literature Reviews; Digital Assets.

I. INTRODUCTION

In 1999, Mood and Walsh were the first to propose an economic view directed to digital assets. In their view, data represented the raw material, information systems (hardware & software) would be the manufacturers and information would be the finished product that would need to be priced [1].

In this study, we sought to understand how monetization in Big Data environments has been suggested in academic literature. Originally defined by Gartner in 2001 as "high-VARIETY data that are received at high VOLUME and at increasingly higher VELOCITY" [2]. This definition came to be known as the 3 Vs of Big Data. After this definition, many others have proposed new Vs to be added to the original definition [3]. At least two new Vs have been accepted as part of this definition: namely Veracity and Value [4]. The concept of each of these dimensions is detailed below [5]:

- Volume is the magnitude of large-scale datasets. The variation in the size of large-scale data relies on the structure and time of data, i.e., volume is the size of distinct types of data acquired from distinct data sources;
- Velocity is the rate at which the data is received and then refined for analytical purposes;
- Variety is a distinct type of data representation such as structured, semi-structured, and unstructured data;
- Veracity refers to the biases, noise, and abnormality in data. Veracity issues arise due to the process uncertainty (randomness in process), data uncertainty (data input uncertainty), and model uncertainty (approximate model);
- Value is another dimension of big data in the business perspective. Business organizations need to notice the value of big data, to increase the profit by minimizing the operational costs to provide better services to the customers;

We will focus our searches on the dimension Value, more specifically on the financial value that can be extracted from a certain datum in a Big Data environment.

For reaching our goal, we sought to find out which methods have been suggested or applied so as to determine the relevance and the value of data in Big Data environments. Additionally, if these methods are based on any kind of information theory, a mathematical theory, originally proposed by Shannon in 1948 [6], studies the quantification, storage and communication of information and ways in which it is applied in different areas.

In order to conduct this research, we applied a formal process of systematic literature review based on the methodology suggested by Kitchenham et al. [7]. This process was set in motion by the definition of the problem we want to solve and by the definition of the research questions, search protocols, selection, extraction and syntheses of the primary studies related to the theme. The process went on with the execution of previously defined protocols in the search for answers.

The results showed that, despite the progress in the theme of Big Data and improvements in the application of analytical methodologies over the last decades, there is not yet a method based on data that can be widely used to determine the value of a certain datum in a Big Data environment. According to the results we found, it is possible to conclude that academic research has given very little attention to the dimension Value, especially when compared to the research done on the other three classical dimensions (Volume, Velocity and Variety) [2]. More specifically, when it comes to financial value, research is even scarcer and the existing papers do not share a common view on the most suitable way to measure it.

If on the one hand, monetization of data in a Big Data environment is still a poorly explored field in academic literature, on the other hand, these intangible assets, the data, grow exponentially and are more and more present in the corporate world. This fact highlights the opportunity to develop studies in search of standards that can be widely accepted and used to this end.

This article is structured as follows: in Section 2, we explore the context that we have adopted in our study related to the topic of Big Data; in Section 3, we provide details on the protocols applied to the review; in Section 4, we present the results; in Section 5, we present the conclusion and suggest further future studies.

II. THEORETICAL FRAMEWORK

After analyzing studies from different sectors and applications with non-specified contexts, theories and designs, we use this section to contextualize both the population and the intervention related to this study.

A. Big Data

In spite of having given a definition to the origin of the term Big Data in the introduction, it is a fact that since its advent it has been used in a number of academic studies and commercial applications without a clear uniform meaning or context.

In a 2016 review comprising over a thousand and five hundred studies that mentioned the term "Big Data", De Mauro et al. [8] proposed the following definition that would be able to bundle most of the assessed texts: "Big Data is the information asset characterized by such a High Volume, Velocity and Variety to require specific Technology and Analytical Methods for its transformation into Value". This definition is the one taken into consideration in our study and what makes the theme of our review even more relevant, once it highlights that the explicit objective of a Big Data environment is to turn digital assets into value.

In our case, we searched for studies that proposed ways in which financial value can be extracted from data in the context herein.

B. The Value of Data as Digital Asset

"Many argue that Facebook did not "purchase" user registrations, but user data and user-generated data are the company's core asset, which led to the largest technology Initial Public Offering (IPO) in history" [1].

The debate on how "value" itself was formed has been going on for millennia, since pre-Christian era, when Aristotle argued that value is based on the need for exchange (Aristotle, 350 BC). This concept is in the core of economic adjustment and is the basis to define what will be produced, how it will be produced and who will produce it.

Another key discussion in economic theory includes questioning the reasons for a product or service to be priced the way it is, that is, how the value of a product or service is determined and how to calculate it correctly.

The theory was formulated and applied in a world where products and services were in their entirety represented by physical assets with well-defined characteristics: raw material, finished products and services provided by physical living beings (humans and animals).

The advent of computers brought the world a new category of assets, digital ones, represented in a discrete numerical way and used in digital devices with computational processing. These digital assets are capable of delivering a new category of products and services: better decisions, increased performance, competitive advantages and they can even be sold directly as a product. It is in this context of "data" as a digital asset and as a product itself that we will study the ways of monetization that have been proposed.

III. METHODS

The formal process of systematic literature review applied in this study was based on the methodology suggested by Kitchenham et al. [7]. Six steps composed our methodology: (1) development of the protocol, (2) identification of the criteria for inclusion and exclusion, (3) search for relevant studies, (4) data extraction, and (5) synthesis.

This review focuses on identifying primary studies that approached techniques that proposed ways for monetizing new data in a Big Data environment. Bearing this goal in mind, the next step was the definition of the problem that would guide the search for primary studies.

According to Eron Kelly, "In the next five years, we'll generate more data as humankind than we generated in the previous 5,000 years" [9]. In this setting, we have defined the problem:

- *How can we monetize new data generated and available in the Market in a Big Data environment?*

Our research questions are presented below. The aim is to discover methods either in use or suggested to determine both relevance and value of the datum in Big Data environments and to observe if any of them considers the information theory in their formation.

A. Research Questions

RQ1. What methods have been suggested or applied to determine the relevance of the datum?

RQ2. What methodologies have been applied to identify the value of a datum?

RQ3. Does the methodology to identify the value use the information theory in its formulation? How?

With the questions well defined, in the following sections we move on to defining the protocols for search, selection, extractions and detailed synthesis.

B. Search Protocol

We chose to perform an automatic selection that would guarantee the feedback of the highest possible number of articles that could answer our research questions. For such, we started by defining the search string. Table I below shows the search string we applied.

TABLE I. SEARCH STRING

	Applied Search String	
	Search Terms	***Rational***
Population	("Big Data")	Studies that approach themes related to Big Data
AND		
Intervention	"data assets" OR "value evaluation" OR "data monetization" OR "data marketplace" OR "information value" OR "data value" OR "business value"	Studies that must be related to monetization of data, that is, the extraction of financial value.

We have selected three (3) academic bases that congregate relevant studies in the context of software engineering and Big Data:

- ACM Digital Library;
- IEEE Xplore;
- ScienceDirect – Elsevier;

In the process of extracting information from the selected bases, the search strings were applied separately in each of them. The searches were conducted between May and June, 2020. The studies were grouped and then examined in search of duplicity. Table II shows the number of studies found in each selected base.

TABLE II. PAPERS SELECT BY DATABASE

Database	Amount of studies
ACM Digital Library	403
IEEE Xplore	162
ScienceDirect – Elsevier	1634

Figure 1 presents the number of studies returned in the search according to the year of publication. It is important to point out that in spite of being a recent theme, as the first studies date from 2012, it has gained increased attention by the year.

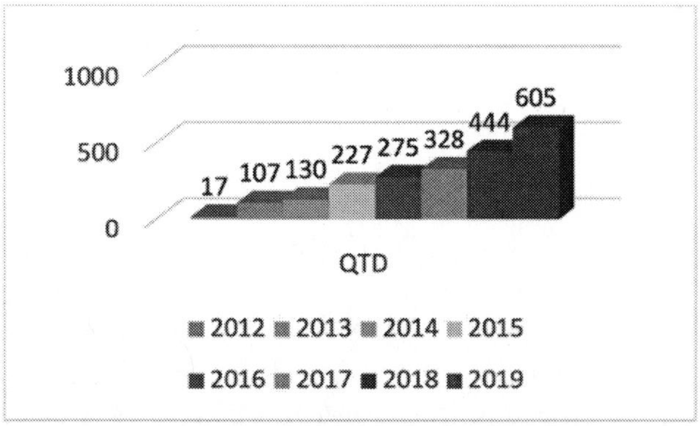

Figure 1. Studies grouped by year of publication.

We have observed a compound annual growth rate of 67% in the number of studies between 2012 and 2019. This shows how this theme has become more and more relevant and coherent with the increase in solutions and demands based on data.

C. *Criteria for Inclusion and Exclusion*

With well-defined string and bases, we focused our selection of articles in the period between 2012 and 2019. The starting point was 2012 for being the year where the first articles related to the theme were published. 2019 was chosen so as to guarantee the replicability of this study in future research (2020 is still ongoing and new articles might still arise for this period in future studies).

On the Criteria for Inclusion and Exclusion, we considered primary studies that would analyze ways of monetizing data, regardless of the context, sector or application.

Criteria for Inclusion: Besides the period of publication, we still defined as criteria for inclusion:

- Primary studies published in English;
- Studies that approach the theme of Big Data and monetization of data;
- Studies that answer at least one of the research questions.

Criteria for Exclusion:

- Academic or teaching-oriented articles;
- Short articles, courses, tutorials and secondary and tertiary studies (reviews);
- Duplicated studies (in these cases, only one version was considered).

D. *Steps of the Selection*

This section describes the selection process from the start by using the strategies described below in order to identify primary studies.

The first step was to obtain studies returned from the search in the databases by using the Zotero [10] and Ryyan platforms [11], both designed for managing publications and supporting reviews. We used these tools to conduct the steps listed below and in Figure 2 in the Results section, showing the number of articles that were filtered through each step until the final selection:

1. Elimination of duplicates and articles written in another language;
2. Search for keywords related to the theme;
3. Reading of the title;
4. Reading of the abstract;
5. Reading of the Introduction and Conclusion, and;
6. Reading of the full article.

In steps 2-6 above, many articles were eliminated for not mentioning ways of monetizing data in the Big Data context either in the title, abstract or keywords, others were also eliminated from the reading of the introduction and conclusion for clearly not approaching the research questions. Finally, in the Reading of the full article step, an additional number of studies were eliminated because, in spite of approaching themes related to the subject of this study, they did not present answers to the research questions.

Figure 2 shows the outcome of the execution of this protocol in the Results section.

E. Extraction and Synthesis Protocol

We used a support form, from the Google Forms tool, to extract the evidence that answered the research question. This evidence was catalogued in a spreadsheet so it could be used in the following synthesis step.

A thematic synthesis was defined to our review, once the contexts, theories and designs of the selected articles do not follow specific standards. This method of synthesis is specially adjusted to these cases, once it allows to identify (codify) and report patterns (themes) based on the data extracted from primary qualitative studies [12].

IV. RESULTS

A. Conducting Search and Selection

The search was performed according to the protocol defined in the previous step and the results are presented in Figure 2.

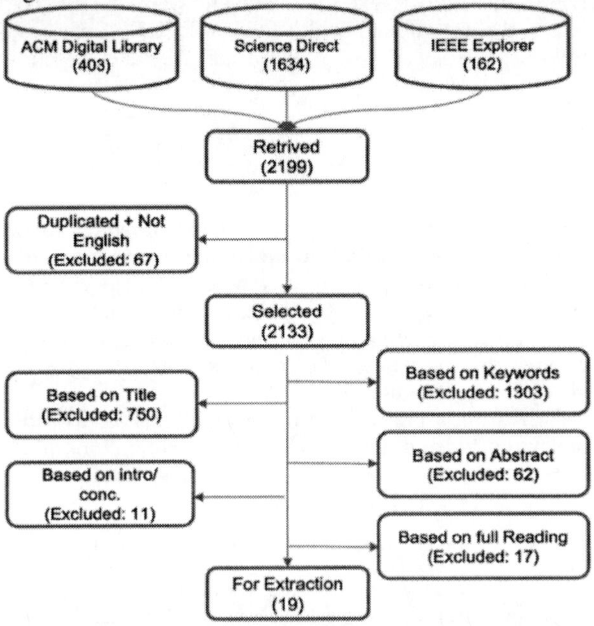

Figure 2. Results of the search and selection process.

A total of 2199 related studies were found in our search string for the defined period and, after the application of the inclusion and exclusion criteria and the steps for selection defined in our protocol, we were left with 19 primary studies to be dealt with in the following extraction and synthesis stages.

Table III presents the number of studies retrieved from each database. It is curious to observe that most of the studies where we found answers to our research questions came from the base that returned the fewest articles in our initial search. In general, at the end of the selection process, only a few studies approached our problem when compared to the original total of results at the beginning. Answers were found in less than 1% of the studies returned from the initial search.

TABLE III. STUDIES ANSWERING RESEARCH QUESTIONS BY DATABASE

Database	Studies for Extraction
ACM Digital Library	2
IEEE Xplore	12
ScienceDirect – Elsevier	5

B. Conduction the Extraction and Synthesis processes

We move on with the conduction of our protocol, now to the extraction and synthesis steps.

Each of the excerpts extracted from the 19 selected articles was codified for a future more detailed synthesis of the theme, according to the thematic synthesis methodology suggested by Cruzes and Dyba [12]. It starts with the identification of keywords in the extracted texts, followed by a process of codification of these texts into higher concepts and, at last, a definition of themes, grouping one or more of the generated codes. In Figure 3, we present the process we applied.

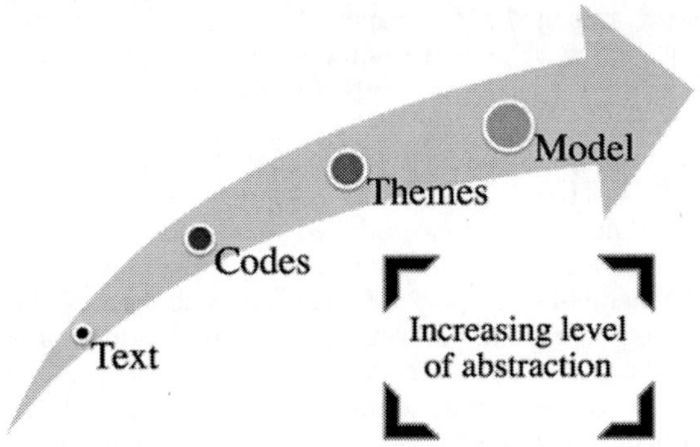

Figure 3. Process of synthesis applied to this study [12].

Table IV presents the answers found in each of the selected articles for each of the research questions.

TABLE IV. QUESTIONS ANSWERED BY ARTICLE

Study	RQ1	RQ2	RQ3	Total
[13]		1		1
[14]	1	1		2
[15]	2	1		3
[16]	1			1
[17]	1			1
[18]		1	1	2
[19]	1	1		2
[20]	1	1		2
[21]	1			1
[22]	1			1
[23]		1		1
[24]	1	1		2
[25]	1			1
[26]		1	1	2
[27]	1	1	1	3
[28]		1		1
[29]	1	1		2
[30]		1	1	2
[1]	1	1		2
Total	**14**	**14**	**4**	**32**

We have found eight studies with answers to one of our questions and in ten other papers we found answers to two of our questions. Only one of the papers was able to answer our three research questions.

C. Answers to the Research Questions

This section approaches a detailed discussion on the results of the systematic review. The subsections provide answers to RQ1 - RQ3 research questions.

After the analysis and extraction steps have been done in primary studies, we were able to identify some aspects related to monetization of data in a Big Data environment based on these studies. The first conclusion is that the theme of monetization of data in a Big Data context is still a recent theme, as two thirds of the answers were found in studies published in the last 3 years. The second conclusion is that few theories and models were developed aiming to approach the theme of this research, once we were left with only 19 studies that were able to answer the research questions. Finally, among the few papers that proposed theories and models to meet the theme of this research, we have not been able to find a model or method that could be considered a standard.

It was surprising to find out that in order to valuate a datum in a Big Data context, techniques based on data are not the most commonly applied. This may sound like a contradiction at first, but it can also be interpreted according to the market law (supply x demand) even in these contexts.

Another hypothesis to justify this observation would be the natural stillness of concepts (inertia), usually applied to physical assets, with characteristics of scarcity, in an approach that would seem more natural in the context of digital assets (using data-based techniques in order to price data).

In this section, we summarize the answers to each of the research questions.

1) RQ1: What methods have been suggested or applied to determine the relevance of the datum?(14 answers)

a) In this review, the most applied methods to determine the relevance of data were the analytical techniques (50% of the findings, 7 cases);

b) Methods that evaluated the relevance of data in a business context were found in 29% of the cases (4 cases);

c) In 2 of the cases (14%) there were methods based in intrinsic characteristics on the data (kinds of data, volume, velocity, etc.);

d) Finally, in 1 of the articles, the use of the datum was applied as a method to determine the relevance of the datum (defined as the number of hits or references to a certain piece of information).

Even among the most used methods, it was not possible to find uniformity, for instance, in the case of the use of analytical techniques to determine the relevance of a datum, where many distinct techniques were applied without the predominance of a specific one.

2) RQ2: What methodologies have been applied to identify the value of a datum? (14 answers)

Table V summarizes the answers to this research question.

TABLE V. BASE FOR VALUE IDENTIFICATION

Way of determining value	**%**
SUPPLY X DEMAND	35.71%
ANALYTICAL TECHNIQUES	21.43%
USE OF THE DATUM (USE/HITS)	14.29%
BOOK VALUE	14.29%
RISK X RETURN	7.14%
INFORMATION THEORY	7.14%

In a simplified way, we have found that the supply x demand market law was the most common reference to determine the value of new data in a Big Data context, followed by analytical techniques (also highlighted in the previous question). Next in line, there were the methods based on the use of data, book value and, finally, a case was based on the price of risk x return and the other based on information theory.

3) Does the methodology to identify the value use the information theory in its formulation? How?

Although in only one of the cases the Information Theory has been used as a method to determine the value of new data, four other studies have referenced this theory in their considerations. Two studies cite entropy as a factor that is directly linked to pricing new data and two others refer to the exchange of information as a trigger to generate value, that is, no exchange, no value.

Many of the studies that proposed methods for valuating a datum considered that, despite the proliferation of the theme of Big Data, research to determine value in this context is still recent in academic literature.

V. CONCLUSIONS AND FUTURE WORK

As we finished the proposed systematic literature review process, in search for answers on how to monetize data in a Big Data context, the first conclusion was that the theme of monetization of data in this context is still recent in academic literature. The first studies that answered our questions in the researched bases dated from 2013 (2 studies) and 75% of the answers we found dated from 2017 on. Another conclusion is that very few theories and models were developed with the specific aim of approaching this theme, since out of 2199 studies in our initial search we ended up with only 19 that were able to address our research questions. In sum, it was possible to observe that less than one percent of the studies answered at least one of our questions. Finally, even among the few papers that proposed theories and models to answer the research questions, we could not find a pattern or method that would be considered a standard or even a most applied one.

The results showed that, despite the progress in the theme of Big Data and in the application of analytical methodologies over the last decades, there is not yet widely used data-based method to determine the value of a datum as a digital asset. Based on the studies we found, it is possible to conclude that very little attention has been given to the dimension Value in academic research when compared to the three classical dimensions (Volume, Velocity and Variety) of the original definition of Big Data. Research is even more scarce in terms of financial value, and the existing studies do not share a common view on the right way of measuring and defining this value.

The most surprising finding was the fact that, in order to valuate a datum in the context of Big Data, techniques based on data are not the most commonly applied. This may sound like a contradiction at first, but it can also be interpreted by the market law (supply x demand) even in contexts or by the natural stillness necessary to a change of approach that seems to be inevitable when considering the characteristics of digital assets.

If on the one hand monetization of data in Big Data environments is a poorly explored field in academic literature, these intangible assets grow exponentially and they are more and more present in the corporate world, which highlights the opportunity to develop research to find standards that can be widely accepted and used to this end. With future studies, we will delve deeper in the theme in search of models and standards for pricing data-based digital assets (analytical techniques).

We can consider as threats to the validity of this research the fact that we have not done manual search for articles and did not include commercial white papers in the scope. The main reason is that it was a first approach to the problem and our intention was to review the theme in academic literature in an automatic manner. Future works will also consider these additional steps.

References

[1] K. Ruan, "Digital Assets as Economic Goods," in *Digital Asset Valuation and Cyber Risk Management*, K. Ruan, Ed. Academic Press, 2019, pp. 1–28.

[2] Oracle, "Oracle: What Is Big Data? Big Data Definition," 2017. [Online]. Available: https://www.oracle.com/br/big-data/what-is-big-data.html. [Accessed: 09-May-2020].

[3] N. Khan, M. Alsaqer, H. Shah, G. Badsha, A. A. Abbasi, and S. Salehian, "The 10 Vs, issues and challenges of big data," in *ACM International Conference Proceeding Series*, 2018, pp. 52–56.

[4] R. Addo-Tenkorang and P. T. Helo, "Big data applications in operations/supply-chain management: A literature review," *Comput. Ind. Eng.*, vol. 101, pp. 528–543, 2016.

[5] T. R. Rao, P. Mitra, R. Bhatt, and A. Goswami, "The big data system, components, tools, and technologies: a survey," *Knowl. Inf. Syst.*, vol. 60, no. 3, pp. 1165–1245, Sep. 2019.

[6] C. E. Shannon, "A Mathematical Theory of Communication," *Bell Syst. Tech. J.*, vol. 27, no. 3, pp. 379–423, 1948.

[7] B. Kitchenham and P. Brereton, "A systematic review of systematic review process research in software engineering," *Inf. Softw. Technol.*, vol. 55, no. 12, pp. 2049–2075, 2013.

[8] A. De Mauro, M. Greco, and M. Grimaldi, "A formal definition of Big Data based on its essential features," *Libr. Rev.*, vol. 65, no. 3, pp. 122–135, 2016.

[9] W. Redmond, "The Big Bang: How the Big Data Explosion Is Changing the World – Microsoft UK Enterprise Insights Blog," *Microsoft*. 2013.

[10] N. L. Karavaev, "Referencemanagement software," *Sci. Tech. Inf. Process.*, vol. 43, no. 3, pp. 184–188, Jul. 2016.

[11] M. Ouzzani, H. Hammady, Z. Fedorowicz, and A. Elmagarmid, "Rayyan-a web and mobile app for systematic reviews," *Syst. Rev.*, vol. 5, no. 1, pp. 1–10, Dec. 2016.

[12] D. S. Cruzes and T. Dybå, "Recommended steps for thematic synthesis in software engineering," *Int. Symp. Empir. Softw. Eng. Meas.*, no. 7491, pp. 275–284, 2011.

[13] H. Maruyama, D. Okanohara, and S. Hido, "Data marketplace for efficient data placement," in *Proceedings - IEEE 13th International Conference on Data Mining Workshops, ICDMW 2013*, 2013, pp. 702–705.

[14] K. Pantelis and L. Aija, "Understanding the value of (big) data," in *2013 IEEE International Conference on Big Data*, 2013, pp. 38–42.

[15] J. Debattista, C. Lange, S. Scerri, and S. Auer, "Linked 'Big' Data: Towards a Manifold Increase in Big Data Value and Veracity," in *Proceedings - 2015 2nd IEEE/ACM International Symposium on Big Data Computing, BDC 2015*, 2016, pp. 92–98.

[16] Y. G. Fu, J. M. Zhu, and N. Zhang, "Analysis on information value of big data in Internet finance," in *2015 International Conference on Logistics, Informatics and Service Science, LISS 2015*, 2015, pp. 1–6.

[17] V. Deolalikar, "How valuable is your data? A quantitative approach using data mining," in *Proceedings - 2015 IEEE International Conference on Big Data, IEEE Big Data 2015*, 2015, pp. 1248–1253.

[18] D. Rao and N. W. Keong, "A Method to Price Your Information Asset in the Information Market," in *2016 IEEE International Congress on Big Data (BigData Congress)*, 2016, pp. 307–314.

[19] D. Rao and W. K. Ng, "Information Pricing: A Utility Based Pricing Mechanism," in *2016 IEEE 14th Intl Conf on Dependable, Autonomic and Secure Computing, 14th Intl Conf on Pervasive Intelligence and Computing, 2nd Intl Conf on Big Data Intelligence and Computing and Cyber Science and Technology Congress(DASC/PiCom/DataCom/CyberSciTech)*, 2016, pp. 754–760.

[20] A. S. Bataineh, R. Mizouni, M. El Barachi, and J. Bentahar, "Monetizing Personal Data: A Two-Sided Market Approach," *Procedia Comput. Sci.*, vol. 83, pp. 472–479, 2016.

[21] H. Li, H. Li, Z. Wen, J. Mo, and J. Wu, "Distributed heterogeneous storage based on data value," in *Proceedings of the 2017 IEEE 2nd Information Technology, Networking, Electronic and Automation Control Conference, ITNEC 2017*, 2018, vol. 2018-Janua, pp. 264–271.

[22] J. Attard, F. Orlandi, and S. Auer, "Exploiting the Value of Data Through Data Value Networks," in *Proceedings of the 10th International Conference on Theory and Practice of Electronic Governance*, 2017, pp. 475–484.

[23] H. Yu and M. Zhang, "Data pricing strategy based on data

quality," *Comput. Ind. Eng.*, vol. 112, pp. 1–10, 2017.

[24] W. Song, Y. Zhang, J. Wang, H. Li, Y. Meng, and R. Cheng, "Research on Characteristics and Value Analysis of Power Grid Data Asset," *Procedia Comput. Sci.*, vol. 139, pp. 158–164, 2018.

[25] C. Lim, K. H. Kim, M. J. Kim, J. Y. Heo, K. J. Kim, and P. P. Maglio, "From data to value: A nine-factor framework for data-based value creation in information-intensive services," *Int. J. Inf. Manage.*, vol. 39, pp. 121–135, 2018.

[26] Z. Li, Y. Ni, X. Gao, and G. Cai, "Value Evaluation of Data Assets: Progress and Enlightenment," in *2019 4th IEEE International Conference on Big Data Analytics, ICBDA 2019*, 2019, pp. 88–93.

[27] Z. Li, Y. Ni, L. Yang, and Y. Gao, "Review and Prospect of Data Asset Research: Based on Social Network Analysis Method," in *2019 IEEE 4th International Conference on Big Data Analytics (ICBDA)*, 2019, pp. 345–350.

[28] Y. Zhang, Y. Huang, D. Zhang, and Y. Qian, "The Importance of Data Assets and Its Accounting Confirmation and Measurement Methods," in *BESC 2019 - 6th International Conference on Behavioral, Economic and Socio-Cultural Computing, Proceedings*, 2019, pp. 1–8.

[29] X. Ma and X. Zhang, "MDV: A Multi-Factors Data Valuation Method," in *Proceedings - 5th International Conference on Big Data Computing and Communications, BIGCOM 2019*, 2019, pp. 48–53.

[30] Y. Shen, B. Guo, Y. Shen, X. Duan, X. Dong, and H. Zhang, "Pricing personal data based on information entropy," in *ACM International Conference Proceeding Series*, 2019, pp. 143–146.

Hotel Quality Evaluation from Online Reviews Using Fuzzy Pattern Matching and Fuzzy Cognitive Maps

Alexandros Bousdekis
Business Informatics Lab, Department of Business Administration, School of Business
Athens University of Economics and Business
Athens, Greece
e-mail: albous@mail.ntua.gr

Dimitris Kardaras
Business Informatics Lab, Department of Business Administration, School of Business
Athens University of Economics and Business
Athens, Greece
e-mail: dkkardaras@yahoo.co.uk

Stavroula G. Barbounaki
Merchant Marine Academy of Aspropyrgos,
Aspropyrgos, Greece
e-mail: sbarbounaki@yahoo.gr

***Abstract*— Online review comments have become a popular and efficient way for sellers to acquire feedback from customers and improve their service quality. These online reviews in the e-tourism era, in the format of both textual reviews (comments) and ratings, generate an electronic Word Of Mouth (eWOM) effect, which influences future customer demand and hotels' financial performance and thus have significant business value. This paper proposes an approach for hotel quality evaluation according to online review comments and ratings using Fuzzy Pattern Matching (FPM) for mining customers' opinions and Fuzzy Cognitive Maps (FCM) for evaluating the attributes that contribute to the review rating. The proposed approach was applied to a 4-star hotels dataset in Athens, Greece and experiments were performed.**

Keywords-e-tourism; data analytics; machine learning; tourism management; service quality.

I. INTRODUCTION

Online comments have become a popular and efficient way for sellers to acquire feedback from customers and improve their service quality [1]. According to a survey, with the increased popularity of online bookings, 53% of travellers state that they would be unwilling to book a hotel that had no reviews, while a 10% increase in travel review ratings would increase bookings by more than 5% [2]. Customer online reviews of hotels have significant business value in the e-commerce and big data era, while they affect room occupancy [3], revenue, prices [4] and market share [5]. These online reviews in the e-tourism era, in the format of both textual reviews (comments) and ratings, generate an electronic Word Of Mouth (eWOM) effect, which influences future customer demand and hotels' financial performance [6].

Hotel owners want to know the details about hotel guests' experiences, to improve the corresponding product and service attributes, and customers' overall evaluation of the hotel stay experience, to obtain a snapshot of the hotel's operational performance and overall customer satisfaction [7][8]. Although the direct measurement of customer ratings in terms of closed-ended survey questions can show overall customer satisfaction in a direct way [7][8], they suffer from confounding the data of customers' true evaluation because of variations in survey design from different approaches [9].

Recently, many studies have focused on textual reviews [8][10]. In contrast to a pre-designed questionnaire survey, online textual reviews have an open-structured form and can show customer consumption experiences, highlight the product and service attributes customers care about, and provide customers' perceptions in a detailed way through the open-structure form [8]. The provided information is free from obvious bias and is helpful in understanding and assessing hotel performance [11]. In addition, such information is inexpensive and efficient to collect [12]. However, the exploitation of online textual reviews is still largely under-explored [8], while there is a lack of advanced data analytics approaches and algorithms for modeling complex dynamics of online hotel review data.

Hotel quality evaluation from online reviews is an emerging research field; however, the vast majority of existing research works have been performed from a tourism management perspective. Therefore, the applied methods and algorithms are limited to descriptive statistics, e.g., using well-established regression models. However, the increasing amount of online reviews as the core means for customers to express their level of satisfaction about a hotel pose significant challenges to the data analytics and computer science community for the development of advanced data analytics models aiming at providing a higher level of intelligence and thus, increased business value.

In this paper, we propose an approach for hotel quality evaluation from online reviews using Fuzzy Pattern Matching (FPM) and Fuzzy Cognitive Maps (FCM). The objective is to provide a unified algorithm, which both: (i) mines customers' opinions from online hotel reviews (review comments and rating); and, (ii) evaluates the hotel performance by identifying how the various attributes (e.g., location, cleanliness, breakfast, etc.) affect the overall review rating. The rest of the paper is organized as follows: Section II presents the related work on methods and approaches for hotel evaluation based on online review comments. Section III describes the research methodology and the proposed approach for hotel quality evaluation from online reviews using FPM and FCM. Section IV presents the results from the adoption of the proposed methodology on a dataset of six

4-star hotels in Athens. Section V concludes the paper and outlines our plans for future work.

II. Related Work

The business value of online consumer reviews has emerged in recent year in the hotel industry aiming at solving the problems confronted by the traditional hotel service quality assessment methods [13]. For example, in [14], the authors performed hierarchical multiple regressions in order to examine the effects of traditional customer satisfaction relative magnitude and social media review ratings on hotel performance and found that social media review rating is a more significant predictor. In the traditional hotel quality assessment, domain experts or customers are asked to fill in a questionnaire and score each evaluation index to be used in a service quality assessment model [15]-[17]. On the contrary, online comments are made by a large amount of customers with actual user experience shortly after the consumption is completed. In addition, the increasing amount of reviews-related data pave the way for the use of advanced data analytics and machine learning algorithms that outperform traditional statistical methods based on sampling [2].

Technical attributes of online textual reviews can explain significant variations in customer ratings and can have a significant effect on customer ratings [18][19]. In this direction, in [8], the authors developed an approach for predicting overall customer satisfaction using the technical attributes of online textual reviews and customers' involvement in the review community. They calculated subjectivity and polarity measurements by using naïve Bayes classifier and sentiment analysis. The research work in [10] investigated the underpinnings of satisfied and unsatisfied hotel customers by applying text mining techniques on online reviews.

The literature is rich of methodologies based on descriptive statistics aiming at providing insights on hotel quality performance for various datasets. In [20], the authors applied statistical methods in order to assess how several characteristics, such as timeliness of the response, length of the response, number of responses, etc., contributes to the hotel's financial performance. The research work in [21] compared the rating dynamics of the same hotels in two online review platforms, which mainly differ in requiring or not requiring proof of prior reservation before posting a review (respectively, a verified vs a non-verified platform). In [22], the authors examined the effect of factors of online consumer review, including quality, quantity, consistency, on the offline hotel occupancy (i.e., how popular the hotel is among consumers).

In [3], the extent to which digital marketing strategies influence hotel room occupancy and revenue per available room and how this mechanism is different for different types of hotels in terms of star rating and independent versus chain hotels was investigated. In [23], the authors examined the determinants of customer satisfaction in hospitality venues through an analysis of online reviews using text mining and content analysis. The research work in [24] investigated the impacts of online review and source features (usefulness, reviewer expertise, timeliness, volume, valence and comprehensiveness) upon travelers' online hotel booking intentions by applying factor analysis and regression analysis. In [11], the authors compared customer satisfaction by classifying several attributes influencing customer satisfaction in: satisfiers, dissatisfiers, bidirectional forces, and neutrals. Reference [25] applied qualitative research methods and extracted six main factors influencing the positive or negative emotions of the comments of travelers staying in the hotel.

Reference [26] conducted a multilevel analysis of factors affecting customer satisfaction, such as service encounter, visitor, visitor's nationality, hotel, and destination. In [27], the authors applied a multi-group analysis and an importance-performance map analysis by means of PLS-SEM in order to differentiate between service quality performance scores and their influences on customer satisfaction across accommodation with a different star grading. Reference [28] assessed social media content produced by customers and related review-management strategies of domestic and international hotel chains with the use of multilevel regression.

As mentioned earlier, the increasing amounts of reviews-related data require advanced data analytics and machine learning methods for exploiting the full potential. To this end, the research work in [2] assessed whether terms related to guest experience can be used to identify ways to enhance hospitality services. They developed a model based on naïve Bayes classifier in order process vast amount of data and to classify reviews of hotels. Reference [29] developed a framework in order to integrate visual analytics and (deep) machine learning techniques, such as clustering for text classification and Convolutional Neural Networks (CNN), to investigate whether hotel managers respond to positive and negative reviews differently and how to use a deep learning approach to prioritize responses. Reference [1] combined fuzzy comprehensive evaluation and fuzzy cognitive maps aiming at identifying the causal relations among evaluation indexes from online comments. Based on this, their proposed approach recommends more economical solutions for improving the service quality by automatically getting more trustworthy evaluation from a large amount of less trustworthy online comments.

III. Research Methodology

Our research methodology consists of three main steps: (i) Extracting the evaluation criteria from online comments; (ii) Mining customers' opinions using FPM; and, (iii) Applying FCM for attributes evaluation. These steps are described in detail in the following sub-sections.

A. Extracting the Evaluation Criteria from Online Comments

The proposed approach utilizes three fields from the online hotel reviews: (i) *review title*; (ii) *review comments*; and, (iii) *review rating*. This step of the methodology processes the *review title* and the *review comments* in order to extract the evaluation criteria from the online comments.

More specifically, based upon an evaluation index for hotel service quality [1], this step identifies the criteria mentioned in the hotel reviews under examination, e.g., location, price, breakfast, room space, etc. In this way, the criteria are defined dynamically out of the pre-defined list, according to the dataset of the available online comments. The extracted evaluation criteria of the previous step play the role of a questionnaire and the online review comments can be considered as the answers to the questionnaire made by customers, so that they can be further processed with the use of Fuzzy Pattern Match Template (FPMT), as we describe in Section III.B. Moreover, along with the review rating, they constitute the concepts of the FCM, as we describe in Section III.C.

B. *Mining Customers' Opinions Using Fuzzy Pattern Matching*

Since online comments are written in natural and informal language, there is the need to mine customers' opinions so that they subsequently feed into the FCM for further processing. FPM, alternatively mentioned as fuzzy string searching or approximate string matching, has been developed in the framework of fuzzy set and possibility theory in order to take into account the imprecision and the uncertainty pervading values, which have to be compared in a matching process [30]. This technique has proved effective for implementing patterns of approximate reasoning in expert system inference engines, and for designing retrieval systems capable of managing incomplete and fuzzy information data bases and vague queries.

In online review comments, different customers may use different words or phrases to express their opinions, while the comments may be vague. For example, poor cleanliness can be expressed as: "The room was too dirty", "Very dirty", etc. Regular expression is an efficient pattern match [31] technology to identify the specific pattern strings from a long text. A simple example of regular expression is "[\s\S]*?[room|bathroom][\s\S]*?dirty[\s\S]*?" that can match "The room was too dirty." However, the regular expression method causes a binary value result: match or not match.

In the proposed approach, we apply FPMT [1] as an effective fuzzy pattern matching method to deal with the vagueness of the free text online comments. FPMT is a set of pattern strings with membership degrees, denoted as:

$$FPMT = \{(p_1, w_1), (p_2, w_2), \ldots, (p_i, w_i), \ldots, (p_n, w_n)\}$$

where p_i is a pattern string described by regular expression, and w_i is the membership degree that a string falls into the object FPMT when the string matches p_i. When a string matches multiple pattern strings at the same time, the max membership degree of these pattern strings will be selected as the final membership degree. Although this method results in some mismatched cases due to the limitation of pattern strings, this causes little impact on the final result, because there are many redundant comments with similar semantics.

The output of customers' opinions mining is a fuzzy evaluation of the extracted criteria. Specifically, first, the extracted evaluation criteria of hotel quality are assigned to a five-level Likert scale (1 – Very Low, 2 – Low, 3- Neutral, 4 – High, 5 – Very High), which serve as an equivalent to responses of a Likert scale questionnaire. Then, following the approach proposed by [32], this step considers the median of the resulting responses in order to represent the magnitude of causality among the evaluation criteria to be used as FCM concepts in Section III.C.

C. *Applying Fuzzy Cognitive Maps for Attributes Evaluation*

This step applies FCM in order to evaluate the quality of the hotels with respect to the extracted evaluation criteria, i.e., attributes, from Section II.A and to identify the effect of each criterion to the review rating. An FCM is a graph consisting of nodes C_i that represent the concepts of the domain in study, connected to each other with weighted arcs $W(i,j)$ showing how concept i is causally affected by concept j. The weights on the arcs connecting two concepts correspond to fuzzy qualifiers, such as 'a little', 'moderately', 'a lot', or fuzzy numbers can be assigned in order to show the extent to which a concept affects another. FCMs are used to model and study perceptions about a domain, to investigate the interrelationships among its concepts and to draw conclusions based on the implications of scenarios. The impact among the concepts of a FCM is estimated using the indirect effect i.e., the impact caused due to the interrelationships among the concepts along the path from a cause variable (X) to an effect variable (Y) and the total effect, i.e., the sum of all the indirect effects from the cause variable X to the effect variable Y [33].

FCMs can be represented by means of an N×N matrix E = [e_{ij}], where N is the number of the concepts in the FCM with i and j representing concepts in the FCM. Every value e_{ij} of this matrix represents the strength and direction of causality between interrelated concepts. The value of causality e_{ij} is assigned values from the interval [-1, +1], as follows [34]:

- $e_{ij} > 0$ indicates a causal increase or positive causality from node i to j.
- $e_{ij} = 0$ there is no causality from node i to j.
- $e_{ij} < 0$ indicates a causal decrease or negative causality from node i to j.

The multiplication between matrices representing FCMs produces the indirect and total effects [35] and allows the study of the impact that a given causal effect D_1 causes. Causal effects can be represented with a 1×N vector [36]. This impact is calculated through repeated multi-plications: $E \times D1 = D2$, $E \times D2 = D3$ and so on, that is, $E \times D_i = D_{i+1}$, until equilibrium is reached, which is the final result of the effect D_1. Equilibrium is reached when the final result equals to zero, i.e., all cells of the resulting vector are equal to zero (0) and there is no any further causal impact caused by any concept. Different thresholds, depending on the modelling needs, restrict the values that result from each multiplication within the range [-1, +1] [32].

The FCM suitability for hotel quality evaluation through online review is argued by considering that a variety of what – if sensitivity simulations can be performed effectively. Through what – if simulations, hotels can identify a set of relevant review factors, pertaining to the customer satisfaction as well as hotel services that need to be improved. In the proposed approach, the FCM concepts matrix consists of the extracted evaluation criteria plus an additional concept referring to the *review rating*. The latter is affected by all the other concepts and does not affect any of them.

The FCM is applied separately for each hotel in order to allow each hotel gaining meaningful insights for its performance. However, there is also the possibility for aggregated results of more than one hotel (e.g., in one region of interest, specific number of stars, same overall review rating, etc.) in the sense of an "augmented topology", thus allowing the combination of multiple FCMs into a single knowledge-based representation. Multiple weighted FCMs are combined into a single averaged FCM by adding their scaled and augmented adjacency weight matrix. This procedure is based on the mathematical transformation of the causal weight matrices [37]. If the FCMs involve different concepts, each causal matrix is augmented by adding a new column and row filled with zeros for each additional concept.

IV. RESULTS

The proposed methodology was applied to a dataset including six 4-star hotels in Athens, Greece. Each hotel had 60 reviews consisting, among others, of the *review title*, the *review comments*, and the *review rating*. The superset of the FCM concepts is shown in Table I. These concepts represent the extracted evaluation criteria from FPMT (C1-C9) along with the review rating (C10).

TABLE I. THE EXTRACTED EVALUATION CRITERIA

ID	Concepts	ID	Concepts
C1	Location	C6	Quiet
C2	Personnel	C7	Parking
C3	Cleanliness	C8	Interior Design
C4	Room Space	C9	Bed
C5	Breakfast	C10	Review Rating

After the fuzzy evaluation of the aforementioned concepts for each hotel, the weight matrix is created and is inserted to the FCM model. Figure 1 depicts the result for one indicative hotel, while Figure 2 depicts the augmented FCM topology of all the six hotels under examination. The C10: Review Rating has been put on the left so that the effect of the various attributes on the review rating is more visible. For these visualizations as well as for experimental purposes, we used the "FCM Expert" software tool [37]. The rest of the experimental analysis deals with the augmented topology, thus providing insights on a regional basis. As shown in Figure 2, the review rating (C10) is mainly affected by Location (C1), Cleanliness (C3), Room Space (C4) and Interior Design (C8).

Table II presents the values related to the degree centrality. It is a local centrality measure determined by only its directed connections. The degree centrality of a node is the summation of its absolute incoming (indegree) and outgoing (outdegree) connection weights. Furthermore, we performed inference using various reasoning rules (Kosko's activation rule, Kosko's activation rule with self-memory, Rescaled activation rule with self-memory) in order to compute the output vector including the weights of the concepts. Figure 3 presents an indicative visualization of our results. Specifically, Figure 3a depicts a chart and Figure 3b depicts a table with the iterations of the algorithm until convergence.

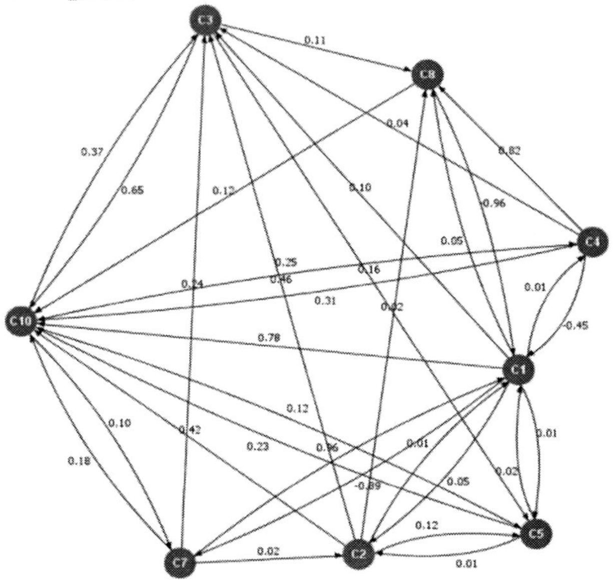

Figure 1. The resulting FCM of one indicative hotel.

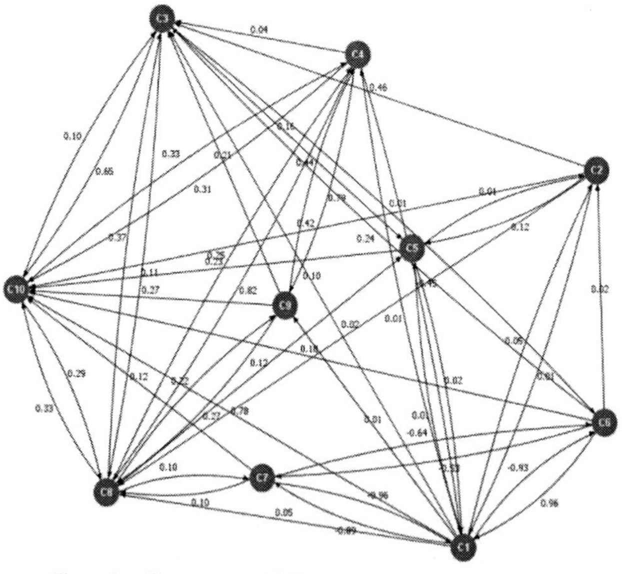

Figure 2. The augmented FCM topology for all the six hotels.

Table III presents and compares the output vector of weights by applying three different unsupervised learning methods using a Hebbian rule, i.e., non-linear Hebbian learning, differential Hebbian learning, and balanced differential Hebbian learning. Hebbian learning constitutes an unsupervised technique initially applied on the training of artificial neural networks [38]. The main feature of this learning rule is that the change of a synaptic is computed by taking into account the presynaptic and postsynaptic signals flow towards each processing unit (neuron) of a neural network [39].

TABLE II. OUTDEGREE, INDEGREE, AND CENTRALITY OF THE FCM

Concepts	Outdegree	Indegree	Centrality
C1	2.06	2.40	4.46
C2	0.64	0.08	0.72
C3	0.49	1.52	2.01
C4	2.78	1.03	3.81
C5	0.03	0.41	0.44
C6	1.75	1.58	3.33
C7	1.70	1.52	3.22
C8	1.44	1.66	3.10
C9	0.92	1.02	1.94
C10	0.72	1.31	2.03

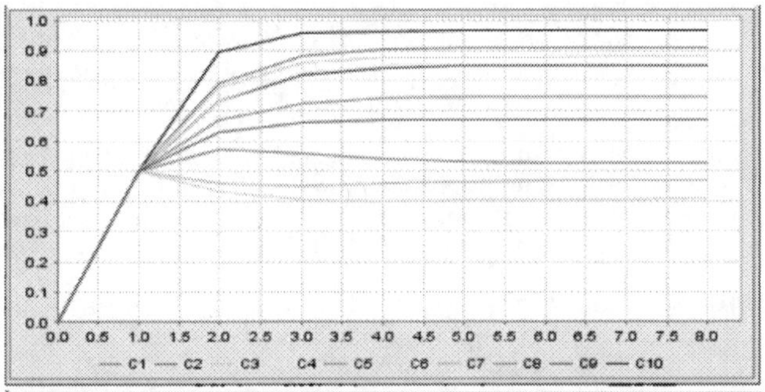

Step	C1	C2	C3	C4	C5	C6	C7	C8	C9	C10
0	0.0	0.0	0.0	0.0	0.0	0.0	0.0	0.0	0.0	0.0
1	0.5	0.5	0.5	0.5	0.5	0.5	0.5	0.5	0.5	0.5
2	0.572	0.6318	0.779	0.734	0.6693	0.4305	0.4601	0.7908	0.733	0.8952
3	0.558	0.6628	0.8576	0.8257	0.7252	0.4042	0.4506	0.8832	0.8165	0.9563
4	0.5406	0.6695	0.8746	0.849	0.7414	0.4026	0.4571	0.9037	0.8414	0.964
5	0.5319	0.6708	0.8781	0.8543	0.7457	0.4052	0.4633	0.908	0.8477	0.9652
6	0.5283	0.6711	0.8789	0.8555	0.7467	0.4068	0.4665	0.9089	0.8491	0.9653
7	0.5269	0.6711	0.879	0.8557	0.7469	0.4075	0.468	0.9091	0.8494	0.9653
8	0.5263	0.6711	0.8791	0.8558	0.747	0.4078	0.4685	0.9092	0.8495	0.9653

Figure 3. Results of inference until convergence: (a) Chart; (b) Table.

As shown in Table III, the outcome of the non-linear Hebbian rule varies significantly compared to the outcomes of differential Hebbian learning and balanced differential Hebbian learning. Non-linear Hebbian learning constitutes an extension of differential Hebbian learning and is able to capture effectively non-linear relationships [40]. However, despite the differences in the estimated weight vector of the criteria, all the aforementioned implementations result in the same order of significance in terms of their impact on the review rating (C10), i.e., C8 – C3 – C4 – C9 – C5 – C2 – C1 – C7 – C6.

TABLE III. COMPARATIVE ANALYSIS FOR THE OUTPUT WEIGHT VECTOR

Concepts	Non-linear Hebbian Learning	Differential Hebbian Learning	Balanced Differential Hebbian Learning
C1	0.5825	0.6466	0.6674
C2	0.6712	0.6624	0.6663
C3	0.8266	0.7079	0.6851
C4	0.8090	0.6942	0.6757
C5	0.7256	0.6740	0.6713
C6	0.4731	0.6131	0.6556
C7	0.5145	0.6211	0.6572
C8	0.8609	0.7133	0.6860
C9	0.8008	0.6920	0.6730
C10	0.9200	0.7542	0.6997

V. CONCLUSIONS AND FUTURE WORK

Hotel quality evaluation from online reviews is an emerging research field, while the use of data analytics and machine learning methods are able to exploit its full potential in an e-tourism context. This paper proposed an approach for hotel quality evaluation according to online review comments and ratings using FPM for mining customers' opinions and FCM for evaluating the attributes that contribute to the review rating. The results show that the proposed approach is able to model the complex dynamics of online hotel review data, which are derived from both the textual nature of the review comments and the uncertain relationships between these comments and the review rating. Regarding our future work, we plan to apply our methodology to further datasets and to investigate the role of user profiling in hotel selection.

REFERENCES

[1] X. Wei, X. Luo, Q. Li, J. Zhang, and Z. Xu, "Online comment-based hotel quality automatic assessment using improved fuzzy comprehensive evaluation and fuzzy cognitive map," IEEE Trans. on Fuzzy Sys., vol. 23, no. 1, pp. 72-84, 2015.

[2] M. J. Sánchez-Franco, A. Navarro-García, and F. J. Rondán-Cataluña, "A naive Bayes strategy for classifying customer satisfaction: A study based on online reviews of hospitality services.," J. of Bus. Res., vol. 101, pp. 499-506, 2019.

[3] P. De Pelsmacker, S. Van Tilburg, and C. Holthof, "Digital marketing strategies, online reviews and hotel performance," Int. J. of Hosp. Man., vol. 72, pp. 47-55, 2018.

[4] Q. Ye, R. Law, B. Gu, and W. Chen, "The influence of user-generated content on traveler behavior: An empirical investigation on the effects of e-word-of-mouth to hotel online bookings," Comp. in Hum. Behav., vol. 27, no. 2, pp. 634-639, 2011.

[5] P. Duverger, "Curvilinear effects of user-generated content on hotels' market share: a dynamic panel-data analysis," J. of Trav. Res., vol. 52, no. 4, pp. 465-478, 2013.

[6] K. L. Xie, Z. Zhang, and Z. Zhang, "The business value of online consumer reviews and management response to hotel performance," Int. J. of Hosp. Man., vol. 43, pp. 1-12, 2014.

[7] A. S. Cantallops and F. Salvi, "New consumer behavior: A review of research on eWOM and hotels," Int. J. of Hosp. Man., vol. 36, pp. 41-51, 2014.

[8] Y. Zhao, X. Xu, and M. Wang, "Predicting overall customer satisfaction: Big data evidence from hotel online textual reviews," Int. J. of Hosp. Man., vol. 76, pp. 111-121, 2019.

[9] Z. Xiang, Q. Du, Y. Ma, and W. Fan, "A comparative analysis of major online review platforms: Implications for social media analytics in hospitality and tourism," Tour. Man., vol. 58, pp. 51-65, 2017.

[10] K. Berezina, A. Bilgihan, C. Cobanoglu, and F. Okumus, "Understanding satisfied and dissatisfied hotel customers: text mining of online hotel reviews," J. of Hosp. Mark. & Man., vol. 25, no. 1, pp. 1-24, 2016.

[11] L. Zhou, S. Ye, P. L. Pearce, and M. Y. Wu, "Refreshing hotel satisfaction studies by reconfiguring customer review data," Int. J. of Hosp. Man., vol. 38, pp. 1-10, 2014.

[12] X. R. Zhao, L. Wang, X. Guo, and R. Law, "The influence of online reviews to online hotel booking intentions," Int. J. of Cont. Hosp. Man., vol. 27, no. 6, pp. 1343-1364, 2015.

[13] E. Boon, M. Bonera, and A. Bigi, "Measuring hotel service quality from online consumer reviews: A proposed method," in Information and Communication Technologies in Tourism, pp. 367-379, Springer, Cham, 2014.

[14] W. G. Kim and S. A. Park, "Social media review rating versus traditional customer satisfaction," Int. J. of Cont. Hosp. Man., vol. 29, no. 2, pp. 784-802, 2017.

[15] J. M. Benitez, J. C. Martín, and C. Román, "Using fuzzy number for measuring quality of service in the hotel industry.," Tour. Man., vol. 28, no. 2, pp. 544-555, 2007.

[16] Y. Yu, W. S. Chen, and M. Li, "Fuzzy comprehensive evaluation methods of hotel product quality," Tour. Sc., vol. 5, 2008.

[17] C. C. Yang, Y. T. Jou, and L. Y. Cheng, "Using integrated quality assessment for hotel service quality," Qual. & Quant., vol. 45, no. 2, pp. 349-364, 2011.

[18] M. Geetha, P. Singha, and S. Sinha, "Relationship between customer sentiment and online customer ratings for hotels-An empirical analysis," Tour. Man., vol. 61, pp. 43-54, 2017.

[19] W. He, X. Tian, R. Tao, W. Zhang, G. Yan, and V. Akula, "Application of social media analytics: a case of analyzing online hotel reviews," Onl. Inf. Rev., vol. 41, no. 7, pp. 921-935, 2017.

[20] K. L. Xie, K. K. F. So, and W. Wang, "Joint effects of management responses and online reviews on hotel financial performance: A data-analytics approach," Int. J. of Hosp. Man., vol. 62, pp. 101-110, 2017.

[21] P. Figini, L. Vici, and G. Viglia, "A comparison of hotel ratings between verified and non-verified online review platforms," Int. J. of Cul., Tour. and Hosp. Res., vol. 14, no. 2, pp. 157-171, 2020.

[22] K. L. Xie, C. Chen, and S. Wu, "Online consumer review factors affecting offline hotel popularity: evidence from tripadvisor," J. of Trav. & Tour. Mark., vol. 33, no. 2, pp. 211-223, 2016.

[23] H. Li, Q. Ye, and R. Law, "Determinants of customer satisfaction in the hotel industry: An application of online review analysis," Asia Pac. J. of Tour. Res., vol. 18, no. 7, pp. 784-802, 2013.

[24] X. R. Zhao, L. Wang, X. Guo, and R. Law, "The influence of online reviews to online hotel booking intentions," Int. J. of Cont. Hosp. Man., vol. 27, no. 6, pp. 1343-1364, 2015.

[25] P. Ye and B. Yu, "Customer Satisfaction Attribution Analysis of Hotel Online Reviews Based on Qualitative Research Methods," in Proceedings of the 2nd International Conference on E-Education, E-Business and E-Technology, pp. 93-98, 2018.

[26] T. Radojevic, N. Stanisic, and N. Stanic, "Inside the rating scores: a multilevel analysis of the factors influencing customer satisfaction in the hotel industry," Cornell Hosp. Quart., vol. 58, no. 2, pp. 134-164, 2017.

[27] R. Nunkoo, V. Teeroovengadum, C. M. Ringle, and V. Sunnassee, "Service quality and customer satisfaction: The moderating effects of hotel star rating," Int. J. of Hosp. Man., 102414, in press, 2019.

[28] M. Schuckert, S. Liang, R. Law, and W. Sun, "How do domestic and international high-end hotel brands receive and manage customer feedback?," Int. J. of Hosp. Man., vol. 77, pp. 528-537, 2019.

[29] C. H. Ku, Y. C. Chang, Y. Wang, C. H. Chen, and S. H. Hsiao, "Artificial Intelligence and Visual Analytics: A Deep-Learning Approach to Analyze Hotel Reviews & Responses," in Proceedings of the 52nd Hawaii International Conference on System Sciences, 2019.

[30] D. Dubois, H. Prade, and C. Testemale, "Weighted fuzzy pattern matching," Fuz. Sets and Sys., vol. 28, no. 3, pp. 313-331, 1988.

[31] C. L. Forgy, "Rete: A fast algorithm for the many pattern/many object pattern match problem," in Readings in Artificial Intelligence and Databases, pp. 547-559, Morgan Kaufmann, 1989.

[32] D. K. Kardaras, B. Karakostas, and X. J. Mamakou, "Content presentation personalisation and media adaptation in tourism web sites using Fuzzy Delphi Method and Fuzzy Cognitive Maps," Exp. Sys. with Appl., vol. 40, no. 6, pp. 2331-2342, 2013.

[33] B. Kosko, "Fuzzy cognitive maps," Int. J. of Man-Mach. Stud., vol. 24, no. 1, pp. 65-75, 1986.

[34] M. Schneider, E. Shnaider, A. Kandel, and G. Chew, "Automatic construction of FCMs," Fuz. Sets and Sys., vol. 93, no. 2, pp 161-172, 1998.

[35] R. Yu and G. H. Tzeng, "A soft computing method for multi-criteria decision making with dependence and feedback," Appl. Math. and Comp., vol. 180, no. 1, pp. 63-75, 2006.

[36] G. A. Banini and R. A. Bearman, "Application of fuzzy cognitive maps to factors affecting slurry rheology," Int. J. of Min. Proc., vol. 52, no. 4, pp. 233-244, 1998.

[37] G. Nápoles, M. L. Espinosa, I. Grau, and K. Vanhoof, "FCM Expert: Software Tool for Scenario Analysis and Pattern Classification Based on Fuzzy Cognitive Maps," Int. J. on Artif. Intell. Tools, vol. 27, no. 7, 1860010, 2018.

[38] S. Haykin, "Neural networks: a comprehensive foundation," Prentice Hall PTR, 1994.

[39] G. A. Papakostas, A. S. Polydoros, D. E. Koulouriotis, and V. D. Tourassis, "Training fuzzy cognitive maps by using Hebbian learning algorithms: a comparative study," in 2011 IEEE International Conference on Fuzzy Systems (FUZZ-IEEE 2011) , pp. 851-858, IEEE, 2011.

[40] W. Stach, L. Kurgan, and W. Pedrycz, "Data-driven nonlinear Hebbian learning method for fuzzy cognitive maps," in 2008 IEEE International Conference on Fuzzy Systems (IEEE World Congress on Computational Intelligence), pp. 1975-1981, IEEE, 2008.

Gendered Data in Falls Prediction Using Machine Learning

Leeanne Lindsay
Institute for Research in Social Sciences
Ulster University
Northern Ireland, UK
email: lindsay-l@ulster.ac.uk

Sonya Coleman
Intelligent Systems Research Centre
Ulster University
Northern Ireland, UK
email: sa.coleman@ulster.ac.uk

Dermot Kerr
Intelligent Systems Research Centre
Ulster University
Northern Ireland, UK
email: d.kerr@ulster.ac.uk

Brian Taylor
Institute for Research in Social Sciences
Ulster University
Northern Ireland, UK
email: bj.taylor@ulster.ac.uk

Anne Moorhead
Institute for Nursing and Health Research
Ulster University
Northern Ireland, UK
email: a.moorhead@ulster.ac.uk

***Abstract*— Adults over the age of 65 years may be considered as a vulnerable population prone to having falls, which may have huge consequences. Machine learning is being explored as an approach to understanding better the specific risk factors for falling. However, most studies use composite population data rather than including data on male or female gender in the analysis. This study focused on using machine learning models utilizing healthcare data to establish whether gendered data gives a more accurate prediction of falling. Splitting the data into male and female gives slightly higher predictive accuracy, however, reducing the size of the dataset is likely to give a lower prediction. Such models could provide useful information to health and social care professionals in their daily decision-making with individuals and families about optimal care arrangements.**

Keywords—machine learning; male; female; falls; prediction.

I. INTRODUCTION

Public Health England reported that a third of the population of adults over 65 years old is likely to fall at least once per calendar year [1]. They also reported that half of the population over 80 years old is likely to fall once per year. It is estimated that 255,000 adults over the age of 65 years old who fall are admitted to hospital in England [2]. Similar to Public Health England, the Health Executive in Ireland reported that 30% of adults over 65 years old in Ireland will fall at least once per year [3].

It is quite common to be defined as being in a vulnerable group of adults if they are over the age of 65 years as they are unfortunately more prone to falls [4]. There is also an increased prevalence of fear of falling in older adults whether or not they have already fallen [5]. With the increased risk of falling in older adults, there is a tendency to lose confidence when living at home independently. There is also a high possibility of losing mobility due to falls, resulting in further injury. Overall, falls affect health and social care services due to the increasing costs that arise [3]. It is estimated that falls cost the National Health Service in England around £2.3 billion per year [6].

Falls affect not only the individual, but may also have implications for the individual's family and decisions by health and social care professionals. After an older person falls, a shared decision between individuals, families and health and social care professionals may be made on whether or not the individual can continue living at home safely [7]. Health and Social Care professionals make these types of decisions every day in order to support the well-being of an older adult. Decisions regarding the elderly are best when they are shared between all parties and ensure an appropriate safe care package is in place [7]. Falls may occur due to factors such as poor eyesight, low blood pressure, medication or cognitive impairment [8]. As humans we all experience positive and negative risks in the world we live in. Generally, older adults encounter more negative risks like burns [9], forgetting to take medication or taking too much medication [10] and falling [11]. Figure 1 illustrates a small number of the categorized risk factors that older adults experience. Figure 1 is based on the health care risk factors that have been based on a review of the literature.

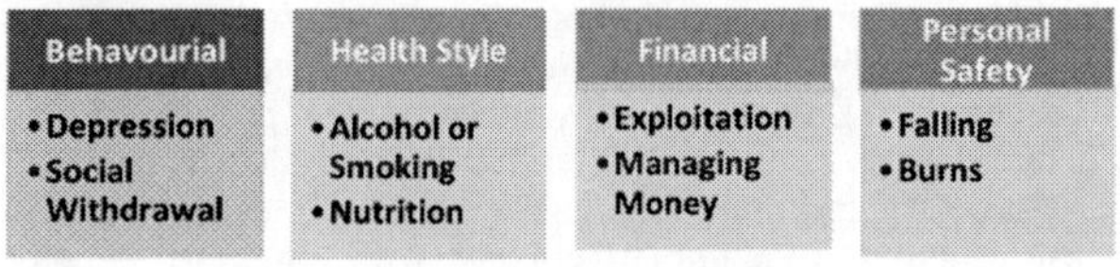

Figure 1. Associated Risks with Older Adults

There is a view that medical research is failing to include gender differences when analyzing data [12]. Therefore, research could potentially be predominantly based on one gender, and generalized over both genders. It is important to include results for both genders in order to implement the best practice for individuals within health and social care research [12]. For example, medical imaging is one field that has implemented gender balance and hence is developing more accurate algorithms in order to help assist medical doctors in diagnosing diseases [13]. Ferrante et al. produced a study, which aims to display the importance of gender balance using medical imaging datasets while training artificial intelligence systems for diagnosis [13]. During the study they found that genders that were underrepresented caused a decrease in performance. To overcome bias, training samples should include the details of the sample in terms of male and female so the data can be used for analysis purposes.

In this study, we utilize machine learning models to estimate the negative risks of falls in older adults as the study techniques allow us to examine the male and female data individually. We, as humans, use our attained knowledge to predict different outcomes on a daily basis. Machine learning helps to analyse, design and develop systems [14] with the ability to learn new trends or patterns within the data [15] in a consistent and objective way, but they are subject to underlying bias in the data from which the models are obtained. Machine learning is becoming popular within the health and social care sector to predict adverse outcomes. With the ability to aid health and social care professionals in decision making, the health sector has adopted machine learning approaches, such as diagnosing respiratory conditions from chest x-rays [16], detecting signs of lung cancer at an early stage [17] and identifying patients who need to be moved to the intensive care unit [18]. Meaningful information can be extracted with machine learning and used to help assist health and social care professionals in their daily job by finding correlations within data that could ideally be used to help improve the level of care and help reduce costs overall within the health sector [19]. The aim of this study was to use machine learning algorithms to predict the likelihood of falls in older adults by performing experiments and analyses on separate male and female data. The paper is organised as follows: Section 2 outlines machine learning methods and the gendered dataset used; the experiments and results are followed in Section 3; the paper is then brought to a conclusion in Section 4 with future work proposed.

II. Machine Learning & Gendered Data

In this study, we explore how different machine learning algorithms work in identifying gender differences in the underlying data. The Waikato Environment for Knowledge Analysis (WEKA) [20] is an open source machine learning software program that has been used for this study. Within WEKA, we have used a number of different machine learning approaches, as detailed below.

Firstly, we use the Naïve Bayes algorithm, which implements Bayes Theorem whereby the probability for each class is calculated from the training data supporting both binary and multiclass classification problems. We also use Support Vector Machines with Support Vector Classification (SVC). SVC manages missing data as well as nominal attributes. Multilayer Perceptron is a class of neural networks and contains one or more hidden layers, which we also use within WEKA. WEKA also contains a number of decision tree-based approaches. Decision trees are supportive of classification and regression and evaluate data by beginning at the root node of a tree and moving down towards the leaves until a prediction can be made. We use PART [20], which builds a partial C4.5 decision tree in each iteration and the best leaf is then made into a rule. A Random Forest classifier [20] is used, which constructs a multitude of trees for classification and regression purposes. Probabilistic approaches such as Bayes Net [20], which is a probabilistic model representing a set of variables and conditional dependencies can also be utilized. Logistic models are also used to predict the probability of a class or event existing by using a logistic function to model binary variables. A Simple Logistic algorithm models the probability of the output in terms of the input. Lastly, Classification via Regression completes classification using regression methods. One regression model is built for each class value. Each of these models will be used in Section III, where experiments and results are presented.

In this study, we use the Irish Longitudinal Study on Ageing (TILDA) dataset along with the WEKA program for falls prediction. The dataset is split into gender-based datasets - male and female. We subsequently use the machine learning algorithms to predict the likelihood of falls for males and females independently and thus determine if gender has an effect on machine learning algorithms prediction accuracy. The TILDA dataset is based on adults over the age of 50 years who live in a community dwelling in Ireland [21]. The dataset is split into three different waves, each collected in different years. Wave 1 consists of data collected from 2009 to 2011. Wave 2 data were collected during 2012 and 2013 and, lastly, Wave 3 data were collected in 2015 and 2016. For the purposes of this study, only Wave 1 data have been utilized. TILDA has been used in numerous studies previously [22].

III. Experiments & Results

A number of machine learning algorithms were selected from WEKA's machine learning environment to form predictions alongside The Irish Longitudinal Study on Aging dataset. These algorithms were used to train models to predict if an individual is likely to fall depending on whether they are male or female. Previous work has identified the risk of an older adult falling using the same dataset [22], but not considering gender differences.

This study presents a deeper analysis of the two genders (male and female) to determine any patterns. There is a number of input factors used in each of the models such as: "Overall health description", "Emotional mental health", "Long-term health issues", "Afraid of falling", "Joint or hip replacements" and any "Previous blackouts or fainting" episodes. A binary classification is the desired target output, corresponding to either fall or no fall. Each input risk factor has been added incrementally to the training inputs of each model to ensure each one is of importance and if not, it was subsequently removed. Each dataset was split into a training and testing set and to remain consistent with previous work this split was defined as 90%/10%. To ensure consistency in the reported classifier accuracy, ten-fold cross validation was used throughout all experiments. Each algorithm used the standard selection of hyperparameter optimization methods, Auto-WEKA does this using a fully automated approach. Table I displays results based on previous work [22], showing accuracies from 56% - 62%. The lowest accuracy of 56% was obtained using the Multilayer Perceptron machine learning technique and the highest accuracy of 62% was obtained using the Classification via Regression algorithm. The results below were based on using the full dataset *n=3242*.

TABLE I. MACHINE LEARNING ALGORITHM PERFORMANCE USING THE FULL DATASET (n=3242) [20]

WEKA Classifier	Correctly Classified %
Naïve Bayes	61
Support Vector Classification	60
PART	60
Random Forest	57
Decision Tree	59
Bayes Net	61
Logistic	60
Multilayer Perceptron	56
Simple Logistic	60
Classification via Regression	62

In Table II, we present results for the same experiment as in Table I using the full dataset except that we have now included gender as another input factor. This enables us to identify if gender has any effect on each of the models and hence determine if there are gender differences.

Table II results demonstrate the significant increase in accuracy when including male and female as a binary input in comparison to Table I. The predictive performance of the algorithms in Table II are higher overall and vary between 57% - 66%. The best performing model is Simple Logistic and Classification via Regression classifying with an accuracy of 66%. The poorest performing algorithm at 57% was again the Multilayer Perceptron. This single model approach has proved to be sufficient in identifying that gender differences exists; the inclusion of gender, enabled all algorithms to classify the data better than when gender was not included (Table I).

TABLE II. MACHINE LEARNING ALGORITHM PERFORMANCE USING THE FULL DATASET (n=3242) INCLUDING MALE AND FEMALE

WEKA Classifier	Correctly Classified %
Naïve Bayes	64
Support Vector Classification	63
PART	61
Random Forest	58
Decision Tree	63
Bayes Net	64
Logistic	64
Multilayer Perceptron	57
Simple Logistic	66
Classification via Regression	66

As gender differences are evident, we investigated this further by separating the dataset into male and female records, in each dataset $n=1364$. However, this results in a reduced number of records per dataset compared with the results presented in Tables I and II. The results n=3242 and n=1364 are not directly half of the full dataset as the full dataset had a random number of both male and females whereas the smaller dataset included the same number of male (n=682) and females (n=682) to total 1364 in the smaller dataset. Results using only male data from the dataset are presented in Table III. There are no significant differences in the performance of each of the machine learning algorithms. The highest classification accuracy was consistently achieved by four algorithms; Support Vector Classification, Logistic, Simple Logistic and Classification via Regression which, all correctly classify 59% of falls and no falls correctly.

TABLE III. MACHINE LEARNING ALGORITHM PERFORMANCE USING MALE DATA (n=1364)

WEKA Classifier	Correctly Classified %
Naïve Bayes	58
Support Vector Classification	59
PART	58
Random Forest	57
Decision Tree	58
Bayes Net	58
Logistic	59
Multilayer Perceptron	57
Simple Logistic	59
Classification via Regression	59

The results for only female data from the dataset are presented in Table IV. The results are again not significantly different in terms of the machine learning algorithms with respect to the best performance. However, we note the overall classification accuracy results are slightly higher than the male only data using the same amount of records as the male dataset $n=1364$. The three algorithms that correctly classified the data with 61% accuracy are Naïve Bayes, Bayes Net and Logistic. The Logistic model remained consistent providing the highest overall accuracy for both the individual male data and individual female data.

TABLE IV. MACHINE LEARNING ALGORITHM PERFORMANCE USING FEMALE DATA (n=1364)

WEKA Classifier	Correctly Classified %
Naïve Bayes	61
Support Vector Classification	60
PART	59
Random Forest	59
Decision Tree	60
Bayes Net	61
Logistic	61
Multilayer Perceptron	59
Simple Logistic	59
Classification via Regression	60

If we compare the results in Tables III and IV with the results in Table II, we can see that the single model, using the gender data, classifies the output more accurately than two individual gender-based models. However, this could be attributed to the fact that there is more than twice as much data used to generate the results in Table II, compared with Tables III and IV. Therefore, for fair comparison with balanced datasets, we re-ran the experiment illustrated in Table II, using only 50% of the dataset (*n=1621*) and the results are presented in Table V. This enables direct comparison with the results in Tables III and IV, and enables a fuller understanding of whether gender is important information and whether inclusion of gender data improves accuracy.

TABLE V. REDUCED DATASET (n=1621) INCLUDING MALE AND FEMALE USING MACHINE LEARNING ALGORITHMS

WEKA Classifier	Correctly Classified %
Naïve Bayes	60
Support Vector Classification	59
PART	57
Random Forest	56
Decision Tree	60
Bayes Net	60
Logistic	61
Multilayer Perceptron	56
Simple Logistic	61
Classification via Regression	60

A comparison of the results in Tables III, IV and V demonstrates the similarity of results. However, the female data in Table IV are slightly better. A comparison of Table V with Table II (the only difference being that Table V uses half the dataset) demonstrates a slight decrease in predictive accuracy due to using fewer records. The use of male and female data as an input variable demonstrates gender differences in the data, and that predictive accuracy can be improved using male and female data as an input variable. The results are not significant enough to justify the use of individual models for gender due to the smaller data set; a single model with gender as an input is sufficient to classify the data. It should be noted that the TILDA dataset is collected through self-declaration and, therefore, performance accuracy of 50%-70% is as high as one would expect for such a dataset that is not collected in a controlled manner.

IV. CONCLUSION

This study has explored ten different machine learning algorithms utilizing the data from The Longitudinal Study on Ageing. The risk factors explored were: Overall Health Description, Long-Term Health, Emotional Mental Health, Afraid of Falling, Joint Replacements and Blackouts or Fainting. The dataset was split into two, separating male data from the female data to find correlations or patterns when comparing against the dataset that included both male and female together. This was an attempt to distinguish whether there were any gender differences. A reduction in the size of the dataset lowers predictive accuracy as expected, but splitting the data into male and female gives slightly higher predictive accuracy in both cases with the female data outperforming the male. The slightly higher predictive accuracy of the female compared to the male data suggests that the risk factors used are slightly more relevant for females than males based on this data. For this data it is apparent that separating male and female was beneficial. To be useful in practice and delivery of services, these computer models must be understandable and acceptable to health and social care professionals as potentially they could be of help in their daily job when guiding and making decisions by individuals and families. It is important that health and social care professionals view males and females differently when looking at risk factors that affect the elderly. Further work proposed is to develop visualization methods to visualize risk to health and social care professionals.

REFERENCES

[1] K. Fenton, "The Human Cost of Falls," 17 July 2014. [Online]. Available: https://publichealthmatters.blog.gov.uk/2014/07/17/the-human-cost-of-falls. [Accessed 09, 2020]

[2] Public Health England, "Public Health Outcomes Framework," 2016. [Online]. Available: www.phoutcomes.info/search/falls. [Accessed on 09, 2020]

[3] Health Service Executive, "Falls," NHS Choices, 13 07 2011. [Online]. Available: https://www.hse.ie/eng/health/az/f/falls/. [Accessed 09, 2020].

[4] I. Johansson, M. Bachrach-Lindström, S. Struksnes & B. Hedelin. Balancing integrity vs. risk of falling – nurses' experiences of caring for elderly people with dementia in nursing homes. 2009. *Journal of Research in Nursing*, vol. *14*(1), pp. 61-73. https://doi.org/10.1177/1744987107086423

[5] Public Health England, "Falls and fracture consensus statement: Supporting commissioning for prevention," England, PHE Publications, 2017.

[6] National Institute for Health and Care Excellence, "Falls in older people: assessing risk and prevention," Clinical Guideline [CG161], England and Wales, 2013.

[7] W. Godolphin, "Shared Decision-Making," *Healthcare Quarterly*, vol. 12, August 2009.

[8] National Health Service Confederation, "Falls Prevention: New approaches to integrated falls prevention services," *Ambulance Service Network Community Health Services Forum*, no. 234, April 2012.

[9] J. R. Oyebode, P. Bradley, and J. L. Allen. Relatives' experiences of frontal-variant frontotemporal dementia. *Qual. Health Res.* 2013; vol. 23(2): pp. 156-166. doi:10.1177/1049732312466294

[10] C. While, F. Duane, C. Beanland, and S. Koch, "Medication management: the perspectives of people with dementia and family carers.," *Dementia (London)*, vol. 12, no. 6, pp. 734-750, 2013.

[11] L. M. Allan, C. G. Ballard, E. N. Rowan, and R. A. Kenny. Incidence and prediction of falls in dementia: a prospective study in older people. *PLoS One*. 2009; vol. 4(5). doi:10.1371/journal.pone.0005521

[12] A. Holdcroft, "Gender bias in research:," *Journal of the Royal Society of Medicine*, vol. 100, no. 1, pp. 2-3, January 2007.

[13] A. J. Larrazabala, N. Nieto, V. Peterson, D. H. Milone, and

E. Ferrante, "Gender imbalance in medical imaging datasets," 2019.

[14] T. Wang, Intelligent Condition Monitoring and Diagnosis System, Frontiers in Artificial Intelligence and Applications, 2003, Volume 93, pp. 132.

[15] P. Parodi. Computational intelligence with applications to general insurance: A review: The role of statistical learning. Annals of Actuarial Science, vol. 6(2), pp. 307-343, 2012. Doi:10.1917/S1748499512000036

[16] P. Rajpurkar, "CheXNet: Radiologist-level pneumonia detection on chest X-rays with deep learning," 2017. [Online]. Available: https://arxiv.org/abs/1711.05225. [Accessed 09, 2020]

[17] D. Ardila, A. P. Kiraly, and S. Bharadwaj. End-to-end lung cancer screening with three-dimensional deep learning on low-dose chest computed tomography. *Nat Med.* 2019; vol. 25(8) pp. 1319. doi:10.1038/s41591-019-0536-x

[18] G. J. Escobar, B. J. Turk, and A. Ragins. Piloting electronic medical record-based early detection of inpatient deterioration in community hospitals. *J Hosp Med.* 2016;vol. 11 pp, S18-S24. doi:10.1002/jhm.2652

[19] H. C. Koh and G. Tan, Data Mining Applications in Healthcare. Journal of healthcare information management : JHIM. vol. 19, pp. 64-72, 2005.

[20] E. Frank, M. A. Hall, and I. H. Witten, "The WEKA Workbench. Online Appendix for "Data Mining: Practical Machine Learning Tools and Techniques"," 2016. [Online] https://www.cs.waikato.ac.nz/ml/weka/index.html [Accessed 09, 2020].

[21] Trinity College Dublin, "The Irish Longitudinal Study on Ageing," The University of Dublin, 20 June 2020. [Online] https://tilda.tcd.ie/data/accessing-data/ [Accessed 09, 2020].

[22] L. Lindsay, S. Coleman, D. Kerr, B. Taylor, and A. Moorhead. (Accepted/In press). *Classification of Health Risk Factors to Predict the Risk of Falling in Older Adults*. Paper presented at International Conference on Risk Analysis and Hazard Mitigation, Stockholm, Sweden.

Technical Indicators for Hourly Energy Market Trading

Catherine McHugh, Sonya Coleman, Dermot Kerr
Intelligent Systems Research Centre (ISRC)
Ulster University
Northern Ireland, UK
e-mail: {mchugh-c24; sa.coleman; d.kerr}@ulster.ac.uk

Abstract—**Financial trading often combines machine learning and technical indicators to accurately predict future market prices. Energy data and financial data have similar features; therefore, this research derives eight electricity price technical indicators to help control spending and reduce trading costs for the Integrated Single Electricity Market in Ireland. The proposed technical indicators were derived from electricity price data, collected on an hourly basis from February until November 2019, and used to train three regression machine learning algorithms (Random Forest, Gradient Boosting, and Extreme Gradient Boosting). The results for each of the regression algorithms were first compared using one model for all trading periods. The Random Forest algorithm was then trained with the same technical indicators for each of the 24 hours periods individually to see if an hourly approach enhanced model performance. The proposed technical indicators accurately predict electricity prices and overall accuracy was greatly improved using separate hourly forecasting models.**

Keywords- Hourly Forecasting; Machine Learning; Technical Indicators; Energy Market.

I. Introduction

Energy data display volatile characteristics that make forecasting in the energy market difficult [1]. Time series models analyse patterns by observing and training with previous prices to predict future values. Price prediction machine learning algorithms are an increasingly popular tool to tackle volatility and reduce trading costs by creating optimal price models [2]. Price fluctuations arise when supply and demand are imbalanced, but price forecasting can optimise unit purchasing especially when short-term forecasting as the relationship is stronger between actual and predicted values [3]. This research centres on day-ahead electricity price prediction to examine energy market trends, with the overall aim of building an innovative system that assists electricity suppliers in future planning to reduce purchasing costs and hence enables consistent pricing for customers.

In the financial trading market, simple machine learning algorithms have been quite effective when used for prediction [4]. Technical indicators originate from historical financial data and are often used as inputs to train machine learning forecasting models. Generally, technical indicators are mostly considered to aid investors in whether it is best to buy or sell in the trading market [5]. This approach could be applied to the day-ahead energy market by developing specific technical indicators that follow electricity price trends and including these derived indicators as inputs in prediction models to forecast future electricity prices. Technical indicators have only recently been applied in the energy market for day-ahead forecasting, therefore existing literature in this area is limited [6]. Energy forecasting models that apply fundamental indicators as inputs (load, weather variables, generation, etc.) have found that same hour input data have robust correlation [7]. This conclusion was also stated when separate 24-hour time-series models were applied to the Spanish electricity price market data, noting that separate hour models were more homogeneous in observing trends than a model that considers all hours [8].

This paper develops eight new technical indicators specifically for the energy market, building on the idea from [6] of calculating the indicators for each hour separately. First, we examine our technical indicators by including them as inputs and using the actual electricity price as output in machine learning regression models. The forecasting performance for day-ahead predictions is evaluated for all techniques and all 24-hours are included in the training models. The model performance accuracies are then compared with the performance of models that are trained only on raw price data as input, denoted as persistence models, to determine if including technical indicators as inputs improves model performance. This research then examines 1-hourly models for each of the 24 hours to determine if technical indicators do follow hourly patterns and are therefore better at matching market trends when split by hour.

This paper is organised as follows: Section II outlines each of the proposed technical indicators for energy market prediction and describes how each is calculated in terms of electricity price. Section III discusses the three regression algorithm modelling techniques. The results are presented and discussed in Section IV highlighting first, the accuracy of each regression 24-hour model, and then displaying the results for each of the individual 24 1-hour Random Forest models. Section V concludes the paper by summarising the key findings of this research.

II. Technical Indicators

Technical analysis is common in stock market trading to capture trends and information on price movement from indicators built using raw stock price [9]. The core indicators for price prediction are: (i) trend, (ii) oscillator, and (iii) momentum [5]. The most complex part of technical analysis is deciding on parameter optimization and the sliding window size is a key feature as it relates to the corresponding number of historical records required for the calculation of each indicator [10]. A new advancement for the island of Ireland is the Integrated Single Electricity Market (ISEM) allowing energy traders greater control. This development has led to the need for novel technical price indicators to aid in forecasting decisions when to buy or sell in the ISEM.

Our research presents eight innovative energy trading technical indicators originating from, but not the same as, the common financial technical indicators. The requirement for the ISEM is day-ahead, therefore this work only focusses on technical price indicators which improve day-ahead prediction accuracy. The individual calculations for each of the indicators used in both the all hours model and separate hourly models are listed below:

1. Percentage Price Change Moving Average (PPCMA): A trend indicator in time-series that, for the energy market, we calculate price change as the difference between the current price ($Price_{Hour\ n}$) and the price from the same time period the day before ($Price_{Lag\ 24}$), all divided by $Price_{Lag\ 24}$. In the all hours model, the moving average percentage price change was calculated for is a rolling 24-hour window (*i*=24). For the hourly models, a pool (*i*) ranging from a rolling 1-hour window (*i*=1) to a 100-hour window (*i*=100) was calculated:

$$PPCMA_i = \sum_i [PPC] \tag{1}$$

where

$$PPC = \frac{Price_{current} - Price_{Lag\ 24}}{Price_{Lag\ 24}} * 100 \tag{2}$$

2. Moving Average Deviation (MAD): A trend indicator that utilises the PPCMA indicator to calculate the deviation rate of the current electricity price from PPCMA. For the hourly models, a pool (*i*) ranges from 1 to 100:

$$MAD_i = \frac{Price_{current} - PPCMA_i}{PPCMA_i} \tag{3}$$

3. Percentage Range (PR): An oscillator indicator that finds a relationship between current electricity price and the highest/lowest prices over a 24-hour window for the all hours model. For the hourly models, a pool (*i*) ranges from 1 to 100 to calculate the highest and lowest prices. This indicator oscillates between 0 and 100, with a value above 80 determined to indicate energy units are oversold and a value below 20 indicating that energy units are overbought:

$$PR_i = \left[\frac{HighestPrice_i - Price_{current}}{HighestPrice_i - LowestPrice_i}\right] * 100 \tag{4}$$

4. Average True Range (ATR): A trend indicator measuring price volatility. Over a 24-hour window, there are three different values calculated for the all hours model: highest price over the 24-hour period minus lowest price over the 24-hour period; highest price over the 24-hour period minus starting electricity price; and lowest price over the 24-hour period minus starting electricity price. The maximum value from these three values is selected for each trading hour and averaged over a rolling 24-hour window. For the hourly models, a pool (*i*) ranging from a rolling 1-hour window to a 100-hour window were used in the calculations:

$$ATR_i = \sum_i MAX\,[A_i, B_i, C_i] \tag{5}$$

$$A_i = HighestPrice_i - LowestPrice_i \tag{6}$$

$$B_i = |\,HighestPrice_i - Price_{current}\,| \tag{7}$$

$$C_i = |\,LowestPrice_i - Price_{current}\,| \tag{8}$$

5. Relative Strength Index (RSI): An oscillator indicator that compares recent price gains to recent price losses. This indicator oscillates between 0 and 100, with a value over 70 determined to indicate that energy units are overvalued and a value below 30 indicating that energy units are undervalued. For the all hours model, Price Up is the average of the previous 24 hours when price difference increased, and Price Down is the average of the previous 24 hours when price difference decreased. For the hourly models, Price Up and Price Down are calculated from the average of the previous *i* hours with *i* ranging from 0 to 100:

$$RSI_i = 100 - \left[\frac{100}{D_i}\right] \tag{9}$$

where

$$D_i = \left(1 - \frac{\sum_i Price\ Up\left[Price_{current} - Price_{Lag\ i}\right]}{\sum_i Price\ Down\left[Price_{current} - Price_{Lag\ i}\right]}\right) \tag{10}$$

6. Average Directional Movement Index (ADX): A trend indicator measuring the strength of the trend, grouping the two directional movement indexes depending whether price change, calculated as current electricity price minus previous 24-hour price (all hours model)/previous i-hour price (hourly models), is grouped as a Price Up (positive) change or Price Down (negative) change. The two indexes are combined and smoothed with a moving average:

$$ADX_i = \left[\frac{\sum_i DX\ Up(a_i) - \sum_i DX\ Down(b_i)}{\sum_i DX\ Up(a_i) + \sum_i DX\ Down(b_i)}\right] * 100 \tag{11}$$

where

$$a_i = \frac{\sum_i Price\ Up[Price_{current} - Price_{Lag\ i}]}{ATR_i} \quad (12)$$

$$b_i = \frac{\sum_i Price\ Down[Price_{current} - Price_{Lag\ i}]}{ATR_i} \quad (13)$$

7. Moving Average Convergence/Divergence (MACD): An oscillator indicator that considers the strength, direction, and duration of the trend as well as price momentum through moving averages of previous price values with rolling window sizes of 12 and 24 for the all hours model and rolling window sizes of 7 and 14 for the hourly models:

$$MACD = \sum_{7} Price\ MA_{Lag\ 7} - \sum_{14} Price\ MA_{Lag\ 14} \quad (14)$$

8. Price Momentum (PMOM): A momentum indicator that measures the power of the market by observing the current electricity price with the previous trading value (1 hour before) for the all hours model. For the hourly models, a pool (i) ranges from 1 to 100 to calculate:

$$PMOM_i = Price_{current} - Price_{Lag\ i} \quad (15)$$

III. Modelling Methodology

Three machine learning algorithms were trained with the eight technical indicators, implemented through SkLearn. A Random Forest regression algorithm is an efficient ensemble technique with many benefits: straightforward tuning, robust to outliers, and expandable for data fitting [11]. During training of a Random Forest, there are multiple trees split at nodes therefore no single tree perceives the complete training dataset [12]. There is transparency with the algorithm as a tuning parameter decides when to split the input data for classifying [13]. After the Random Forest is built a prediction value is outputted, which is the average of each individual regression tree's prediction [14]. In this research, a Random Forest regression algorithm was implemented with 1000 trees and no pruning. Criterion measure of split was set to Mean Squared Error (MSE) with minimum sample split set to 2 and minimum sample leaf node set to 1.

Sequential learning, used in boosting algorithms, combines weak learner models to create one strong learner model [15]. In a Gradient Boosting regression algorithm, a prediction model is built from weak learners through optimizing a loss function [16]. Another boosting regression algorithm is the Extreme Gradient Boosting (XGBoost) that works through ensemble sequential learning with weighted predictors [16]. This is an advanced machine learning algorithm due to speed and the ability to train large data [17]. In this research, an XGBoost algorithm was implemented with 1000 trees, the fraction of column to be a random tree sample was set to 0.6, the fraction of observations to be random tree subsample was set to 0.8, the maximum depth of tree was set to 4, with a learning rate of 0.05.

The hourly models contain different technical indicator parameters depending on the hour (0-23). As a pool of indicators ranging from 1 to 100 were created for this part of the research, selecting the optimal indicators for each hour is the first step. Hyperparameters n and s represent the lag factor and span respectively. This approach of finding an optimal n and s was taken from the work presented in [6]. In our research, n was utilized in the creation of five of our novel technical indicators (PR, ATR, RSI, ADX, and PMOM) and s was utilized in the creation of two of our novel technical indicators (PPCMA and MAD). To find the optimal n and s for each hour, the model which provided the lowest Root Mean Square Error (RMSE) during the Random Forest algorithm testing set was selected. This is calculated in terms of electricity price as the difference between actual and predicted price values. Optimization was implemented on SkLearn by creating a list with all possible combinations for n and s and ranking the RMSE for each combination in order from lowest to highest RMSE.

TABLE I. Optimal n and s For Hourly Models

Hour	Optimal n	Optimal s
0	48	45
1	100	42
2	61	74
3	59	5
4	59	76
5	74	75
6	100	99
7	99	75
8	91	93
9	2	97
10	87	82
11	75	76
12	78	77
13	41	7
14	95	97
15	83	71
16	87	82
17	106	80
18	87	94
19	102	99
20	102	106
21	56	38
22	81	81
23	55	55

Table I displays the optimal n and s values for each of the 24 1-hour models. During the selection, the Random Forest algorithm was applied and the corresponding technical indicators were chosen based on optimal n and s. For instance, the optimal technical indicators for Hour 0 are PPCMA45, MAD45, PR48, ATR48, RSI48, ADX48, MACD, and PMOM48. If n or s reached the maximum value of 100 the indicator pool range was increased to 150 to ensure the optimal model was selected.

IV. RESULTS

For the experiments, we use hourly ISEM electricity price data ranging from 1st February 2019 until 01st December 2019 retrieved from SEMOpx website [18]. The technical indicators derived from the raw price data, outlined in Section II, were first calculated using all data and a sliding window of 24 hours. Additionally, the indicators were calculated for each hour separately and this time a sliding window pool i from 1 to 100 was utilised for each indicator to find the optimal n and s. The calculated technical indicators were applied as training inputs for the three machine learning models.

The data for the 24-hour machine learning models were split 85% for training (04th February - 16 October 2019) and 15% for testing (17th October – 30th November 2019). The input data were the eight technical indicators and the output data was the actual electricity price for the same timeframe, time T. To put this research work into context, a persistence model with raw electricity price data as input was observed as a baseline at time T and output price data at time T+24. Table II presents comparative results for both persistence and technical indicator 24-hour models for Random Forest, Gradient Boosting, and XGBoost. The most predictive indicators were MAD and Percentage Range.

TABLE II. SUMMARY RESULTS FOR 24-HOUR MODELS

Algorithm	Persistence Models		Technical Indicators	
	Testing Accuracy	Testing RMSE	Testing Accuracy	Testing RMSE
Gradient Boosting	75.44%	13.18	86.90%	6.66
Random Forest	73.21%	16.30	91.57%	6.77
XGBoost	75.02%	14.39	89.70%	5.34

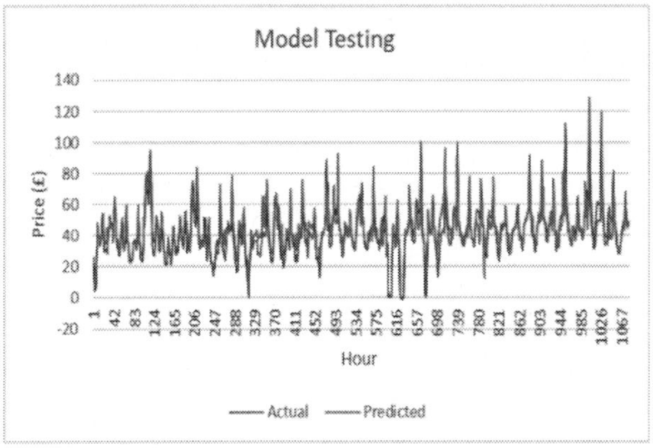

Figure. 1. Random Forest 24-Hour Model Testing

Testing model accuracy percentage is computed as model error, chosen as the Root Mean Squared Log Error (RMSLE), subtracted from 100. The RMSLE metric was chosen for the accuracy calculation as it is robust to outliers, only observes relative error, and gives a larger penalty for underestimating [19]. From Table I, the testing accuracy ranged between 73% and 76% for the persistence models and ranged between 86% and 92% for the technical indicator models highlighting that using technical indicators as inputs improves model performance. RMSE evaluates the model performance of the test set, the closer the value is to zero the better the prediction. During model testing, XGBoost provided the lowest RMSE value of 5.34. However, the model accuracy was the highest at 91.57% using the Random Forest. Figure 1 illustrates the actual electricity price values plotted against the predicted price values for the Random Forest testing phase. The figure exhibits a good-fit for the majority of predicted values especially at the beginning of the testing period, but the fit is less accurate during the last few hours of the testing period.

TABLE III. SUMMARY RESULTS FOR RANDOM FOREST HOURLY OPTIMAL MODELS

Hour	Testing Accuracy	Testing RMSE
0	88.16%	1.55
1	98.17%	0.98
2	90.26%	0.81
3	84.78%	0.77
4	86.28%	0.87
5	89.33%	0.75
6	91.16%	3.16
7	98.74%	1.28
8	99.32%	0.74
9	98.92%	1.19
10	98.46%	1.99
11	98.64%	1.69
12	98.82%	1.47
13	98.02%	2.38
14	97.89%	2.42
15	98.50%	1.74
16	98.04%	3.24
17	94.62%	11.86
18	97.65%	4.6
19	98.58%	1.79
20	98.70%	1.44
21	98.32%	1.95
22	98.32%	1.59
23	86.87%	1.75

The next stage of this work was to split the data by hour before calculating separate hourly technical indicators to determine if models are better trained as 24 separate 1-hour prediction models. As well as hourly technical indicators, there was also a pool of indicators with varying *n* and *s* for each hour in order to select the optimal hourly models. The technical indicators were calculated from data ranging between February and December 2019 and used as model inputs. From the previous work, it was clear that no matter which machine learning algorithm was used, the use of technical indicators improved prediction performance. Therefore, we only create hourly models using the Random Forest algorithm as it presented the highest model accuracy in Table II. The Random Forest hourly models used 85% of the dataset for training (11th May - 31 October 2019) and 15% for testing (01st November – 01st December 2019). Each Random Forest hourly model had the technical indicators as input at time *T* and output price data at time *T*+1 (day-ahead).

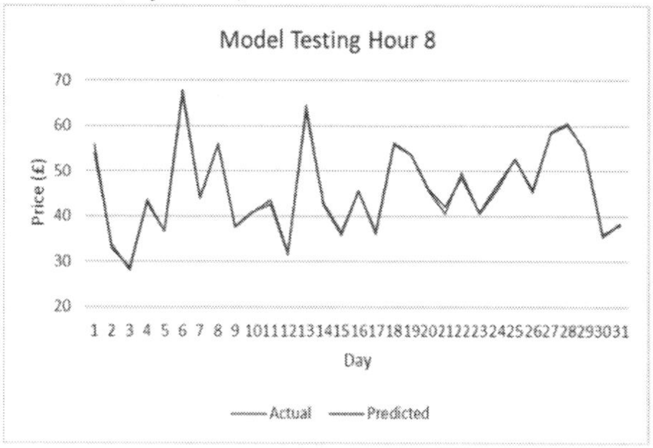

Figure. 2. Random Forest Hour 8 Model Testing

Table III presents the optimal model testing accuracy and RMSE values for each hour separately. Overall, the testing accuracy ranged from 84% to over 99% and most of the testing RMSE values were below 3. This is a significant improvement from the testing results shown in Table II. Hour 8 had the most promising results with a testing accuracy of 99.32% and a RMSE value of 0.74. The visual output of the actual and predicted electricity prices for this hour are displayed in Figure 2 illustrating an excellent fit. As this plot is for a 1-hour model (Hour 8) the x-axis (Figure 2) is the same hour in each day in the testing period, whereas in the all hours technical indicator model the x-axis (Figure 1) is every hour in the testing period.

V. CONCLUSION

Eight technical indicators (PPCMA, MAD, PR, ATR, RSI, ADX, MACD, and Price Momentum) were specifically derived from raw data for energy trading and tested on three machine learning regression models (Random Forest, Gradient Boosting, and XGBoost) to forecast electricity prices. The technical indicators were first calculated using an all hours approach and then they were re-calculated when split by hour to find an optimal hourly electricity price forecasting model.

In both approaches, the model data were split 85% for training and 15% for testing. In the 24-hour model approach, the results were compared with a baseline persistence model which was tested with raw price data only. The three algorithms accuracy ranged between 73% and 76% for the persistence models and ranged between 86% and 92% for the technical indicator models. These results confirmed that including technical indicators as model inputs improved overall performance.

In the next experiment stage, 24 separate 1-hour prediction models were generated using the Random Forest algorithm. Random Forest was selected here as in previous results it resulted in the highest model accuracy. Optimal *n* and *s* were required for each of the 24 1-hour Random Forest models split by hour and chosen through running each indicator pool combination and selecting the hyperparameters which result in the lowest RMSE. The testing accuracy ranged between 84% to over 99% for each of the 24 1-hour models and the majority had a RMSE value below 3. These promising results indicate that having individual hour models are more homogeneous and beneficial for energy trading.

To conclude, energy traders should consider technical indicators in price prediction models, especially individual models that have been optimised for each hour of the day, to capture market trends and enable accurate predictions, thus reducing purchasing costs. Further work will consider adding other energy related factors, such as wind generation to the optimal models to determine if model accuracy can be further improved.

ACKNOWLEDGMENT

This research was supported by DfE CAST scholarship in collaboration with Click Energy.

REFERENCES

[1] H. Mosbah and M. El-Hawary, "Hourly Electricity Price Forecasting for the Next Month Using Multilayer Neural Network," in *Canadian Journal of Electrical and Computer Engineering*, 2016, vol. 39, no. 4, pp. 283–291.

[2] G. Gao, K. Lo, and F. Fan, "Comparison of ARIMA and ANN Models Used in Electricity Price Forecasting for Power Market," *Energy Power Eng.*, vol. 09, no. 04, pp. 120–126, 2017.

[3] N. Pandey and K. G. Upadhyay, "Different price forecasting techniques and their application in deregulated electricity market : A comprehensive study," in *International Conference on Emerging Trends in Electrical , Electronics and Sustainable Energy Systems (ICETEESES)*, 2016, pp. 1–4.

[4] E. A. Gerlein, M. McGinnity, A. Belatreche, and S. Coleman, "Evaluating machine learning classification for financial trading: An empirical approach," in *Expert Systems with Applications*, 2016, vol. 54, pp. 193–207.

[5] M. T. Ã and S. Tokuoka, "Adaptive use of technical indicators for the prediction of intra-day stock prices," in *Statistical Mechanics and its Applications*, 2007, vol. 383, pp. 125–133.

[6] S. Demir, K. Mincev, K. Kok, and N. G. Paterakis, "Introducing technical indicators to electricity price forecasting: A feature engineering study for linear, ensemble, and deep machine learning models," *Appl. Sci.*, vol. 10, no. 1, p. 255, 2019.

[7] P. Li, F. Arci, J. Reilly, K. Curran, and A. Belatreche, "Using Artificial Neural Networks to predict short-term wholesale prices on the Irish Single Electricity Market," in *2016 27th Irish Signals and Systems Conference (ISSC)*, 2016, pp. 1–10.

[8] C. García-Martos, J. Rodríguez, and M. J. Sánchez, "Mixed models for short-run forecasting of electricity prices: Application for the Spanish market," *IEEE Trans. Power Syst.*, vol. 22, no. 2, pp. 544–552, 2007.

[9] J. Diego, J. Ignacio, J. Francisco, and L. Jose, "Multiobjective

Optimization of Technical Market Indicators," in *Proceedings of the 11th Annual Conference Companion on Genetic and Evolutionary Computation Conference*, 2009, pp. 1999–2004.

[10] Y. Shynkevich, T. M. McGinnity, S. A. Coleman, A. Belatreche, and Y. Li, "Forecasting price movements using technical indicators: Investigating the impact of varying input window length," in *Neurocomputing*, 2017, vol. 264, pp. 71–88.

[11] J. Mei, D. He, R. Harley, T. Habetler, and G. Qu, "A random forest method for real-time price forecasting in New York electricity market," *IEEE Power Energy Soc. Gen. Meet.*, vol. 2014-Octob, no. October, pp. 1–5, 2014.

[12] L. Khaidem, S. Saha, and S. R. Dey, "Predicting the direction of stock market prices using random forest," vol. 00, no. 00, pp. 1–20, 2016.

[13] K. Mulrennan, J. Donovan, D. Tormey, and R. Macpherson, "A data science approach to modelling a manufacturing facility's electrical energy profile from plant production data," *Proc. - 2018 IEEE 5th Int. Conf. Data Sci. Adv. Anal. DSAA 2018*, pp. 387–391, 2018.

[14] J. Pórtoles, C. González, and J. M. Moguerza, "Electricity Price Forecasting with Dynamic Trees: A Benchmark Against the Random Forest Approach," *Energies*, vol. 11, no. 6, p. 1588, 2018.

[15] R. Gandhi, "Boosting Algorithms: AdaBoost, Gradient Boosting and XGBoost," 2018. [Online]. Available: https://hackernoon.com/boosting-algorithms-adaboost-gradient-boosting-and-xgboost-f74991cad38c. [Retrieved: June, 2020].

[16] S. Dey, Y. Kumar, S. Saha, and S. Basak, "Forecasting to Classification : Predicting the direction of stock market price using Xtreme Gradient Boosting Forecasting to Classification : Predicting the direction of stock market price using Xtreme Gradient Boosting," no. October, pp. 1–10, 2016.

[17] M. Pathak, "Using XGBoost in Python," 2019. [Online]. Available: https://www.datacamp.com/community/tutorials/xgboost-in-python. [Retrieved: June, 2020].

[18] SEMOpx, "Day-Ahead Electricity Price." [Online]. Available: https://www.semopx.com/market-data/market-results/. [Retrieved: March, 2020].

[19] S. Saxena, "What's the Difference Between RMSE and RMSLE?," *Analytics Vidhya*, 2019. [Online]. Available: https://medium.com/analytics-vidhya/root-mean-square-log-error-rmse-vs-rmlse-935c6cc1802a. [Retrieved: July, 2020].

A Comprehensive Study of Recent Metadata Models for Data Lake

Redha Benaissa*†‡, Omar Boussaid†, Aicha Mokhtari‡, and Farid Benhammadi§
*§ DBE Laboratory, Ecole Militaire Polytechnique, Bordj el Bahri, Algiers, Algeria
† ERIC, Universite de Lyon, Lyon 2, France
‡ RIIMA Laboratory, USTHB University, Algiers, Algeria
Email: *benaissa.redha@gmail.com, †omar.boussaid@univ-lyon2.fr, ‡amokhtari@usthb.dz, §fbenhammadi2008@gmail.com

***Abstract*—In the era of Big Data, an unrepresented amount of heterogeneous and unstructured data is generated every day, which needs to be stored, managed, and processed to create new services and applications. This has brought new concepts in data management such as Data Lakes (DL) where the raw data is stored without any transformation. Successful DL systems deploy efficient metadata techniques in order to organize the DL. This paper presents a comprehensive study of recent metadata models for Data Lake that points out their rationales, strengths, and weaknesses. More precisely, we provide a layered taxonomy of recent metadata models and their specifications. This is followed by a survey of recent works dealing with metadata management in DL, which can be categorized into level, typology, and content metadata. Based on such a study, an in-depth analysis of key features, strengths, and missing points is conducted. This, in turn, allowed to find the gap in the literature and identify open research issues that require the attention of the community.**

Keywords–Metadata; Metadata models; Data Lakes; Big Data.

I. INTRODUCTION

In the era of Big Data, data has become more and more unstructured rendering traditional data storage models, such as Relational Data-Bases and their Management Systems (RDBMS) ill-adapted to meet these new needs. Indeed, traditional DBMS models are only suitable for applications having limited volume with relatively infrequent updates. Such systems, for instance, are unable to meet the exponentially growing data processing requirements for giant IT (Information Technology) companies, such as Google, Facebook, and Amazon. These limitations emphasize the need to review the methods of storing and processing this massive data and how to extract the relevant information. As a result, the concept of Data Lake (DL) has emerged. Within Data Lakes, massive heterogeneous data coming from different sources, is stored in its raw format without any transformation in order to accommodate multiple use-cases and applications. This, however, introduces new challenges to the management of these data with regards to discovery, storage, query, and construction of the catalog, as can be seen from Figure 1. To address such issues, metadata techniques are deployed within Data Lakes to reorganize and store data. The extraction of metadata from different heterogeneous data sources allows the construction of the DL catalog, which is essential for querying the DL. Within a Data Lake, a metadata catalog is a metadata management system, i.e., a formal system, which provides authority information on the structure and semantics of each element ingested within the Data Lake. It provides for each element the definition, the qualifiers associated with it, as well as the correspondences with equivalents in other languages or other diagrams, and finally the reference of the physical location of this element for retrieval data. Nevertheless, the extraction of the right metadata to build the catalog remains a challenging issue.

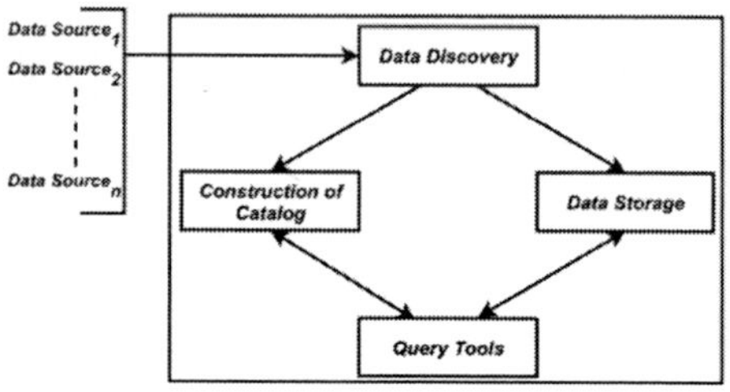

Figure 1. Data management process in a Data Lake.

This paper presents a comprehensive study of recent metadata models for Data Lake that points out their rationales, strengths, and weaknesses. More precisely, we provide a layered taxonomy of recent metadata models and their specifications. This is followed by a survey of recent works dealing with metadata management in DL, which can be categorized into level, typology, and content metadata. Based on such a study, an in-depth analysis of key features, strengths, and missing point is conducted. This, in turn, allowed to find the gap in the literature and identify open research issues that require the attention of the community.

The remainder of this paper is organized as follows: in Section 2, we detail and discuss existing metadata management methods on Data Lake, which can be categorized into three categories namely level, typology, and content metadata. In Section 3, we study some metadata management models and systems that support the description and semantics of data ingested in the Data Lake. In Section 4, we present some limits of different metadata management existing models that have been identified and may be the subject of research directions to explore. The paper ends in Section 5 with conclusions and future directions.

II. METADATA IN DATA LAKE

With the emergence of Data Lakes, which refer to a massively scalable storage repository that contains a large amount of raw data [1], and for good management of heterogeneous data sources, only metadata can guarantee efficient management and effective interoperability of data sources [2]. However, until now, the representation and management of metadata on Data Lakes remains an open research area. In this section, we detail and discuss existing metadata management methods on Data Lake, which can be categorized into three categories namely level, typology, and content metadata, as can be seen from Figure 2.

A. Metadata Level

This category encompasses three models [3] [4] namely technical metadata, operational metadata, and business metadata, detailed below.

1) Technical metadata: Technical metadata [3] describes the technical aspects of data sets. It is used by the ingestion engine to determine the type of data encoding and to automatically convert the data sets into encodings according to the need or specification of the format and the type of encoding used in the ingestion target. It includes the type and format of the data (text, images, JSON, etc.) and the structure or the schema [5]. This latter reports the names of the sources, their data types, their lengths, and whether they can be empty or not.

2) Operational metadata: Operational metadata [5] contains information on the quality and origin of the data. It includes information about the source and target locations of the data, file size, number of records, and the number of records rejected during data preparation. Operational metadata can come in two forms [3]:

- Run-Time operational metadata: Reflects the state of the data sets each time a record is added, modified, or deleted.
- On-boarding metadata: Describes the cycle and life expectancy of data sets attributes provided by the ingestion phase.

3) Business metadata: Business metadata [3] provides meaning and semantics to technical metadata to give more knowledge of the data sets. It provides information about the data providers and source systems. This type of metadata [5] covers management rules, such as setting an upper/lower limit on wages or determining the data that must be deleted from certain jobs for security and confidentiality reasons, for instance.

B. Metadata Typology

Defining a model for Data Lakes also involves identifying the data to be considered. Six key functionalities, expected by a metadata system from a Data Lake, have been identified by Sawadogo [6], which can be summarized as follows:

- *Semantic enrichment (SE)*, to generate a description of the context of the data, with interpretable and understandable tags based on ontologies.
- *Data indexing (DI)* consists in setting up a data structure essential for the recovery of data sets via specific characteristics (keywords or models). This requires the construction of forward or reverse indices.
- *Link generation and conservation (LG)* is the process of discovering similarity relationships or integrating relationships between data sets.
- *Data polymorphism (DP)* as storing multiple representations of the same data.
- *Data version (DV)* refers to the ability of the metadata system to handle data changes while keeping the previous states.
- *Usage tracking (UT)* saves the interactions between users and the Data Lake.

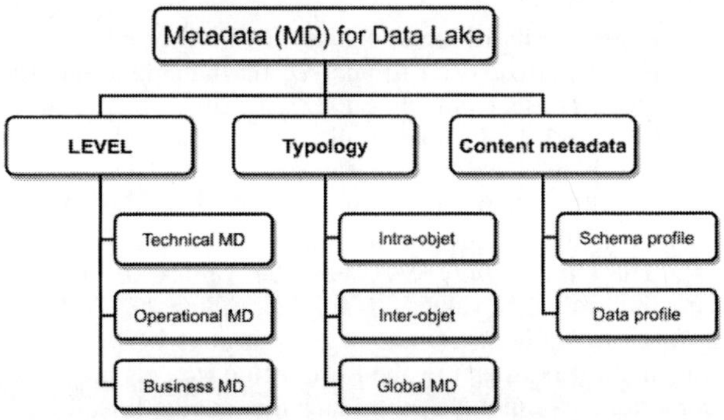

Figure 2. Metadata categories in Data Lake.

Besides, Sawadogo and al. [6] also proposed a typology of metadata, which categorizes it into intra-object, inter-object and global metadata. The following subsections detail each one of them.

1) Intra-object metadata: This category identifies *properties, summaries and previews, versions, and semantic metadata* associated with a given object. The properties provide a general description of an object, in the form of key/value pairs, obtained from the file system (the title of the object, size, date of the last modification, path, etc.). Summaries and previews provide an overview of the content or structure of an object. They can take the form of a data schema in the context of structured or semi-structured data, or a word cloud for text data. On the other hand, the creation of new versions of the initial data follows updates to the raw data in the Data Lake. Likewise, raw data (especially unstructured data) can be reformatted, inducing the creation of new representations of an object. Finally, semantic metadata are annotations that help to understand the meaning of the data (descriptive tags, text descriptions, or professional categories), useful for detecting object relationships.

2) Inter-object metadata: Inter-object metadata describes the relationships between at least two objects and has two main elements namely object groupings and similarity links. The former organizes objects into collections, which are derived from semantic metadata. Besides, properties like format or language can be used to group objects. The latter refers to the intrinsic properties of objects, such as their content or structure. It measures the compatibility of the diagrams of two structured or semi-structured objects, or other measures of common similarity.

3) Global metadata : Global metadata concern the entire Data Lake. They provide a contextual layer to the Data Lake that is essential for its analysis. Also, two new types of global metadata are presented. Semantic resources are essentially knowledge bases (ontologies, taxonomies, thesauri, dictionaries) used to generate other metadata and improve analyzes. Generally, they come from external sources such as ontologies. Furthermore, indexes are data structures that help find an object rapidly, and logs are used to track user interactions with the Data Lake.

C. Content metadata

According to [7], content metadata is the representation of all possible types of profiles in the Data Lake. Indeed, when analyzing raw data, the discovery of structural models and statistical distributions is based on the extraction and profiling patterns of traditional data [8]. Ontology alignment techniques [9] are used to analyze the metadata and schema extracted. These techniques use *schema metadata and data profile metadata* to match different attributes of different datasets, generating the information profile. A *schema profile* describes the schema of datasets, e.g. the number of attributes, the names of the attributes and their data types [7]. The *data profile* describes the values of the dataset, i.e., the statistics values of single-attribute [7]. Information profiles are called metadata of relationships between datasets. Information profiles use the data profile models and schemas. For example, annotating attributes that can be linked based on the approximate similarity of data distributions and data types. The ingestion of data in the Data Lake allows the construction of the metadata catalog that offers added value to the enormous amount of data stored in DL. The metadata catalog describes this data and allows querying to extract hidden knowledge from data sources ingested in the Data Lake.

III. METADATA MANAGEMENT SYSTEMS IN A DATA LAKE

In a Data Lake, the extraction of knowledge is based and articulated on metadata, which describes the sources of ingested data. It may have other data from other sources that satisfy the request, and building semantic bridges between metadata will increase the performance of querying the DL. In this section, we study of recent metadata management models and systems that support the description and semantics of data ingested in the Data Lake.

A. Network-based model for Data Lake

In the model presented in [10], the aim is to offer an approach for the extraction of complex knowledge schemes from concepts belonging to structured, semi-structured and unstructured sources in a Data Lake. In [10], the term complex knowledge model is used to indicate a semantic relationship (specifically, a synonymy or part of a relationship), that focuses on the semantics of data sources, and, therefore, only business metadata is considered. They include the business names and descriptions assigned to the data fields. They also cover business rules, which can become integrity constraints for the corresponding data source. This model adopts a typical notation of XML, JSON and many other semi-structured models to represent business metadata. The proposed approach [10] is based on an appropriate network, which represents all the sources of Data Lakes. It builds a structured representation of keywords, generally flat, used to represent unstructured data sources. Formally, a complex knowledge model consists of a logical succession $x_1, x_2, ..., x_w$ of w objects. With this uniform and network-based representation of sources in the Data Lake, the extraction of complex knowledge models can be carried out by using tools based on graphs. It consists in constructing suitable paths going from the first node (ie, x_1) to the last node (ie, x_w) of the succession expressing the patterns. The proposed approach seeks an appropriate path (if it exists) connecting x_1 to x_w. Since x_1 and x_w can belong to different sources, the approach considers the possible presence of synonymies between concepts belonging to different sources, and should model these synonymies by means of an appropriate form of arcs (cross arcs or *c-arcs*), and should include both intra-source arcs (internal arcs or *i-arcs*) and c-arcs in the path connecting x_1 to x_w and representing the complex knowledge model of interest.

In addition, there are cases where synonymies are not sufficient to find a complex knowledge model from x_1 to x_w. In such cases, the proposed approach makes two other attempts in which it first tries to imply similarities in chains and, even if these properties are not sufficient, partial relationships. If neither the synonymies, the similarities of strings, nor the partial relations allow the construction of a path from x_1 to x_w, the proposed approach concludes that, in the Data Lake considered, a complex knowledge model of x_1 to x_w does not exist.

The biggest difficulty concerns unstructured data because a consistent flat representation by a simple element, for each keyword provided to designate the content of the source, is not recommended. In fact, this type of representation would make it very difficult to reconcile and next integrate an unstructured source with the other sources (semi-structured and structured) of the Data Lake. Therefore, it is necessary (at least partially) to "structure" unstructured data. To solve this problem, the proposed approach creates a complex element to represent the source as a whole and a simple element for each keyword. The approach exploits the lexical and string similarities. In particular, the lexical similarity is considered by declaring that there is an arc of the node n_{k1}, corresponding to the keyword $k1$, to the node n_{k2}, corresponding to the keyword $k2$ (and vice versa). It is possible if $k1$ and $k2$ have at least one common lemma in an appropriate thesaurus. To this end, the approach adopts the ontology or multilingual semantic network BabelNet [11]. The chain similarity is applied via an appropriate chain similarity metric on $k1$ and $k2$, is "sufficiently high". In this case, N-Grams [12] is used as a chain similarity metric.

B. MEDAL

MEtadata model for DAta Lakes (MEDAL) [6] adopts a logical representation of metadata based on a hypergraph, a nested graph and the concepts of assigned graph. An object is represented by a hypernode containing various elements (versions and representations, properties, etc.). The hypernodes can be located between them (similarity, groupings, etc.). Objects can take the form of structured data (relational database tables, CSV files, etc.), semi-structured (JSON, XML, YAML, etc.) and unstructured (images, text documents, videos, etc.). The metadata, obtained on the typology, are subdivided into three components: $M = (M_{intra}, M_{inter}, M_{glob})$, where M_{intra} is the set of intra-object metadata, M_{inter} is the set of inter-object metadata and M_{glob} is the set of global metadata.

Each hypernode contains *representations*, associated with an object. There is at least one representation per hypernode, corresponding to the raw data of the Data Lake. Other representations all derive from this initial representation. Each representation corresponds to a node carrying simple or complex attributes. The *transition* from one representation to another is done via a transformation, formalized by an oriented edge, which also carries attributes or properties describing the transformation process (complete script or description, in case of manual transformation). A hypernode may also contain *versions* associated with nodes with attributes to manage data revolution of the lake over time. Indeed, a hypernode contains a tree whose nodes are representations or versions and the oriented edges are transformations or updates. One representation (resp. Version) is derived from another by a transformation (resp. Update), as can be seen from Figure 3a.

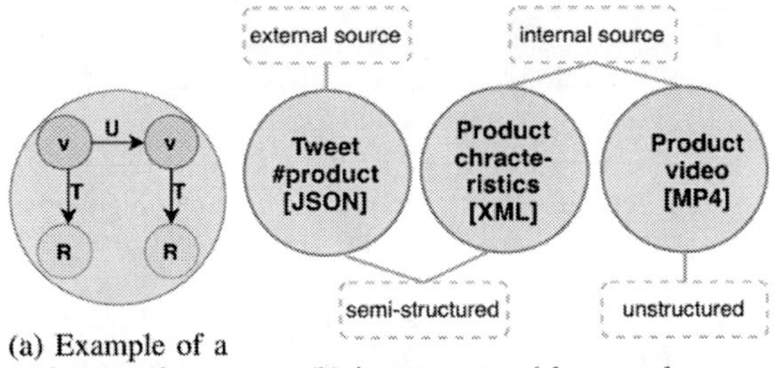

(a) Example of a hypernode.
(b) interconnected hypernodes.

Figure 3. Hypergraph representation of MEDAL [6].

So, the root of the tree is the initial raw representation of the hypernode and each version has its own representation subtree.

A group of objects is modeled by a set of undirected hyper-edges, i.e., edges, which can connect more than two (hyper) nodes. Each hyper-edge corresponds to a collection of objects. This grouping is performed on a hypernode attribute depicted in Figure 3b. A similarity link between two hypernodes is represented by an undirected edge with attributes: the value of the similarity metric, the type of the metric used, the date of the metric, etc. A hypernode can be derived from other hypernodes via a parental link. To translate this relation, a directed hyper-edge is used from all hypernodes "parents" towards the hypernode "child". Hypernodes are grouped in relation to a given parameter (often an attribute) and by parental relations.

The global metadata gravitate hypernodes and operated, as required, that is to say almost always, especially logs and indexes.

C. A generic and extensible classification of metadata-based System

In [13], metadata can help users find data that matches their needs, accelerates data access, verifies the origin of the data and treatment history to find relevant data and thereby enriches their analysis. The proposed metadata classification [13] has the advantage of integrating both intra-metadata and inter-metadata for all data sets or datasheets.
For Inter-metadata, the classification of [14] [See Section 2] is completed by subcategories. *Dataset Containment* indicates a containment relationship between the datasets. *Partial overlap* expresses the overlap of certain attributes in certain datasets. *Provenance* means that one dataset is the source of another dataset. *Logical clusters* mean that certain datasets are in the same domain. *Content similarity* finds common attributes shared between different datasets.
For Intra-metadata, the classification of [15] is extended to include access, quality and security. *Data characteristics* includes information such as the identification, name, size, type of structure and date of creation of the data sets. *Definition metadata* specifies the meaning of data sets. They are classified into semantic and schematic metadata. Semantically, structured and unstructured data sets can be described by text or by certain key words (vocabularies). Schematically, a structured dataset can be presented by a database schema. Other characteristics are described such as Navigation metadata, which relates to the location of data sets, Lineage, which presents the life cycle of the data, Access metadata, which presents access

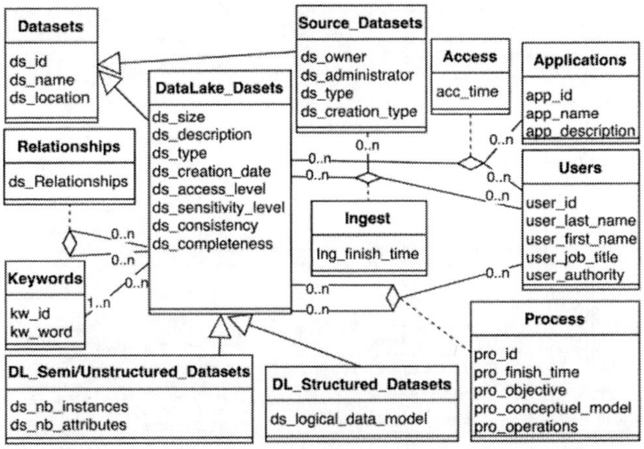

Figure 4. Scheme of the proposed conceptual metadata [13].

information, Quality metadata, which is the consistency and completeness of the data to ensure the reliability of the data sets and Security metadata, which includes data sensitivity and level of access.
Based on the classification in [13], a conceptual metadata schema, shown in Figure 4, is presented. A structured or unstructured dataset is ingested from one or more sources by one or more users. Datasets can be processed by users to transform into new datasets. Users can access datasets for their analyzes with certain tools. Datasets stored in a Data Lake can have relationships.

D. Model for integrating evolving heterogeneous data sources

In [16], a metadata model is proposed to describe the schemas and additional properties of datasets or datasets extracted from sources and transformed to obtain integrated data in order to perform the analysis in a flexible way. In addition, it keeps all changes that occur in the system. To collect metadata on the structure of data sources and to keep information on the changes that occur there, the conceptual model [16], presented in Figure 5, shows the metadata used.

In this section, we focus on the model classes that describe the schemas of the data sources and pipeline levels of data processing shown in Figure 5. The *Data Set class* is used to represent a collection of Data Items that are individual pieces of data. The *Data Set class* is divided into three subclasses according to the type and format. *Structured data Set* represents a relational database table where the data elements correspond to the columns of the table. *Semi-structured data* reflects the files in which the data elements are organized in a schema, which is not predefined. The *Type* attribute of a data element embedded in such a data source indicates its position in the schema. *Unstructured Data Sets* include data that has no recognized organization or schema, such as text files, images, other multimedia content, etc. A dataset can be obtained from a *Data Source* where it can be part of a *Highway Level* data processing pipeline level. In addition, information about the speed at, which data in the dataset is collected or updated by assigning one of the speed types and frequency attribute to the *Data Set class*.

In general, there are relationships between data elements in the same data set or between different data sets determined by the format of these data sets. These relationships are

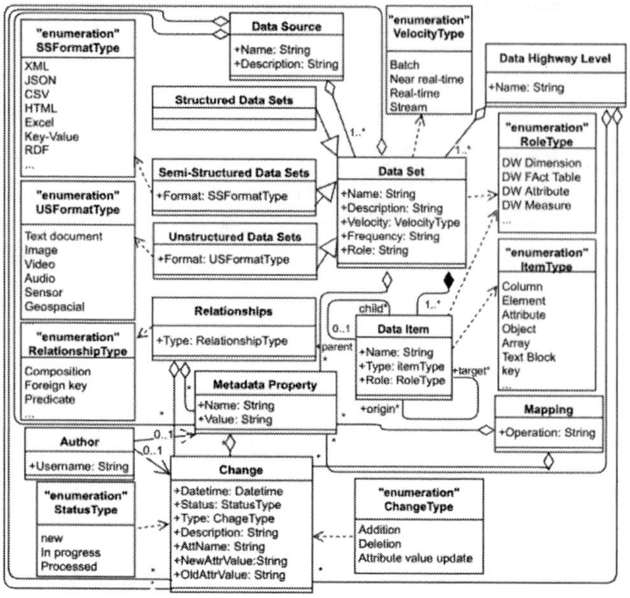

Figure 5. Conceptual diagram of the proposed metadata [16].

modeled by a *Relationship* association class that connects the child and parent data elements and assigns the corresponding relationship type. The *Equality* relationship type is assigned if two different dataset elements contain the same data.
To maintain the metadata of provenance of the data sets within the data processing pipeline and allow their lineage to be followed, a *Mapping* association-class has been introduced to define the way in which a target data element is derived from the elements of original data by a transformation that indicated in the *Operation* attribute of the *Mapping* class.
In the event that revolution is caused by a change in the value of an attribute of a model element, including the metadata property, the name of the attribute is saved as attribute $AttrName$ of the class *Change* and both the value before the modification ($OldAttrValue$ attribute) and after ($NewAttrValue$ attribute).

IV. Summary and Open Research Issues

According to the study carried out on these different metadata management existing models, some limits have been identified and may be the subject of research directions to explore.

A. Limits of existing models

Concerning the work of Paolo et al. [10], who propose a model based on a network or graph to represent and manage the data sources of a Data Lake:

- In terms of lexical similarity between keywords describing the data ingested within the Data Lake, the approach adopts the BabelNet [11] multilingual semantic network or ontology. As a result, the choice of the ontology domain depends on ingested data within the Data Lake.
- The relevance of the similarity measure in relation to the choice of ontology impacts the semantic representation of the Data Lake data. The weighted aggregation, the measure of similarity, and the choice of ontology contribute to the improvement of the semantic representation.
- The approach exploits the lexical similarities of character strings to carry out the mapping between the attributes that describe the data sources or the N-Grams measurement is used. Other metrics can be used (Cosine, Minkowski distance, etc.).
- The extraction of knowledge in this work is to find an optimal path in the graph representing result. This graph is evaluated with the metric (average local coefficient, density and transitive). Other metrics (Betweenness centrality, Closeness centrality, etc.) can be used.

When it comes to MEDAL [6], according to the classification of metadata relating to the typology category:

- Compared to intra-object metadata:
  - The change in values is represented by transformation, however, the updates concerning the structure of the data ingested in the Data Lake is not supported.
  - The risk of repetition of descriptive tags between the different representations is true for structured data (update of BD), but not for semi or unstructured data. For a better analysis, it is necessary to save the history of the data ingested in the DL.
- Compared to inter-object metadata:
  - The grouping of hypernodes is based on functions and, therefore, the choice of the latter is essential and impacts the categorization of hypernodes (in this case, some criteria have been cited (the origin of the data source, the type of the latter (structured, semi or unstructured)).
  - The possible relationships between metadata are represented by parental type. Indeed, it is possible to extend this relationship by other types, such as include, friend, and equal, which will be based on similarity measures.
- Compared to global metadata:
  - Requirement of tools to identify semantic sources to add them to the DL metadata representation graph.

However, there is no system that automatically extracts inter or intra-metadata from different types (structures, semi-structures, non-structures) of datasets. With regard to the system proposed [13], based on a generic and extensible classification of metadata:

- Compared to intra-object metadata:
  - Unstructured data sources have no schema and, therefore, of according to the definition metadata, will not have schematic metadata.
  - Furthermore, under the proposed definition of metadata, semantic metadata is based solely on descriptive text and requires tools for the extraction of descriptive tags.
- Compared to inter-object metadata:

- ◦ The similarity of the content is based only on the same attributes shared by the different data sets, hence the need to measure the similarity between attributes to further expand this similarity.
- ◦ The conceptual schema of metadata offers [13] takes into account the structural aspect of data sources or datasets. It does not deal with the semantic aspect intra or inter datasets because it is limited to the identification of the same attributes that appear in these datasets.

Finally, in [16], the model for the integration of evolving heterogeneous data sources, used to store metadata, describing the schemas of the implied data sets and their changes, is one of the central components of the data warehouse architecture in the context of Big Data.

- Within this model, there may be a link between an unstructured data set and structured / semi-structured data. These relationships are modeled by an association class Relationship, which is limited to two types: Parent-children or Equality. Equality happens when two elements of different data sets contain the same data, but the case of synonymous or equivalent data elements is not considered.
- In the case where the data set revolution is produced and is caused by a modification of the value of an attribute of an element of the model, the names of the old and new attributes are represented, but there is no change in the scheme, ie. the structure remains unchanged.

B. Summary and challenges (Open research)

In this context of metadata management within a Data Lake and to overcome the limitations mentioned above, research work can be oriented to:

- Enrich the possible relationships between the concepts that describe the data sources, based on the similarity measure score. Several types of relations can be exploited, such as Include, Friend, Equal, Assigned, according to these scores (at intervals for each relationship type).
- Compared with textual descriptions of data sources, extracting relevant descriptive tags enhances the semantic representation of ingested data within the Data Lake.
- Several similarity measures can be used to compare descriptive tags of the sources ingested within the Data Lake.
- Model a meta-metric that merges the results obtained according to several similarity measurement metrics.

V. CONCLUSION

In this paper, we have presented a comprehensive study of recent metadata models for Data Lake that points out their rationales, strengths, and weaknesses. Specifically, we have provided a layered taxonomy of recent metadata models and their specifications. Afterward, a study of recent work dealing with DL metadata management models was conducted to classify metadata in 3 categories: by level, typology, and content. Based on such a study, an in-depth analysis of the main characteristics, strengths, and missing points is presented. Consequently, we have bridged the gap in the literature and identified open research issues that require community attention. As future work, we plan to propose a meta-metric that merges the results obtained according to several similarity measurement metrics to enrich the possible relationships between the concepts that describe the data sources ingested in Data Lakes.

REFERENCES

[1] N. Miloslavskaya and T. Alexander, "Big data, fast data and data lake concepts," Procedia Computer Science, vol. 88, 2016, pp. 300–305.

[2] I. Suriarachchi and B. Plale, "Crossing analytics systems: A case for integrated provenance in data lakes," in e-Science (e-Science), 2016 IEEE 12th International Conference on. IEEE, 2016, pp. 349–354.

[3] S. Badih, G. Gregory, and Y. Q. Herman, "Metadata-driven data management platform," Sep. 6 2018, uS Patent App. 15/909,833.

[4] C. Diamantini, G. Paolo, L. Musarella, P. Domenico, E. Storti, and D. Ursino, "A new metadata model to uniformly handle heterogeneous data lake sources," in European Conference on Advances in Databases and Information Systems. Springer, 2018, pp. 165–177.

[5] Oram, "Managing the data lake," in Managing the Data Lake OReilly, Sebastopol, CA, USA, 2015. IEEE, 2015.

[6] P. N. Sawadogo, S. Etienne, F. Ccile, F. Eric, L. Sabine, and D. Jrme, "Metadata systems for data lakes: Models and features," in ADBIS 2019 Short Papers, Workshops BBIGAP, QAUCA, SemBDM, SIMPDA, M2P, MADEISD and Doctoral Consortium Bled, Slovenia, September, 811, 2019, Proceedings. IEEE, 2019, p. 440.

[7] A. Alserafi and O. R. A. Abello, "Towards information profiling: Data lake content metadata management," in 2016 IEEE 16th International Conference on Data Mining Workshops (ICDMW). IEEE, 2016, pp. 178–185.

[8] F. Naumann, "Data profiling revisited," ACM SIGMOD Record, vol. 42, no. 4, 2014, pp. 40–49.

[9] R. Hauch, A. Miller, and R. Cardwell, "Information intelligence: metadata for information discovery, access, and integration," in Proceedings of the 2005 ACM SIGMOD international conference on Management of data, 2005, pp. 793–798.

[10] P. L. Giudice, L. Musarella, G. Sofo, and D. Ursino, "An approach to extracting complex knowledge patterns among concepts belonging to structured, semi-structured and unstructured sources in a data lake," vol. 478. Elsevier, 2019, pp. 606–626.

[11] R. Navigli and S. Ponzetto, "Babelnet: The automatic construction, evaluation and application of a wide-coverage multilingual semantic network," in Artificial Intelligence, vol. 193, IEEE. Elsevier, 2012, pp. 217–250.

[12] W. H. Gomaa, A. A. Fahmy et al., "A survey of text similarity approaches," vol. 68, no. 13. Citeseer, 2013, pp. 13–18.

[13] F. Ravat and Y. Zhao, "Metadata management for data lakes," in European Conference on Advances in Databases and Information Systems. CCIS, vol. 1064. Springer, Cham., 2019, pp. 37–44.

[14] H. Alon, K. Flip, N. N. Fridman, O. Christopher, P. Neoklis, R. Sudip, and W. S. Euijong, "Managing google's data lake: an overview of the goods system." IEEE Data Eng. Bull., vol. 39, no. 3, 2016, pp. 5–14.

[15] B. Bilalli, A. Abelló, T. Aluja-Banet, and R. Wrembel, "Towards intelligent data analysis: The metadata challenge." in IoTBD, 2016, pp. 331–338.

[16] D. Solodovnikova, L. Niedrite, and A. Niedritis, "On metadata support for integrating evolving heterogeneous data sources," in European Conference on Advances in Databases and Information Systems. Springer, 2019, pp. 378–390.

An Intelligent Recommender System for E-learning Process Personalization: A Case Study in Maritime Education

Stefanos I. Karnavas
Merchant Marine Academy of Oinousses
Oinousses, Greece
e-mail: stefkarnavas@gmail.com

Alexandros Bousdekis
Business Informatics Lab, Department of Business Administration
School of Business, Athens University of Economics and Business
Athens, Greece
e-mail: albous@mail.ntua.gr

Stavroula Barbounaki
Merchant Marine Academy of Aspropyrgos
Aspropyrgos, Greece
e-mail: sbarbounaki@yahoo.gr

Dimitris K. Kardaras
Business Informatics Lab, Department of Business Administration
School of Business, Athens University of Economics and Business
Athens, Greece
e-mail: dkkardaras@yahoo.co.uk

***Abstract*—The lockdown due to the pandemic of COVID-19 led to an unprecedented impact on education. Higher education institutions were forced to shift rapidly to distance and online learning. On the one hand, this fact revealed the weaknesses of adoption and utilization of e-learning strategies and technologies, but, on the other hand, it resulted in a digital revolution in education. However, the wide adoption of e-learning strategies and technologies and the complete transformation of the physical learning process to a virtual one pose the challenge of personalization of the learning process. This paper proposes a recommender system for supporting the professors in higher education in understanding their students' needs so that he/she adapts the e-learning process accordingly. To do this, it utilizes learning profile theory and it implements k-means clustering and Bayesian Networks (BN) The proposed approach was applied to a maritime educational institution.**

Keywords-learning profiles; learning styles; higher education; k-means clustering, Bayesian network; classification.

I. INTRODUCTION

According to a European Commission's report on digital skills in education in 2013, an average of 65% of students in EU countries never used digital textbooks, exercise software, broadcasts/podcasts, simulations or learning games [1]. Since then, higher education institutions have shown a persistent concern with enhancing students' academic performance through the use of innovative technologies that offer new ways of delivering and producing university education [2]. From an economic point of view, the industry of e-learning has developed considerably in the last decade. The market of e-learning all over the world will be over 243 billion dollars in 2022 [3].

The pandemic of COVID-19 led most of the governments around the world to impose lockdown, social/physical distancing, avoiding face-to-face teaching-learning, and restrictions on travelling and immigration [4]. It caused the closing of classrooms all over the world and forced 1.5 billion students and 63 million educators to suddenly modify their face-to-face academic practices [3]. This closure led to an unprecedented impact on education. Higher education institutions were forced to shift rapidly to distance and online learning. On the one hand, this fact revealed the weaknesses of adoption and utilization of e-learning strategies and technologies [4] [5]; but, on the other hand, it resulted in a digital revolution through online lectures, teleconferencing, digital open books, online examination, and interaction at virtual environments [6].

E-learning is the use of new multimedia technologies and the Internet to improve the quality of learning by facilitating access to resources and services, as well as remote exchange and collaboration [7] [8]. It has a great potential from the educational perspective and it has been one of the main research lines of educational technology in the last decades [3]. Particular attention has been given on understanding the adoption factors related to e-learning services satisfaction and acceptance by students and tutors [5] [7] [9].

However, the wide use of e-learning due to COVID-19 demonstrated inequalities as a result of previously underestimating the potential of e-learning and its exclusion from the digital education projects of educational institutions [3]. A considerable amount of literature has investigated inequalities between developed and developing countries [3] [10]. However, the wide adoption of e-learning strategies and technologies and the complete transformation of the physical learning process to a virtual one pose the challenge of personalization according to different learning profiles [11], a research area rather underexplored. E-learning provides people with a flexible way to learn allowing learning on demand and reducing the associated costs [7]. E-learning personalization is emerged as a major challenge [11] [12], especially in today's fast adoption of this alternative way of learning.

Despite the large amount of research works dealing with learning profiles in physical classrooms, these models should be further investigated and validated in the virtual classrooms, during the e-learning process. To this end, the contribution of e-learning to several learning factors according to the learning profiles has the potential to reveal the acceptance of e-learning by different learning profiles and to result in e-learning process personalization in order to mitigate the respective inequalities.

The objective of the current paper is to develop an intelligent recommender system for supporting the professors in higher education in understanding their students' needs so that he/she adapts the e-learning process accordingly. In addition, the proposed recommender system is able to classify new records (i.e. students) to the appropriate learning profiles, e.g., in order to support the organization of the class groups. The proposed approach was applied to a maritime educational institution. The rest of the paper is organized as follows: Section II presents the related work on methods and approaches for evaluating students' acceptance of the e-learning process as well as learning profile models for learning personalization. Section III describes the research methodology and the proposed approach for the development of an intelligent recommender system for e-learning process personalization. Section IV presents the results from the adoption of the proposed methodology on a dataset of 268 students in the maritime education. Section V concludes the paper and outlines our plans for future work.

II. RELATED WORK

Existing literature is quite rich on evaluating students' experience, satisfaction and acceptance of the e-learning process. In general, earlier studies focused more on content, customization and technology, while more recent studies focused on students' attitude and interaction, expectations, acceptance and satisfaction [9] [13]. To this end, there is an emerging trend towards the identification of the key factors for the adoption of e-learning strategies and technologies.

Several studies have used the original version of the classic model, the DeLone & McLean (D&M) IS Success Model [14] to measure and evaluate the success of e-learning systems [15]-[17]. The use of virtual learning environments in addition to classroom study (blended learning), were surveyed by [18]. They concluded that the students' performance of the virtual learning environment support had better results than those having only face to face learning. The identified key satisfaction factors are information quality, system quality, instructor attitude toward e-learning, diversity in assessment, and learner perceived interaction with others.

The authors in [7] identified clear governance structure and the need of organized distribution of planning responsibilities and implementation as the main adoption factors. In [19], the authors concluded that perceived usefulness, ease of use, perceived enjoyment, network externality factor, system factor, individual factors, and social factors are the main e-learning acceptance predictors. Student interface, learning community, content, and customization as well as ease of use of web courses have also been identified to have a significant impact on e-learning acceptance [20] [21].

In [22], the authors concluded that student e-learning adoption and attitudes in the university context are academic achievements mediated by digital readiness and academic engagement. In [23], the authors proposed an e-learning tools acceptance model in order to examine the level of acceptance and critical factors of virtual learning tools among university students in developing countries. Results confirm a strong relation between the perceived usefulness and the instructor preparation and autonomy in learning, as well as between the ease of use and the perceived self-efficacy perception. The reseach work of [24] developed a Technology Acceptance Model (TAM) for e-learning. The results indicated that system quality, computer self-efficacy, and computer playfulness have a significant impact on perceived ease of use of e-learning system. Furthermore, information quality, perceived enjoyment, and accessibility were found to have a positive influence on perceived ease of use and perceived usefulness of e-learning system.

The authors in [25] applied process mining methods in order to discover students' self-regulated learning processes during e-learning. They identified a high presence of actions related to forum-supported collaborative learning among the students who finally passed the exams and an absence of those in their failing classmates. The research work of [5] concluded that the main factors affecting the usage of e-learning are: technological factors, e-learning system quality factors, trust factors, self-efficacy factors and cultural aspects. Therefore, apart from the challenges related to the technological infrastructure, change management, course design, computer self-efficacy and financial support are also issues of outmost importance.

Learning personalization is an important topic in educational sciences. Since different people learn in different ways, it is important to create and adapt the e-learning process in order to maximize and speed up the learning process [11]. The need to adapt teaching strategies to the student's preferences is a reality in classrooms, be they physical or virtual [26] [27]. However, this does not mean that a method should be created for each student in a classroom, but that the best form of interaction for each of them be identified, building groups of learners with common characteristics [28]. Learning styles are cognitive, affective and psychological traits that determine how a student interacts and reacts in a learning environment [29]. The idea is to identify the marked characteristics of a given learner so that these traits influence his learning process.

Several learning profile models have been developed in the literature, such as the Myers-Briggs Type Indicator – MBTI, Kolb's Experiential Learning Model, the Hermann Brain Dominance Instrument (HBDI), the Dunn and Dunn Model, the Felder-Silverman Model, and the Honey and Mumford Model [26] [27]. With the wide adoption of e-learning strategies and technologies, there is the need for applying and validating learning profile models in the digital and online learning era. For example, in [11], the authors investigated the e-learning personalization aiming at keeping students motivated and engaged. To that end, they proposed the use of k-means algorithm to cluster students based on 12 engagement metrics divided into two categories: interaction-related and effort-related. The research work of [27] presented the architecture of a system that realizes an evaluation of learning profiles based on categories of student preferences. The profile models were built according to categories of student preferences based on the proposal of learning styles put forward by [29].

III. RESEARCH METHODOLOGY

A. Data Collection and Learning Profile Model Selection

The data was collected in the form of an online questionnaire of 80 questions addressed to students of higher educational institution. Each question was in the form of Likert scale (1: Strongly Disagree – 5: Strongly Agree) and it was related to one out of the four learning styles as defined by the Honey and Mumford Model [30]: *activist, reflector, pragmatist*, and *theorist*. For example, in an ideal scenario that a student has answered 5: Strongly Agree to all the questions matching to the "activist" learning profile and 1: Strongly Disagree to all the others, he/she is classified as "activist".

Activist refers to an individual's preference for active involvement in the learning activity (through problem solving, discussion, creating their own models). *Reflector* learns best by watching and thinking about what is happening. The reflector responds more positively to learning activities where there is time to observe, reflect and think and work in a detailed manner. *Pragmatist* wants to know how to put what they are learning into practice in the real world. They experiment with theories, ideas, and techniques and take the time to think about how what they've done relates to reality. *Theorist* seeks to understand the theory behind the action. They enjoy following models and reading up on facts to better engage in the learning process.

B. Classification for Structuring the Learning Profiles

The classification of the student to the learning profiles is not straightforward (like in the aforementioned ideal scenario) since they may have characteristics of more than one profile. Therefore, according to the given answers, the k-means clustering algorithm was applied in order to assign the respondents to 4 clusters ($k=4$) matching to the aforementioned learning profiles.

k-means clustering is a method of vector quantization that aims to partition n observations into k clusters in which each observation belongs to the cluster with the nearest mean (cluster centers or cluster centroid) [31]. k-means clustering minimizes the within-cluster variances (squared Euclidean distances). Given a set of observations $(x_1, x_2, ..., x_n)$, where each observation is a d-dimensional real vector, k-means clustering aims to partition the n observations into k ($\leq n$) sets $S=\{S_1, S_2, ..., S_k\}$ so as to minimize the within-cluster sum of squares (WCSS) (i.e. variance). Formally, the objective is to find:

$$\underset{\mathbf{S}}{\arg\min} \sum_{i=1}^{k} \sum_{\mathbf{x} \in S_i} \|\mathbf{x} - \boldsymbol{\mu}_i\|^2 = \underset{\mathbf{S}}{\arg\min} \sum_{i=1}^{k} |S_i| \operatorname{Var} S_i \tag{1}$$

where $\boldsymbol{\mu}_i$ is the mean of points in S_i. This is equivalent to minimizing the pairwise squared deviations of points in the same cluster:

$$\underset{\mathbf{S}}{\arg\min} \sum_{i=1}^{k} \frac{1}{2|S_i|} \sum_{\mathbf{x},\mathbf{y} \in S_i} \|\mathbf{x} - \mathbf{y}\|^2 \tag{2}$$

The equivalence can be deduced from the identity:

$$\sum_{\mathbf{x} \in S_i} \|\mathbf{x} - \boldsymbol{\mu}_i\|^2 = \sum_{\mathbf{x} \neq \mathbf{y} \in S_i} (\mathbf{x} - \boldsymbol{\mu}_i)(\boldsymbol{\mu}_i - \mathbf{y}) \tag{3}$$

Because the total variance is constant, this is equivalent to maximizing the sum of squared deviations between points in different clusters (Between-Cluster Sum of Squares, BCSS), which follows from the law of total variance.

C. Modelling the Relationships between Learning Profiles and E-learning Preferences

Subsequently, the proposed approach models the relationships between the learning profiles and e-learning contribution to learning factors as derived from the questionnaire. To do this, a Bayesian Network (BN) is applied aiming at identifying these causal and uncertain relationships. A BN, also known as belief network, is defined as a pair $B = (G, \Theta)$. $G = (V, E)$ is a Directed Acyclic Graph (DAG) where $V = \{v_1, ..., v_n\}$ is a collection of n nodes, $E \subset V \times V$ a collection of edges and a set of parameters Θ containing all the Conditional Probabilities (CP) of the network [32]. Each node $v \in V$ of the graph represents a random variable X_V with a state space $\boldsymbol{X_V}$ which can be either discrete or continuous. An edge $(v_i, v_j) \in E$ represents the conditional dependence between two nodes v_i, $v_j \in V$ where v_i is the parent of child v_j. If two nodes are not connected by an edge, they are conditional independent. Because a node can have more than one parent, let π_v the set of parents for a node $v \in V$.

Therefore each random variable is independent of all nodes $V \setminus \pi_v$. For each node, a Conditional Probability Table (CPT) contains the CP distribution with parameters $\theta_{xi|\pi i} := P(x_i|\pi_i) \in \Theta$ for each realization x_i of X_i conditioned on π_i. The joint probability distribution over V is visualized by the BN and can be defined as:

$$P(X_1, \ldots, X_n) = \prod_{i=1}^{n} P(X_i|\pi_i) \tag{4}$$

With BN, inference for what-if analysis can be supported, either top-down (predictive support) or bottom-up (diagnostic support). If a random variable which is represented by a node is observed, the node is called an evidence node; otherwise, it is a hidden node [33]. Based on the learning profiles derived from the questionnaire, a BN with two layers was developed: at the top layer (i.e. learning profiles), there are 4 parent nodes matching to the respective clusters of students.

At the bottom layer (i.e. e-learning contribution to learning factors), there are 9 child nodes referring to 9 e-learning factors grouping the questions. In this way, the model identifies the preferences of each learning profile by assessing the impact of e-learning on the learning process of each profile. Therefore, according to the learning profile, the user is able to select the appropriate learning strategies aiming at personalizing the e-learning process.

D. *Predicting the Class Attribute of E-learning Impact*

At any time, the user of the recommender system is able to make queries in order to investigate particular relationships along with their associated CPTs. Moreover, the model incorporates a Naïve Bayes classifier for predicting the class attribute of a learning profile as soon as new records of students' responses are inserted into the database.

Naïve Bayes classifier is highly scalable, requiring a number of parameters linear in the number of variables in a learning problem. Maximum-likelihood training can be done by evaluating a closed-form expression, which takes linear time, rather than by expensive iterative approximation as used for many other types of classifiers [34]. Prediction of the class attribute can be performed even if the questionnaire is not completely answered.

IV. RESULTS

The proposed approach was applied on a dataset of 268 students of a maritime higher educational institution in Greece. The transformation of maritime from highly labour- to capital-intensive industry contributed to the presence of tertiary education in maritime studies [35]. However, the learning process in maritime education faces additional challenges due to the structure of their programs, the tendency of undergraduate students to combine studies and work, the internationalization, specialization, and standardization [35]-[37]. These make maritime education an interesting case study for the validation of e-learning process personalization.

The implementation and execution of the experiments were performed using the sklearn.cluster library of Python [38] for the k-means clustering algorithm and the BN functionalities of the pgmpy (Probabilistic Graphical Models using Python) package [39]. After having structured the learning profiles of the respondents, the BN is created and the CPTs are calculated, as shown in Figure 1. Table I presents the highest and the lowest CPs of the e-learning contribution to learning factors given the learning profiles. Therefore, the highest CP is the one of a student being activist given the answers of the second row that is 38.6%. The lowest CP is the one of a student being activist given the answers of the last row that is 5.6%. According to the queries posed by the user, various calculations can be done. As already mentioned, the model can also serve as a classifier for predicting the class attribute of learning factors as soon as new records of students are received and classified through the k-means clustering algorithm.

TABLE I. CPS OF THE E-LEARNING CONTRIBUTION TO LEARNING FACTORS GIVEN THE LEARNING PROFILES

	E-learning contribution	Learning profile	CP
Highest CPs	F1={Neutral}, F2={Agree}, F3={Disagree}, F4={Agree}, F5={Strongly Disagree}, F6={Disagree}, F7={Neutral}, F8={Strongly Disagree}, F9={Agree}	Activist	0.386
	F1={Disagree}, F2={Disagree}, F3={Agree}, F4={Strongly Disagree}, F5={ Disagree}, F6={Agree}, F7={Neutral}, F8={Neutral}, F9={Disagree}	Theorist	0.295
Lowest CPs	F1={Stongly Agree}, F2={Disagree}, F3={Strongly Agree}, F4={Neutral}, F5={ Disagree}, F6={Strongly Disagree}, F7={Neutral}, F8={Strongly Disagree}, F9={Disagree}	Reflector	0.081
	F1={Agree}, F2={Strongly Disagree}, F3={Agree}, F4={Strongly Disagree}, F5={Strongly Agree}, F6={Neutral}, F7={Agree}, F8={Agree}, F9={Strongly Disagree}	Activist	0.056

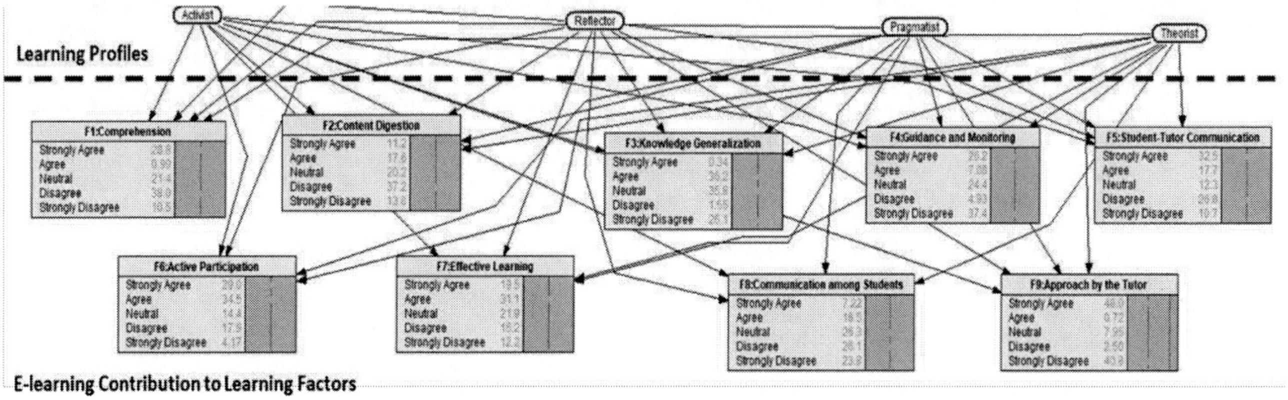

Figure 1. The Bayesian Network structure for modelling the relationships between learning profiles and e-learning contribution to learning factors.

In order to evaluate its classification effectiveness, we inserted additional records, derived from more questionnaires addressed to students of the maritime educational institution, and we created the confusion matrix according to Table II in order to estimate the precision and the recall of the classifier using the (5) and (6) [40].

TABLE II. CONFUSION MATRIX

	Predicted Positive	Predicted Negative
Actual Positive	True Positive (TP) = 31	False Negative (FN) = 6
Actual Negative	False Positive (FP) = 4	True Negative (TN) = 22

$$Precision = \frac{TP}{TP + FP} = \frac{31}{31 + 4} = 88.57\% \quad (5)$$

$$Recall = \frac{TP}{TP + FN} = \frac{31}{31 + 6} = 83.78\% \quad (6)$$

The Precision results are quite satisfactory, while the Recall results can be further improved. We should also take into account that modelling human behavior, such as the learning process, has a high degree of uncertainty [41]. Moreover, the BN model sticks to the initially identified relationships, i.e., the ones that have been mined during the model training. Therefore, when new relationships, not previously identified, are added, they are not classified correctly. These records include values that are not frequent, so they are not critical for decision making.

V. CONCLUSIONS AND FUTURE WORK

During the last years, e-learning has been gaining an increasing attention in higher education. Especially during the last months, higher education institutions were forced to shift rapidly to distance and online learning. On the one hand, this fact revealed the weaknesses of adoption and utilization of e-learning strategies and technologies, but, on the other hand, it resulted in a digital revolution in education. A major challenge was to apply e-learning strategies and technologies for supporting e-learning personalization. In this paper, we proposed an intelligent recommender system for e-learning process personalization.

The proposed approach is based on the Honey and Mumford Model of learning profiles and utilized k-means clustering and BNs in order to classify the students to learning profiles and to reveal relationships with the contribution of e-learning to several learning factors. The proposed approach was applied to a dataset of 268 students in maritime education and we presented indicative examples of queries. We also validated the model in terms of its precision and recall in predicting the learning profile when new records are inserted into the database.

Regarding our future work, we plan to incorporate additional learning factors with respect to the e-learning impact. Moreover, we plan to apply more machine learning and data analytics methods, with an emphasis on fuzzy methods, in combination with different learning profile models. Finally, we will plan to expand our research to various universities in order to obtain more generalized results.

REFERENCES

[1] D. Gubiani, I. Cristea, and T. Urbančič, "Introducing e-learning to a traditional university: a case-study." in Qualitative and Quantitative Models in Socio-Economic Systems and Social Work, pp. 225-241, Springer, Cham, 2020.

[2] H. J. Kim, A. J. Hong, and H. D. Song, "The roles of academic engagement and digital readiness in students' achievements in university e-learning environments," Int. J. of Educ. Tec. in Hig. Educ., vol. 16, no. 1, pp. 21-29, 2019.

[3] J. Valverde-Berrocoso, M. D. C. Garrido-Arroyo, C. Burgos-Videla, and M. B. Morales-Cevallos, "Trends in Educational Research about e-Learning: A Systematic Literature Review (2009–2018)," Sust., vol. 12, no 12, pp. 5153, 2020.

[4] N. Kapasia, P. Paul, A. Roy, J. Saha, A. Zaveri, R. Mallick, and P. Chouhan, "Impact of lockdown on learning status of undergraduate and postgraduate students during COVID-19 pandemic in West Bengal, India," Child. and Youth Serv. Rev., vol. 116, pp. 105194, 2020.

[5] M. A. Almaiah, A. Al-Khasawneh, and A. Althunibat, "Exploring the critical challenges and factors influencing the E-learning system usage during COVID-19 pandemic," Educ. and Inf. Tech., vol. 1, 2020.

[6] T. Gonzalez et al., "Influence of COVID-19 confinement in students performance in higher education," arXiv preprint arXiv:2004.09545, 2020.

[7] W. M. Al-Rahmi, N. Alias, M. S. Othman, A. I. Alzahrani, O. Alfarraj, A. A. Saged, and N. S. A. Rahman, "Use of e-learning by university students in Malaysian higher educational institutions: a case in Universiti Teknologi Malaysia," IEEE Acc., vol. 6, pp. 14268-14276, 2018.

[8] E. R. Vershitskaya, A. V. Mikhaylova, S. I. Gilmanshina, E. M. Dorozhkin, and V. V. Epaneshnikov, "Present-day management of universities in Russia: Prospects and challenges of e-learning," Educ. and Inf. Tech., vol. 25, no. 1, pp. 611-621, 2020.

[9] W. A. Cidral, T. Oliveira, M. Di Felice, and M. Aparicio, "E-learning success determinants: Brazilian empirical study," Comp. & Educ., vol. 122, pp. 273-290, 2018.

[10] E. Vázquez-Cano, M. León Urrutia, M. E. Parra-González, and E. López Meneses, "Analysis of interpersonal competences in the use of ICT in the Spanish University Context," Sust., vol. 12, no. 2, pp. 476, 2020.

[11] A. Moubayed, M. Injadat, A. Shami, and H. Lutfiyya, "Student engagement level in e-learning environment: Clustering using k-means," Amer. J. of Dist. Educ., pp. 1-20, 2020.

[12] J. Shailaja and R. Sridaran, "Taxonomy of e-learning challenges and an insight to blended learning," in 2014 International Conference on Intelligent Computing Applications,pp. 310-314, IEEE, 2014.

[13] H. J. Chen, "Clarifying the impact of surprise in e-learning system design based on university students with multiple learning goals orientation," Educ. and Inf. Tech., pp. 1-20, 2020

[14] W. H. Delone and E. R. McLean, "The DeLone and McLean model of information systems success: a ten-year update," J. of Man. Inf. Syst., vol. 19, no. 4, pp. 9-30, 2003.

[15] C. W. Holsapple and A. Lee-Post, "Defining, assessing, and promoting e-learning success: An information systems perspective," Dec. Sci. J. of Innov. Educ., vol. 4, no. 1, pp. 67-85, 2006.

[16] H. F. Lin and G. G. Lee, "Determinants of success for online communities: an empirical study," Beh. & Inf. Tech., vol. 25, no. 6, pp. 479-488, 2006.

[17] H. F. Lin, "Measuring online learning systems success: Applying the updated DeLone and McLean model," Cyberpsyc. & Beh., vol. 10, no. 6, pp. 817-820, 2007.

[18] D. Stricker, D.Weibel, and B. Wissmath, "Efficient learning using a virtual learning environment in a university class," Comp. & Educ., vol. 56, no. 2, pp. 495-504, 2011.

[19] Y. M. Cheng, "Antecedents and consequences of e-learning acceptance," Inf. Sys. J., vol. 21, no. 3, pp. 269-299, 2011.

[20] Y. S. Wang (2003). Assessment of learner satisfaction with asynchronous electronic learning systems. Information & Management, 41(1), 75-86.

[21] H. M. Selim, "An empirical investigation of student acceptance of course websites," Comp. & Educ., vol. 40, no. 4, pp. 343-360, 2003.

[22] H. J. Kim, A. J. Hong, & H. D. Song, "The roles of academic engagement and digital readiness in students' achievements in university e-learning environments," Int. J. of Educ. Tech. in High. Educ., vol. 16, no.1, pp. 21, 2019.

[23] A. Valencia-Arias, S. Chalela-Naffah, and J. Bermúdez-Hernández, "A proposed model of e-learning tools acceptance among university students in developing countries," Educ. and Inf. Tech., vol. 24, no. 2, pp. 1057-1071, 2019.

[24] S. A. Salloum, A. Q. M. Alhamad, M. Al-Emran, A. A. Monem, and K. Shaalan, "Exploring students' acceptance of e-learning through the development of a comprehensive technology acceptance model," IEEE Acc., vol. 7, pp. 128445-128462, 2019.

[25] R. Cerezo, A. Bogarín, M. Esteban, and C. Romero, "Process mining for self-regulated learning assessment in e-learning," J. of Comp. in High. Educ., vol. 32, no. 1, pp. 74-88, 2020.

[26] C. Heaton-Shrestha, C. Gipps, P. Edirisingha, and T. Linsey, "Learning and e-learning in HE: the relationship between student learning style and VLE use," Res. Pap. in Educ., vol. 22, no. 4, pp. 443-464, 2007.

[27] L. A. Zaina, and G. Bressan, "Classification of learning profile based on categories of student preferences," in 2008 38th Annual Frontiers in Education Conference, pp. F4E-1, IEEE, 2008.

[28] N. A. Fabio, J. A. Self, and S. P. Lajoie, "Modeling the process, not the product, of learning," Comp. as Cogn. Tools, vol. 2, pp.133-162, 2000.

[29] R. M. Felder and R. Brent, "Understanding student differences," J. of Eng. Educ., vol. 94, no. 1, pp. 57-72, 2005.

[30] P. Honey and A. Mumford, "The learning styles helper's guide," Maidenhead: Peter Honey Publications, 2000.

[31] H. P. Kriegel, E. Schubert, and A. Zimek, "The (black) art of runtime evaluation: Are we comparing algorithms or implementations?," Knowl. and Inf. Sys., vol. 52, no. 2, pp. 341-378, 2017.

[32] J. Pearl, "Probabilistic reasoning in intelligent systems: networks of plausible inference," Elsevier, 2014.

[33] T. D. Nielsen and F. V. Jensen, "Bayesian networks and decision graphs," Springer Science & Business Media, 2009.

[34] T. Hastie, R. Tibshirani, and J. Friedman, "The elements of statistical learning: data mining, inference, and prediction," Springer Science & Business Media, 2009.

[35] A. A. Pallis and A. K. Ng, "Pursuing maritime education: an empirical study of students' profiles, motivations and expectations," Marit. Pol. & Manag., vol. 38, no. 4, pp. 369-393, 2011.

[36] Y. Y. Lau & A. K. Ng, "The motivations and expectations of students pursuing maritime education," WMU J. of Marit. Aff., vol. 14, no. 2, pp. 313-331, 2015.

[37] X. Chen, X., Bai, and Y. Xiao, "The application of E-learning in maritime education and training in China," TransNav: Int. J. on Mar. Nav. & Saf. of Sea Transp., vol. 11, no. 2, 2017.

[38] F. Pedregosa et al., "Scikit-learn: Machine learning in Python," J. of Mach. Learn. Res., vol. 12, pp. 2825-2830, 2011.

[39] A. Ankan and A. Panda, "pgmpy: Probabilistic graphical models using python," in Proceedings of the 14th Python in Science Conference (SCIPY 2015), Citeseer, vol. 10, 2015.

[40] C. Goutte and E. Gaussier, "A probabilistic interpretation of precision, recall and F-score, with implication for evaluation," in European conference on information retrieval, pp. 345-359, Springer, Berlin, Heidelberg, 2005.

[41] A. A. Chaaraoui, P. Climent-Pérez, and F. Flórez-Revuelta, "A review on vision techniques applied to human behaviour analysis for ambient-assisted living," Exp. Sys. with Appl., vol. 39, no. 12, pp. 10873-10888, 2012.

Hybrid Transactional and Analytical Processing Databases: A Systematic Literature Review

Daniel Hieber
Dept. of Computer Science
Aalen University
Aalen, Germany
Email: daniel.hieber@hs-aalen.de

Gregor Grambow
Dept. of Computer Science
Aalen University
Aalen, Germany
Email: gregor.grambow@hs-aalen.de

***Abstract*—Hybrid Transactional and Analytical Processing databases (HTAP, OLxP) are an emerging sector of databases combining Online Transactional Processing and Online Analytical Processing in the same system. Such databases yield many advantages like the reduction of the total cost of ownership or the elimination of redundant data sets for analytical and live data. Therefore, both Gartner and Forrester Research see disruptive potential in HTAP databases. While following a common goal, the database architectures of HTAP databases are quite diverse. The solutions range from scaled-up single server systems, using Multi Version Concurrency Control to keep their data consistent while at the same time executing thousands of queries, to scaled-out clusters of many servers using last writer wins approaches to allow even faster transactional processing. The development of HTAP databases resulted in various advances in the database sector like the creation of new index and data structures or improvements of existing concurrency control implementations. This paper provides a comprehensive summary of these implementations, giving an overview of the last decade of research on the emerging sector of HTAP Processing databases and discussing fundamental involved technologies.**

***Keywords*—Hybrid Transactional Analytical Processing; HTAP; Database; Literature Study; OLxP.**

I. INTRODUCTION

The need to analyse data in realtime and not to rely on copies of old databases combined with the growing wish of companies to gather all data in one database lead to the rise of Hybrid Transactional Analytical Processing, a term coined by Gartner [1] in 2014. But, even before that there has already been active research in the area. This systematic literature review summarizes the research on HTAP over the past 10 years.

Solving the problems of keeping data in two separated databases and at the same time reducing the total cost of ownership by introducing one unified system instead, HTAP efficiently combines Online Transactional Processing and Online Analytical Processing capabilities in one system. Therefore, both Gartner [2] and Forrester Research [3] see disruptive potential in HTAP.

In this review, the basics of the different fundamental architectures for HTAP database systems like HyPer [4] and SAP HANA [5] are explained. Further different approaches regarding the concrete implementations and optimization approaches are introduced. The aim of this systematic literature review is to reflect the current state of research in an ordered way, as well as to highlight important decisions leading to todays implementations.

This remainder of this paper is organized as follows: Section 2 provides background on database processing paradigms covered in this paper. Section 3 describes the underlying literature review process in detail. Section 4 discusses the findings and provides a comprehensive overview of the current development and research state of HTAP. Finally, Section 5 summarizes the provided work, supplying all required information in a short form.

II. BACKGROUND

This section provides some background information regarding the database processing paradigms covered in this paper.

A. Online Transaction Processing

Online Transaction Processing (OLTP) describes a category of data processing that is focused on transaction-oriented tasks. The workload is heavily write oriented, consisting of insert, update and delete operations. The size of data involved is usually relatively small, while the amount of transactions can be massive.

Features like normalization and ACID (Atomicity, Consistency, Isolation, Durability) are required by OLTP to function efficiently. Besides fast processing and highest availability, data consistency is also one of the most important features of OLTP databases.

B. Online Analytical Processing

Online Analytical Processing (OLAP) is focused on complex queries for dataset analysis. The workload is read heavy and can include enormous datasets. In order to efficiently analyse such big amounts of data, intelligent indexing and fast read times are necessary. OLAP workloads are resource heavy and require high performance systems.

C. Hybrid Transactional Analytical Processing

Hybrid Transactional Analytical Processing (HTAP) combines both OLTP and OLAP in one database. Therefore, writing and analyzing data is efficiently handled in the same database, removing the need to run two separate systems and thereby reducing implementation efforts, maintenance and cost. However, the resource intensive workload of OLAP

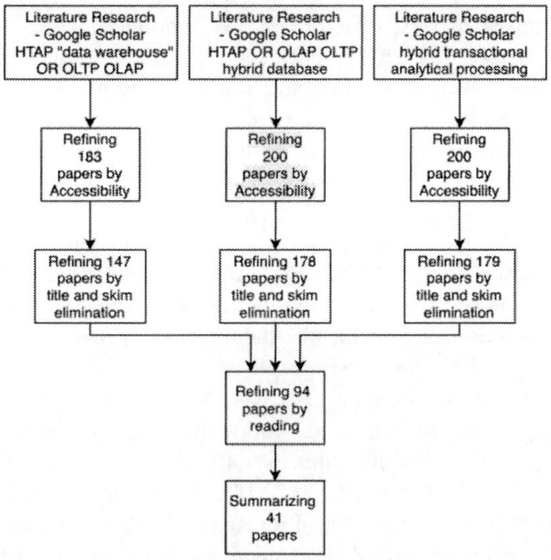

Figure 1. Literature Review Process.

queries and the required high availability of OLTP compete with each other and require new solutions to work on the same system.

III. Literature Review Methodology

Despite the existence of the term HTAP since 2014, many researchers still did not adopt it. To ensure a comprehensive and high-quality literature base for the review, several searches were carried out.

In the study, Kitchenham's systematic review procedure [6] was employed. The following steps were pursued:

1) Determining the topic of the research
2) Extraction of the studies from literature considering exclusion and inclusion criteria
3) Evaluation of the quality of the studies
4) Analysis of the data
5) Report of the results

The reviewing process (Figure 1) was conducted via Google Scholar as this search engine provided far more results than other search engines, which also included most results of the other engines. Searches with other engines did not return the desired quantity of material with the used queries, preventing a sophisticated review of the topic.

Using Google Scholar, the volume was appropriate but the quality was still lacking, mainly because the term HTAP is still not used by all research conducted on this topic. To counter this, three different searches were conducted all using different search terms to gain a sufficient literature base regarding quantity and quality. Quality in this context refers to the overall consistency of the provided content and the adherence to scientific standards.

The search was carried out using (1) "htap" "data warehouse" OR "OLTP" "OLAP" (returning 183 entries), (2) HTAP OR OLAP OLTP hybrid database (returning 200 entries) and (3) hybrid transactional analytical processing (returning 200 entries). Only publications from 2010 or later were considered. The latter queries returned more papers, but were reduced to the 200 most recommended papers, since quality and relevance were continuously decreasing.

Only papers accessible without additional fees and written in German or English were taken into account. Further, theses were not considered in this paper. These criteria left 147 (1), 178 (2) and 179 (3) papers to refine further. With title and abstract based elimination, the papers lacking a combination of required key words or only mentioning HTAP as a side note were excluded. After that step, 55 (1), 44 (2) and 56 (3) papers were left for further analysis. This leaves a total of 94 papers (deducted duplicated paper from the different queries) for a final review.

Of these 94 papers, 15 were found to be of insufficient quality and 19 did not focus on the topic of HTAP databases or on fundamental technologies for those. The 60 papers, which were found scientifically significant and fulfilling the quality requirements were finally reduced to 41, deducting papers providing only outdated non-fundamental information.

IV. Findings and Discussion

The methods to create HTAP databases, their functionality and their optimizations take many different approaches. The contents of the papers were organized into the following sections according to the kind of information provided.

A. Fundamental Architecture

HTAP databases build up a new database sector and there are many databases which were newly developed for this workload, e.g., [4][7][8]. However, some existing databases also have been upgraded to handle HTAP workloads like SAP HANA [5], initially an OLAP database, and PostgreSQL [9], initially an OLTP database, proving that existing databases can be extended to handle HTAP.

Comparing the reviewed database architectures, two main storage paradigmas can be clearly identified with the reviewed solutions: (1) heavily main memory focused databases, keeping all of their (hot) data in memory like HANA [10], HyPer [4], BatchDB [8] and Hyrise [11], as well as (2) cloud/shared disk data stores, keeping some data in memory but relying on a persistent out of memory data store accessible by all instances, e.g., Wildfire [12] and Janus [13].

Further, a Non-Uniform Memory Access (NUMA) architecture is a base requirement for most main memory HTAP databases like SAP HANA [10], AIM [14], BatchDB [8], Hyrise [11] and HyPer [4] enabling multiple cores to access each others memory.

1) Scaling out and up: Another big difference in HTAP databases is their scaling approach. Systems like HyPer [4] (commercialized by Tableau) or Hyrise [11] are deployed on single servers utilizing NUMA to scale-up onto multiple cores, thus creating multiple nodes. This approach can reduce processing time as no data transfer between different servers is required and all data can be accessed in memory. As a downside however, large systems require a strong server with a large main memory. Both HyPer and Hyrise also provide scale-out approaches, normally keeping their OLTP processing on the main server, e.g., ScyPer [15].

Like Hyrise and HyPer - SAP HANA [16] keeps the OLTP workload on one machine, utilizing NUMA to use as many cores as required and available, but implements scaling the OLTP workload out to other servers as a base feature. Using HANA Asynchronous Parallel Table Replication (ATR) the database distributes its data amongst multiple replicas enabling a more efficient OLAP approach.

BatchDB [8] also handles the OLTP workload on the main server. The OLAP workload can be either executed on a different node of the same machine, or an entirely different server.

Contrarily, Wildfire [17] (commercialized as IBM BD2 Event Store) utilizes a fully distributed approach. Heavily relying on Apache Spark, all requests pass Sparks API and get distributed across multiple Spark executors. These executors delegate the transactional and analytical requests to the Wildfire engine daemons. All daemons use their main memory as well as solid-state drives (SSDs) and are connected to one shared data storage, e.g., a cloud data store. With this approach more throughput can be achieved, but ACID on the other hand is no longer possible. The latest research on the Wildfire system, Wildfire-Serializable (WiSer) [18] also offers high availability besides HTAP. It is furthermore optimized for Internet of Things workloads.

Like Wildfire, SnappyData [19] also uses Spark as a core component to scale out the system to a database cluster. Therefore, the system enables more information to be kept in memory without the need for one expensive server.

Janus [13] also uses a distributed setup but implements the query distribution on its own with execution servers. These delegate the query to a corresponding row partitioned server for OLTP workloads or a column partitioned server for OLAP workloads.

2) Data/Table Structure: When dealing with OLTP and OLAP workloads, finding the right table format can be difficult. HTAP databases therefore employ different table and data structures. Wildfire [17] exclusively uses column oriented tables since they are the most efficient solution for OLAP workload.

SAP HANA [10] implements a row-store query engine and a column-storage engine to combine the advantages of both technologies. Thus, it is possible to save data in row or column tables. The column layout is the default, more optimized, option.

HyPer [20] and Hyrise [11] both use columnar stores with self implemented data models. Hyrise further presented a hybrid column layout in an older version [21], combining simple one-attribute-columns with rows. This is planned to be implemented again in the new version, but has low priority and is work in progress.

Opposed to this, PostgreSQL [9] continues to use its row data storage for OLTP, but has a column store extension for OLAP workloads, merging the delta from the row store continuously in the column store.

SnappyData [19] follows a hybrid approach, where the fresh data is stored in an in-memory row-store and is moved in an on-disk column-store after aging.

The Cloud data store Janus [13] is fully hybrid, utilizing row partitions for OLTP and column partition for OLAP. Via a redo-log inspired batching approach and a graph-based dependency management, the delta from the row replicas can be merged into the column replicas.

The Casper prototype [22] uses a tailored column layout to support mixed read/write workloads more efficiently. With this approach, runtime column adaptations are possible.

Flexible Storage Model (FSM) [23] presented a tile based architecture to allow a transition from OLTP optimized tables to OLAP optimized tables depending on the hotness of data. The data is saved in a row oriented manner at the beginning and, depending on the hotness, is tile-wise transitioned to an OLAP column oriented tile structure.

3) Saving and Partitioning Data: For scale-up focused databases, removing data from main memory to larger, more cost efficient stores (e.g., hard drives), or efficiently compressing its size, is crucial. HyPer uses horizontal partitioning and saves its hot data uncompressed on the main memory. The cold data can also be kept in memory. Instead of evicting data to a disk, the data is compressed into self implemented Data Blocks [20] and kept in main memory. However, it is possible to evict them to secondary storage solutions if preferred (e.g., Non-volatile random-access memory) and use them as persistent backups. The compression technique is chosen based on the data actually saved in the Data Block.

Utilizing Small Materialized Aggregates (SMAs) including meta data like min and max values, irrelevant compressed data can easily be skipped in searches. If data cannot be skipped on SMA basis, Positional SMAs (PSMAs), another lightweight indexing structure developed by the HyPer team, can be used. These help to determine the range of positions in the Data Block were the relevant values are located.

Hyrise [21] solves this problem using horizontal partitioning and by saving data in 2 kinds of columns: Memory-Resident Columns for hot data in memory, allowing fast access, and uncompressed row-oriented Secondary Storage Column Groups for cold data on hard drives. As the cold data is saved uncompressed, the cost of accessing it is reduced in comparison to classical compressed approaches.

Furthermore, the data is organized in so-called chunks [11] similar to Data Blocks. Chunks can be mutable as long as they are not full. As soon as they reach their capacity they transition to an immutable append-only container. They also have indexes and filters on a per chunk basis like Data Blocks, allowing faster search and access operations.

Smart Larger Than Memory [24] stores cold data in files on the hard drive decoupled from the database. Modifications to the data are no longer possible. The entries can only be deleted. This happens via removing the reference entry in memory without accessing the cold data and thereby saving time. Updating cold data is possible, but the update is a hidden delete of the cold data index and an insert of new hot data. To fully take advantage of SmartLTM the read operations always check the main memory entries first. If the data cannot be found, cuckoo filters or SMAs are used to locate the data in the files on the hard drive.

Finally, partitioning workloads in an intelligent manner without extra statistical data structures is possible, too. As presented by Boissier and Kurzynski [25], physical horizontal data partitioning as well as the adapted aggressive data skipping approach can skip up to 90% of data on OLAP queries.

B. Concurrency

Handling multiple versions of data is a crucial part of all HTAP databases. Current OLTP and OLAP operations require a solution to parallelize data access.

The most common approach is Multi Version Concurrency Control (MVCC). It is utilized in combination with a delta by PostgreSQL [9], SAP HANA [10] and in new versions of HyPer [26].

Hyrise [27] is also using MVCC, but is following a look free commit approach, replacing the delta.

SnappyData and BatchDB [8] also use MVCC oriented approaches. SnappyData [7] relies on GemFire to handle concurrent access and snapshots, while BatchDB [8] uses MVCC on its OLTP replica, while updating the isolated OLAP replica batch-wise.

Although HyPer is now using MVCC with delta, it initially used the fork systemcall to create multiple isolated in-memory snapshots [28]. Utilizing a copy on write approach to reduce memory consumption OLAP queries could be executed on snapshots while the OLTP operations updated the main memory entries.

In addition to the MVCC on its main OLTP replica, SAP HANA [16] further uses ATR with a replication log system to synchronize its multiple server architecture. This synchronizes data with sub-second visibility delay between the replicas.

Wildfire [17] chooses speed over concurrency as already mentioned. Therefore, a simple last writer wins approach is used by the Wildfire engine.

While most systems nowadays use some implementation of MVCC, research on more efficient snapshotting techniques is still being carried out, e.g., [29]. Inspired by earlier HyPer implementations, another research project on snapshotting, AnKer [30], uses a customized Linux kernel with an updated fork system call. This updated fork, called vm_snapshot, enables high frequency snapshotting. Through vm_snapshot the researchers are able to snapshot only the used columns. This significantly outperforms the default fork used initially by HyPers implementation, providing a possible alternative to MVCC systems.

Wait free HTAP (WHTAP) [31] utilizes snapshotting for concurrency as well. In this dual snapshot engine approach data for OLAP and OLTP are stored in different replicas, using a five state process and two deltas. In this process, the deltas form the OLAP and OLTP replicas are switched and the old OLTP delta is merged into the OLAP replica which takes effect without slowing the analytical queries down.

C. Garbage Collection

MVCC implementations require performant garbage collection to prevent large amounts of versions to slow down the transactions on the database. SAP HANA [10] uses timestamps and visibility bits to track versions of their data. Data gets created/edited with a timestamp. When all active transactions can see this version the timestamp is replaced with a bit indicating the visibility. If the row is no longer visible to any snapshot, it can be deleted with the next delta merge.

HyPers garbage collector Steam [26] follows a similar approach. The main difference is that the garbage collector is called with every new transaction instead of being a background task like with SAP HANA. This approach called eager pruning removes all versions not required by any transaction. This happens by checking every time the chain is extended whether all versions included in the version chain are used by a transaction. With eager pruning the version chain can only be as long as the amount of different queries.

Due to its heavily distributed architecture with many data sets saved in main memory and SSDs on the different servers, Wildfire follows a different solution and implements a lazy garbage collection approach [17]. When performing lazy garbage collection, data is only deleted if there is no possibility that a query could require it. However, the concrete implementation is not explained.

D. Query Handling

The ways to access the concurrent data differ significantly from database implementation to implementation.

1) Query Handling in Scale-up Systems: The systems HyPer [32] and Hyrise [11], primarily engineered for scale-up solutions working on one dataset, implemented the query operators as C++ code in their database. The missing variables are inserted via just in time compilation. After the insertion, the code is compiled to LLVM assembler code, allowing fast query execution. As mentioned before, the two databases also have prototype scale-out options, but focus on the scale-up approach.

Another approach is to dynamically schedule memory and computing resources actively [33]. With this approach, the cores are assigned to the OLAP or OLTP workload as required, always trying to maximize productivity and the database throughput.

2) Query Handling in Scaled-out Systems: Scale-out systems are separated in two groups: On the one hand, systems keeping the OLTP workload on one server, scaling only the OLAP workload to other servers, as e.g., SAP HANA [16] or BatchDB [8]. On the other hand, systems distributing OLTP and OLAP workloads over multiple servers, e.g., Wildfire [12][17] and SnappyData [7][19].

BatchDB [8] and HANA [16] both handle their OLTP workload on a single server, scaling-up via NUMA as described earlier. For OLAP workloads they are able to scale out onto multiple servers working on replicas of the main data.

Wildfire [12] and SnappyData [19] contrarily scale out via Apache Spark, allowing OLTP and OLAP transactions to be executed on a cluster of nodes dealing with big data and streaming workloads. Wildfire [12] executes OLTP queries on the fresh data on Wildfire daemons. OLAP workloads can be executed via Spark Executor as requests to the daemons or directly accessing the shared data of the Wildfire database cluster. With this approach, old data can be consumed from the shared file system without slowing down OLTP throughput while the latest data can still be received if required.

3) Query Language: While the databases offer many new functionalities to access and modify data, Structured Query Language (SQL) is still commonly supported. The database systems SAP HANA [5], Wildfire [17], Hyrise [11], HyPer [4], SnappyData [7] and AIM [14] all enable basic SQL queries to interact with the database. However, many of them further provide new optimized ways to interact with the data.

Wildfire [17] and SnappyData [7] provide data access via an extended version of the SparkSQL API. SnappyData also further extends the Spark Streaming API.

SAP HANA [5] provides more specific access through SQL Script and Multidimensional Expressions (MDX). The database is also is natively optimized for the ABAP language and runtime. This allows to bypass the SQL connectivity stack by directly accessing special internal data representations via Fast Data Access (FDA). The Native For All Entries (NFAE) technique further modifies the ABAP runtime to allow even more performance improvements.

Hyrise [11] provides a command-line interface which allows SQL queries but also provides additional visualization and management functions. Furthermore, the wire protocol of PostgreSQL allows access through common PostgreSQL drivers and clients.

HyPer [32] uses HyPerScript as its query language. HyPerScript is a SQL-based query language and therefore allows base SQL statements as well. The features consist of passing whole tables as query parameters and providing the possibility to use query results in a later part of the query, removing the need to query the same value multiple times.

E. Indices

To allow efficient data access and querying on multiple servers and/or different versions of data, the right index structure is of special importance in HTAP databases. Wildfire's multi-version multi-zone index Umzi [34] employs a LSM-like structure with multiple runs. It divides index runs in multiple zones and implements efficient evolve operations to handle zone switches of data. Further Umzi uses a multi-tier storage using SSDs and memory caching with self-updating functionality for fast execution while persisting the indexes on Wildfires shared data.

HyPer developed the Adaptive Radix Tree (ART) [32] based on the radix tree. ART uses four different node types that can handle 4, 16, 48 and 256 entries. The maximum height for the tree is k for k-byte trees. To further reduce the tree height and required space, the tree is build lazily, saving single leaf branches higher in the tree. Additionally, path compression is used to remove common paths and to insert them as a prefix of the inner node thereby removing cache inefficient one-way node chains.

SAP HANA [10] and Hyrise [11] both use B-Trees. Hyrise further supports the ART index from HyPer [32] and a group-key-index, implemented by the Hyrise project.

BatchDB utilizes a simplified version of the look-free Bw-Tree [8]. The version relies on atomic multi-word compare-and-swap updates.

In 2019, a predictive indexing approach [35] was introduced to cope with the dynamic demands of a HTAP database. Predictive indexing increases the throughput by up to 5%. In this approach, a machine learning system calculates the optimal index structure for the data according to the workload.

The Multi-Version Partitioned B-Tree (MV-MBT) [36] is another recent research in the indexing sector for HTAP databases from 2019. This extension of partitioned B-Tree creates a version aware index, able to maintain multiple partitions within a single tree structure, sorted in alphanumeric order.

Likewise proposed in 2019, the Parallel Binary Tree (P-Tree) [37] is an extension of a balanced binary tree relying on copy-on write mechanisms to create tree copies on updates. With this approach, the indices become the version history without requiring other data structures.

F. Big Data on HTAP Databases

Wildfire was created with big data as its primary use case [17]. Through the distributed design of its big data platform, Wildfire is able to concurrently handle high-volumes of transactions as well as execute analytics on latest data. At the same time, the system is able to scale onto many machines because of its close integration of Apache Spark. The usage of an open data format further enables compatibility with the big data ecosystem. Nowadays, the commercial version IBM Db2 Event Store is capable of handling more than 250 billion events per day [38]. SnappyData [19] is an analogically capable big data platform with an architecture similar to Wildfire.

The SAP HANA database can be used as part of the SAP HANA data platform to handle big data workloads [39]. Using a combination of different SAP products, namely SAP Synbase ESP and SAP Synbase IQ, as well as smart data access frameworks as Hadoop, Teradata or Apache Spark, the SAP HANA data platform is a fully functional big data system with SAP HANA in its core.

HyPerInsight [40] provides big data capabilities in the area of data exploration on the HyPer database. The goal is to minimize the required user expertise with the dataset while simultaneously supporting the user with the formulation of queries. The support for lambda functions in SQL queries allows user defined code to be executed within the queries. In combination with the HTAP HyPer system as the database, data mining on real-time data is possible.

G. Recovery and Logging

As many HTAP databases rely on volatile main memory as primary storage and the other systems utilize distributed data sets, recovery in case of failure is of special importance. Data loss has to be prevented and downtime must be minimized.

SAP HANA instances log data persistently on the local drive for recovery on failure or restart purposes [5]. The logging approach is inspired by SAP MaxDB.

As already explained, HANA works with ATR in its distributed architecture [16]. Following the store-and-forward approach, the data is replicated to multiple servers. An algorithm then compares the record version IDs of the incoming data and stored data, requesting the resend of lost log entries if deviations occur.

Recovery for the latest version of Hyrise is still work in progress [11], but recovery for older versions of Hyrise was explained [27]. The database dumps the main partition of the table as a binary dump on the disk and records the delta to a log via group commits to hide the latency. At checkpoints, the delta partitions are also saved as a binary dump on the drive. If recovery is required, the main dump and delta dump from a checkpoint are restored and an eventually existing delta log is replayed on the table, restoring the old state.

BatchDB logs successful transactions on its OLTP replica in batches via command logging on durable storage [8]. In case of a failure, the database can recover from these logs. The OLAP replica itself has no durable logging and has to recover from the main OLTP replica on failure.

SnappyData [7] uses Apache Sparks logging and recovery mechanisms, logging transformations used to build Sparks Resilient Distributed Datasets (RDDs). Saving RDDs to storage is also possible. In SnappyData the combination with GemFire however allows Spark to save the RDDs in GemFires storage instead of the persistent storage of the server. Small recoveries can be handled directly by GemFires eager replication, leaving batched and streaming recovery to Spark, in combination with the GemFire storage.

Further, a peer-to-peer (p2p) approach is used in SnappyData clusters. Any in-memory data can be synchronously replicated from the cluster. Additional to the replication via the p2p approach, data is always replicated to at least one other node in the cluster.

H. Benchmarking

The combination of OLTP and OLAP workloads on one database also created the need for new benchmarks covering this sector. In 2011, CH-benCHmark [41] was introduced. The CH-benCHmark is based on the TPC-C and TPC-H benchmarks. It executes a transactional and analytical workload in parallel on a shared set of tables on the same database. The benchmark can also be used for single workload databases.

In 2017, HTAPBench [42] was published. This benchmark is able to compare OLTP, OLAP and hybrid workloads on the database. Its main difference to CH-benCHmark lies in its Client Balancer, controlling the coexisting OLAP and OLTP workloads.

Hyrise [11] implements a special benchmark runner to easily execute benchmarks.

I. Stream Processing

Streaming as a special case of OLTP is an emerging use case for HTAP database systems. In 2016 scientists from ETH Zürich in cooperation with Huawei presented AIM [14], which is a high performance event-processing and real time analytics HTAP database. The three-tiered multi node system processes events at one tier, stores the data at a central tier and finally analyses the processed data in real time on the third tier. AIM however, is optimized for a special streaming use case from the telecommunications industry.

In early 2019, the research team around HyPer compared modified versions of HyPer with AIM and Apache Flink [43] in order to determine the current state of streaming capabilities of main memory database systems (MMDB). While MMDBs are still inferior to dedicated streaming frameworks like Flink, the HyPer team was confident, that HTAP databases could catch up with some adjustments, even implementing some of those on HyPer. The main areas requiring improvement are network optimization, parallel transaction processing, skew handling and a strong distributed architecture.

SnappyData aims to solve OLTP, OLAP and streaming all in one product [19] with their tight integration of Apache Spark and GemFire. In an evaluation, SnappyData was able to outperform both Spark on TPC-H queries as well as MemSQL on all kinds of throughput. The focus with SnappyDatas stream processing lies on complex analytical queries on streams, which are not possible with default stream processor solutions [7].

SAPs approach for big data, SAP Big Data [39], supports streaming as well. Since it uses other SAP products to achieve it and is not a part of the base SAP HANA database infrastructure, but rather is built on top of it, it is not further discussed in this paper.

J. Future

HTAP databases are a new sector which has evolved over the past 10 years. On an annual basis, companies and researchers contribute new ideas to lift their database above the competition. Currently, the newest trends tend to lead into three directions:

1. Heterogenous HTAP (HHTAP/H2TAP): with new hardware supporting heterogenous parallelism, HHTAP becomes a possibility. In this approach, CPUs and GPGPUs can access shared memory and divide the workload between both. Complex OLAP queries are solved on the GPGPUs, leaving the OLTP workload for the CPUs. The Caldera [44] prototype proved the feasibility for HHTAP. Early 2020, the data store GridTables [45] was published and proved the concept again.

However, in their summary, the authors of GridTables pointed out that there are still many research issues left to be solved. Further, early in 2020, a paper was published about GPU accelerated data management [46] explaining how to fully exploit hardware isolation between CPUs and GPUs and presenting a SemiLazy access method to reduce the required data transfer.

2. Streaming workloads: as described in detail in the previous section, stream processing is a possible use case for HTAP databases. Because of the optimization for high OLTP throughput and the ability to analyse these data streams in the same system, HTAP databases are an emerging alternative to current stream processing solutions. While still inferior to dedicated stream processors, the research on such solutions saw an increase in interest over the last years, e.g., by the HyPer team [43] and dedicated streaming HTAP databases like SnappyData [19] and AIM [14].

3. Optimization: while the bigger part of the 2010s was spent on researching for new systems [4][5][27], the last quarter focused on their optimization. Few new database systems were proposed and research started optimizing existing systems even further [26][30][37].

Further solutions using machine learning are slowly emerging. These allow databases to adapt on their own according to current workload and requirements. However, there is still not enough research to speak of an own trend and it can rather be viewed as another kind of optimization research. An example for such research is the presented predictive indexing approach [35].

K. Open Source and Free Versions

Some of the database systems summarized in this paper provide open source and/or free solutions. SnappyData [47] is available with a getting started guide covering the basic usage. The source code can be found on GitLab. The project is licensed with the Apache License, Version 2.0.

MemSQL [48], is available, well documented and can be used for smaller projects up to 4 nodes for free. Many extensions are available at the official GitHub account.

Hyrise [49] is available under the MIT license. However, as it is a research database, breaking changes may occur more frequently.

The free MemSQL version and a basic SnappyData setup can already be used on low end systems, naming 8GB main memory as their minimal requirement to operate efficiently.

To try a HTAP database without a setup process, HyPer can be used. The HyPer research version is provided as a simple web tool for exploration and testing [50]. This version, however, is running on a low end system and cannot be used in production.

V. Conclusion

In this paper, we have shown that HTAP databases are nowadays serious alternatives to traditional database solutions. The existence of a market for commercial products like SAP HANA, IBM Db2 Event Store and Tableau further reinforces our findings. Moreover, we have highlighted differences of existing approaches regarding key properties like the fundamental architecture, concurrency, or big data capabilities. Thus, this study can aid both researchers and practitioners in the process of selecting a matching HTAP solution. Finally, by providing a comprehensive overview of current research approaches as well as productive solutions, this study helps to identify trends and point out directions for future research. The following paragraphs provide a brief summary of our findings.

Open source and free HTAP products place HTAP databases on the same level as current database systems, allowing the integration in other products and exploring this new technology without financial risks.

The combination of OLTP and OLAP queries on one database efficiently reduces the total cost of ownership and allows a narrower tech stack for companies. The possibility to analyse data in real time further validates HTAP databases as a productive solution with a great added value compared to conventional databases.

Many different implementations, providing different advantages, are available and can be used as required by the costumer. Solutions using main memory as a primary/sole storage as well as solutions relying on shared data storages exist and are both valid options. Powerful single server database systems allow a slim tech stack while still being faster than most traditional OLTP and OLAP optimized databases. Distributed multi server clusters allow more fail-safe and easier to scale solutions, while at the same time requiring less performant machines. SnappyData and MemSQL, for example, can already be executed on machines with 8GB of memory, scaling up from there.

Over the last years, new indices, filters, data structures and replication techniques were developed, optimizing performant HTAP systems even further. The future seems to be heading in three main directions: HHTAP - utilizing new heterogenous hardware to include the GPUs in HTAP databases and allow even more efficient architectures.

Streaming - HTAP databases optimized for streaming are making a combination with external stream processors unnecessary, further reducing the total cost of ownership and reducing the size of the required tech stack.

Optimization - while the bigger part of the 2010's was spent on developing the base technologies and databases themselves, the last quarter was primarily spent on optimization, still leaving much room for improvement.

Machine learning for self adapting databases also could be an emerging sector in the future, but currently there is not enough research in this direction to call it a trend.

References

[1] R. Nigel, F. Donald, P. Massimo, and E. Roxane, "Hybrid transaction/analytical processing will foster opportunities for dramatic business innovation," 2014.

[2] U. Joseph *et al.*, "Predicts 2016: In-memory computing-enabled hybrid transaction/analytical processing supports dramatic digital business innovation," 2015.

[3] Y. Noel and G. Mike, "Emerging technology: Translytical databases deliver analytics at the speed of transactions," 2015.

[4] A. Kemper and T. Neumann, "Hyper: A hybrid oltp olap main memory database system based on virtual memory snapshots," in *2011 IEEE 27th International Conference on Data Engineering*, 2011, pp. 195–206.

[5] F. Färber *et al.*, "The sap hana database - an architecture overview," *Bulletin of the Technical Committee on Data Engineering / IEEE Computer Society*, vol. 35, no. 1, pp. 28–33, 2012.

[6] B. Kitchenham, "Procedures for performing systematic reviews," *Keele, UK, Keele Univ.*, vol. 33, 08 2004.

[7] B. Mozafari, "Snappydata," in *Encyclopedia of Big Data Technologies*, S. Sakr and A. Y. Zomaya, Eds. Springer, 2019. [Online]. Available: https://doi.org/10.1007/978-3-319-63962-8_258-1

[8] D. Makreshanski, J. Giceva, C. Barthels, and G. Alonso, "Batchdb: Efficient isolated execution of hybrid oltp+olap workloads for interactive applications," *Proceedings of the 2017 ACM International Conference on Management of Data*, 2017.

[9] M. Nakamura *et al.*, "Extending postgresql to handle olxp workloads," in *Fifth International Conference on the Innovative Computing Technology (INTECH 2015)*, 2015, pp. 40–44.

[10] N. May, A. Böhm, and W. Lehner, "Sap hana – the evolution of an in-memory dbms from pure olap processing towards mixed workloads," in *Datenbanksysteme für Business, Technologie und Web (BTW 2017)*, B. Mitschang, D. Nicklas, F. Leymann, H. Schöning, M. Herschel, J. Teubner, T. Härder, O. Kopp, and M. Wieland, Eds. Gesellschaft für Informatik, Bonn, 2017, pp. 545–546.

[11] M. Dreseler *et al.*, "Hyrise re-engineered: An extensible database system for research in relational in-memory data management," in *EDBT*, 2019.

[12] R. Barber *et al.*, "Evolving databases for new-gen big data applications," in *CIDR*, 2017.

[13] V. Arora, F. Nawab, D. Agrawal, and A. E. Abbadi, "Janus: A hybrid scalable multi-representation cloud datastore," *IEEE Transactions on Knowledge and Data Engineering*, vol. 30, no. 4, pp. 689–702, 2018.

[14] L. Braun *et al.*, "Analytics in motion: High performance event-processing and real-time analytics in the same database," in *Proceedings of the 2015 ACM SIGMOD International Conference on Management of Data*, ser. SIGMOD '15. New York, NY, USA: Association for Computing Machinery, 2015, p. 251–264. [Online]. Available: https://doi.org/10.1145/2723372.2742783

[15] T. Mühlbauer, W. Rödiger, A. Reiser, A. Kemper, and T. Neumann, "Scyper: elastic olap throughput on transactional data," in *DanaC '13*, 2013.

[16] J. Lee *et al.*, "Parallel replication across formats in sap hana for scaling out mixed oltp/olap workloads," *Proc. VLDB Endow.*, vol. 10, no. 12, p. 1598–1609, Aug. 2017. [Online]. Available: https://doi.org/10.14778/3137765.3137767

[17] R. Barber, V. Raman, R. Sidle, Y. Tian, and P. Tözün, *Wildfire: HTAP for Big Data*. Germany: Springer, 2019.

[18] R. Barber *et al.*, "Wiser: A highly available HTAP DBMS for iot applications," in *2019 IEEE International Conference on Big Data (Big Data), Los Angeles, CA, USA, December 9-12, 2019*. IEEE, 2019, pp. 268–277. [Online]. Available: https://doi.org/10.1109/BigData47090.2019.9006519

[19] R. Jags *et al.*, "Snappydata: Streaming, transactions, and interactive analytics in a unified engine," 2016.

[20] H. Lang *et al.*, "Data blocks: Hybrid oltp and olap on compressed storage using both vectorization and compilation," in *SIGMOD '16*, 2016.

[21] M. Boissier, R. Schlosser, and M. Uflacker, "Hybrid data layouts for tiered htap databases with pareto-optimal data placements," in *2018 IEEE 34th International Conference on Data Engineering (ICDE)*, 2018, pp. 209–220.

[22] M. Athanassoulis, K. S. Bøgh, and S. Idreos, "Optimal column layout for hybrid workloads," *Proc. VLDB Endow.*, vol. 12, no. 13, p. 2393–2407, Sep. 2019. [Online]. Available: https://doi.org/10.14778/3358701.3358707

[23] J. Arulraj, A. Pavlo, and P. Menon, "Bridging the archipelago between row-stores and column-stores for hybrid workloads," in *Proceedings of the 2016 International Conference on Management of Data*, ser. SIGMOD '16. New York, NY, USA: Association for Computing Machinery, 2016, p. 583–598. [Online]. Available: https://doi.org/10.1145/2882903.2915231

[24] P. R. P. Amora, E. M. Teixeira, F. D. B. S. Praciano, and J. C. Machado, "Smartltm: Smart larger-than-memory storage for hybrid database systems," in *SBBD*, 2018.

[25] M. Boissier and D. Kurzynski, "Workload-driven horizontal partitioning and pruning for large htap systems," in *2018 IEEE 34th International Conference on Data Engineering Workshops (ICDEW)*, 2018, pp. 116–121.

[26] J. Böttcher, V. Leis, T. Neumann, and A. Kemper, "Scalable garbage collection for in-memory mvcc systems," *Proc. VLDB Endow.*, vol. 13, no. 2, p. 128–141, Oct. 2019. [Online]. Available: https://doi.org/10.14778/3364324.3364328

[27] D. Schwalb, M. Faust, J. Wust, M. Grund, and H. Plattner, "Efficient transaction processing for hyrise in mixed workload environments," in *IMDM@VLDB*, 2014.

[28] F. Funke, A. Kemper, T. Mühlbauer, T. Neumann, and V. Leis, "Hyper beyond software: Exploiting modern hardware for main-memory database systems," *Datenbank-Spektrum*, vol. 14, no. 3, pp. 173–181, 2014.

[29] L. Li *et al.*, "A comparative study of consistent snapshot algorithms for main-memory database systems," *ArXiv*, vol. abs/1810.04915, 2018.

[30] A. Sharma, F. M. Schuhknecht, and J. Dittrich, "Accelerating analytical processing in mvcc using fine-granular high-frequency virtual snapshotting," in *Proceedings of the 2018 International Conference on Management of Data*, ser. SIGMOD '18. New York, NY, USA: Association for Computing Machinery, 2018, p. 245–258. [Online]. Available: https://doi.org/10.1145/3183713.3196904

[31] L. Li, G. Wu, G. Wang, and Y. Yuan, "Accelerating hybrid transactional/analytical processing using consistent dual-snapshot," in *Database Systems for Advanced Applications*. Cham: Springer International Publishing, 2019, pp. 52–69.

[32] K. Alfons *et al.*, "Transaction processing in the hybrid oltp&olap main-memory database system hyper," *IEEE Computer Society Data Engineering Bulletin*, vol. Special Issue on "Main Memory Databases", 2013.

[33] A. Raza, P. Chrysogelos, A. G. Anadiotis, and A. Ailamaki, "Adaptive HTAP through elastic resource scheduling," in *Proceedings of the 2020 International Conference on Management of Data, SIGMOD Conference 2020, online conference [Portland, OR, USA], June 14-19, 2020*. ACM, 2020, pp. 2043–2054. [Online]. Available: https://doi.org/10.1145/3318464.3389783

[34] C. Luo *et al.*, "Umzi: Unified multi-zone indexing for large-scale htap," in *EDBT*, 2019.

[35] A. Joy, X. Ran, M. Lin, and P. Andrew, "Predictive indexing," 2019.

[36] C. Riegger, T. Vinçon, R. Gottstein, and I. Petrov, "Mv-pbt: Multi-version index for large datasets and htap workloads," *ArXiv*, vol. abs/1910.08023, 2020.

[37] Y. Sun, G. Blelloch, W. S. Lim, and A. Pavlo, "On supporting efficient snapshot isolation for hybrid workloads with multi-versioned indexes," *Proc. VLDB Endow.*, vol. 13, pp. 211–225, 2019.

[38] IBM, "Ibm db2 event store," last visited: 12.10.2020. [Online]. Available: https://www.ibm.com/de-de/products/db2-event-store

[39] N. May *et al.*, "Sap hana - from relational olap database to big data infrastructure," in *EDBT*, 2015.

[40] N. Hubig *et al.*, "Hyperinsight: Data exploration deep inside hyper," *Proceedings of the 2017 ACM on Conference on Information and Knowledge Management*, 2017.

[41] R. L. Cole *et al.*, "The mixed workload ch-benchmark," in *DBTest '11*, 2011.

[42] F. Coelho, J. Paulo, R. Vilaça, J. Pereira, and R. Oliveira, "Htapbench: Hybrid transactional and analytical processing benchmark," in *Proceedings of the 8th ACM/SPEC on International Conference on Performance Engineering*, ser. ICPE '17. New York, NY, USA: Association for Computing Machinery, 2017, p. 293–304. [Online]. Available: https://doi.org/10.1145/3030207.3030228

[43] A. Kipf *et al.*, "Scalable analytics on fast data," *ACM Trans. Database Syst.*, vol. 44, no. 1, Jan. 2019. [Online]. Available: https://doi.org/10.1145/3283811

[44] A. Raja, K. Manos, P. Danica, and A. Anastasia, "The case for heterogeneous htap," *8th Binnial conference on Innovative Data Systems Reseach (CIDR '17)*, 2017.

[45] M. Pinnecke, G. Campero Durand, D. Broneske, R. Zoun, and G. Saake, "Gridtables: A one-size-fits-most h2tap data store: Vision and concept," *Datenbank-Spektrum*, 01 2020.

[46] A. Raza *et al.*, "Gpu-accelerated data management under the test of time," in *CIDR*, 2020.

[47] SnappyData. Snappydata 1.2.0 - getting started in 5 minutes or less. Last visited: 12.10.2020. [Online]. Available: https://snappydatainc.github.io/snappydata/quickstart/

[48] MemSQL. Memsql documentation. Last visited: 12.10.2020. [Online]. Available: https://docs.memsql.com/v7.1/introduction/documentation-overview/
[49] Hyrise, "Hyrise github," last visited: 12.10.2020. [Online]. Available: https://github.com/hyrise/hyrise
[50] HyPer, "Hyper online interface," last visited: 12.10.2020. [Online]. Available: http://hyper-db.de/interface.html